Heritage Studies

Heritage Studies

Editor
Marie-Theres Albert

Volume 4

Perceptions of Sustainability in Heritage Studies

Editor
Marie-Theres Albert

DE GRUYTER

United Nations
Educational, Scientific and
Cultural Organization

UNESCO Chair
in Heritage Studies
University of Cottbus-Senftenberg, Germany

The following volumes have been published in the Heritage Studies Series:

Volume 1: Understanding Heritage – Perspectives in Heritage Studies, 2013
Volume 2: 40 Jahre Welterbekonvention – Zur Popularisierung eines Schutzkonzeptes für Kultur- und Naturgüter, 2015
Volume 3: 40 Years World Heritage Convention – Popularizing the Protection of Cultural and Natural Heritage, 2015

For further information please consult the following websites:
http://www.heritagestudies.de
http://www.b-tu.de/heritagestudies

The Editor and the Editorial Advisory Board would like to thank the Sparkasse Spree-Neisse for their generous financial support and Dr. Hans-Joachim Aubert for his continuing backing of the Heritage Studies Series by providing the third cover photo free of charge from his documentation of UNESCO World Heritage sites.

ISBN 978-3-11-041513-1
e-ISBN (PDF) 978-3-11-041527-8
e-ISBN (EPUB) 978-3-11-041557-5
ISSN 2196-0275

Library of Congress Cataloging-in-Publication Data
A CIP catalog record for this book has been applied for at the Library of Congress.

Bibliographic information published by the Deutsche Nationalbibliothek
The Deutsche Nationalbibliothek lists this publication in the Deutsche Nationalbibliographie; detailed bibliographic data are available on the internet at http://dnb.dnb.de

Editing: Stefan Simon
Copyediting: Caroline Lawrence and Judith Andreyev
Typesetter: LVD Gesellschaft für Datenverarbeitung mbH, Berlin
Printer: Hubert & Co. GmbH & Co. KG, Göttingen
Printed in Germany

www.degruyter.com

Scientific Peer Review Committee

The Editor of this book and the Editorial Advisory Board were supported by an independent Scientific Peer Review Committee composed of recognized experts in the field of heritage research. We therefore wish to thank ElArabi Emara, Klaus Hüfner, D. Fairchild Ruggels and Franziska Schaaf. The committee reviewed, evaluated, ranked and rated the research papers based on internationally established procedures and guidelines.

Content

Introduction

Perceptions of the Contributors[1]

Marie-Theres Albert

Background

The perceptions of the contributing authors on the issues of *sustainability* and *heritage* are structured into four parts. Following the *Introduction* and Part 1: *Introductory Reflections;* Part 2: *History and Documents* presents three contributions dealing with the history of natural heritage, cultural landscapes and intangible cultural heritage, introducing the paradigmatic discourse that is pursued in Part 3: *Paradigms;* while Part 4: *Theory, Methods and Practices* brings this discussion to a close.

Introductory Reflections

In her paper on *Mission and Vision of Sustainability Discourses in Heritage Studies* Marie-Theres Albert opens the discussion in this publication by introducing the missions of our world at the beginning of the twenty-first century and the corresponding visions on sustainable development on a global scale. She points out the need for developing new concepts of sustainability, especially for protecting and using heritage and World Heritage. On the other hand, as she illustrates, a populist exploitation of the discourse on sustainability can be observed. It has changed the essence of the issue and in many cases created a 'false labeling' of sustainability. Concluding her perceptions, she proposes a more conceptual understanding of sustainability by including concepts of justice, "governing the commons" or empowerment.

The emergence and evolving history of the concepts of culture, heritage and sustainability, including the aspect of World Heritage and underlying theoretical underpinnings and practical execution are discussed in detail in the introductory commentaries by Minja Yang, President of the Raymond Lemaire International Centre for Conservation of the Catholic University of Leuven, and Francesco Bandarin, former Assistant Director General of UNESCO. In her paper *Culture in Moving the MDGs to the Post-2015 Development Agenda,* Yang offers some reflections on the role of living heritage for sustainable development and the cultural dimension of development. She stresses the vital role of culture as an enabler of social cohesion and peace, recalling UNESCO's Constitution and the 2001 Universal Declaration on Cultural Diversity. One

1 I would like to take this opportunity to thank Shina Erlewein, who was mainly responsible for compiling this excellent summary of the articles in our *perception of contributors.*

of her key messages is the leading role of local authorities and cities in fostering sustainable development. She also draws attention to the integration of culture in local development policies and practices.

The sustainability discourse as it relates to the World Heritage Convention is presented in a paper by Francesco Bandarin, *Sustainability in the World Heritage Convention: The Making of a Policy Framework*, where he examines the integration of culture into the Post-2015 Development Agenda and the alignment of the World Heritage Convention with current strategic orientations in international culture and development policy. Reviewing among others the outcome document of the Rio+20 UN Conference on Sustainable Development, UN General Assembly resolutions and UNESCO's recent policy focusing on culture and development, the author perceives a trend towards recognizing culture as a vehicle for sustainable development. The paper concludes with the argument that the prerequisite for future heritage conservation and preservation endeavours is an active heritage coalition with local communities under the aegis of a sustainable development policy framework.

History and Documents

Part 2 addresses the main topic of this publication in the context of UNESCO Conventions and programmes. It includes rationales for the perception of heritage and sustainability in the course of historical developments and adaptations to them, as well as the application of the documents at different stages.

In her paper *Natural Heritage and Sustainable Development – A Realistic Option or Wishful Thinking?*, Barbara Engels discusses World Heritage policy instruments as a discursive shift from conservation to development. She points out that in the absence of tools ensuring sustainable resource use and development and in conjunction with ineffective management, human activities currently pose serious threats to the integrity and value of the sites, particularly in the context of natural World Heritage sites.

In her contribution *The Landscape Approach – A Global Context for Sustainability*, Mechtild Rössler presents recent debates concerning a Global Landscape Convention, including discussions on the European Landscape Convention, as well as the Recommendation on Historic Urban Landscape. The paper describes UNESCO's role in fostering the global landscape debate and related protection measures since the early 1960s. It gives an overview of the historical trajectory of the concept of landscape as it has been approached on the basis of numerous international legal instruments. She finally argues that "landscape" can provide a holistic framework for future activities to address the worlds' ever-growing challenges and thereby facilitate sustainable development perspectives that integrate both durable conservation and development.

Shina Erlewein presents in her paper *Sustainable Development and Intangible Cultural Heritage: Integrating Culture into Development* the interrelation of sustainable development and intangible cultural heritage, reflecting both UNESCO's 2003 Convention for the Safeguarding of the Intangible Cultural Heritage and recent international activities, debates and documents on the matter. She argues for the need to give special attention to the current drafting of a new chapter on sustainable development within the Operational Directives to the Convention. Analysing the 2012 UN report *Realizing the Future We Want For All*, which builds on a three-pillar model of sustainable development and highly influenced the draft version of the new Directives, the paper finally encourages further reflection stressing the importance of conceptualizing culture as an independent goal.

Paradigms

Part 3 addresses normative aspects of heritage and sustainability by focusing on the intentions and constructs associated with heritage conventions and the related perceptions. The aim is to proffer concepts that can preserve the future viability of heritage and sustainability as they pertain to transformation processes.

The opening paper is Giovanni Boccardi's *From Mitigation to Adaptation: A New Heritage Paradigm for the Anthropocene*. This is an urgent plea to the heritage community to expand its sphere of influence and look beyond the limits of specific heritage sites. Such an approach is required to confront today's most urgent challenges – the irrevocable effects of human activities on the environment and ensuing future consequences for all humanity. In dealing with the *Anthropocene*, the author argues that the viability of heritage conservation needs to be questioned and its guiding principles reframed accordingly. In particular, the related mitigation strategy aiming to prevent damage to heritage needs to give way to a new paradigm: the adaptation approach. This concept emphasizes heritage as a 'quality' that can convey cultural values, which needs to join forces with modern sciences and reach out to the world community in order to achieve a balance between symbolic and worldly issues, and thereby potentially enabling both cultural continuity and sustainability.

The paper *Social Sustainability of the Historic Urban Landscape* by Michael Turner provides a historical overview of cities and their transformation over time. The author contemplates the notion of sustainable development and emphasizes the need for a holistic and dynamic approach. Reflecting Karl Mannheim's conceptualization of generation as a sociological phenomenon, he stresses that our understanding of generations from a rather socio-historical perspective needs to extend beyond mere temporal chronology. This perception allows several generations to exist simultaneously. He argues that in addition to the historical aspect, geographical realities also need to be considered when dealing with sustainability in urban environments, with particular emphasis on coexistence, compromise and social inclusion.

With her paper on *Urban Heritage and Sustainable Development in South Asia: A Plea for a Heritage-Aware Approach*, Jyoti Hosagrahar develops a new paradigm, a heritage-aware approach. She discusses preservation and management of World Heritage properties in urban areas, focusing particularly on the Indian and wider South Asian context. It first engages in a historical review of heritage conservation practice and law in South Asia, further outlining the adverse effects of rapid urbanization, modernization and development particularly to historic cities and urban areas. The paper then covers the concepts of cultural heritage and sustainable development, arguing for integrative solutions that recognize heritage as a resource for sustainable development. Subsequently, she identifies a variety of challenges and finally presents six normative policy recommendations advocating a heritage-aware approach to sustainable development.

Robert Rode discusses the *Recognition of Indigenous Peoples' Sacred Natural Sites and the Cultural Dimension of Sustainable Development* through a transformation of the sustainability discourse and change in conservation policies and practices in these particular areas. Although indigenous communities and international organizations have been successful in strengthening the role of culture in sustainable development, there is a risk that this discourse might be devalued by political narratives of nature conservation that could reinforce misrepresentations of indigenous peoples. The paper presents a paradigm shift that purposefully emphasizes their diversity.

In *Culture, Heritage and Solidarity in the Context of Sustainable Development*, Manuel Peters considers the significance of culture and cultural heritage from different but convergent points of view. He argues that the introduction of culture into the debate might help us to better assess proposed sustainable development measures. Against this background, the author emphasizes how a better understanding of the contributions of cultural heritage can further promote sustainable development, for instance by identifying alternative ways of international world-making approaches to a sustainable future. He is thus seeking to interject the concept of solidarity as a new paradigmatic framework.

Theory, Methods and Practices

Part 4 captures the diversity of heritage and sheds light on various theoretical and methodological frameworks, presenting case studies in order to concretize its underlying theories. Essentially, it deals with the new disciplinary and interdisciplinary insights that can be gained from a better understanding of heritage and related epistemological and/or methodological approaches. Part 4 is divided into two sections, *Disciplinary and Epistemological Perceptions* and *Sustainability in Heritage Management Strategies*.

Disciplinary and Epistemological Perceptions presents papers that reflect on urban planning strategies. The first, *Cultural Landscapes: Heritage Preservation as a Foundation for Sustainable Regional Development* by Joaquim Sabaté and Mark Warren, presents an overview of the construct of cultural landscape and describes the conceptual shifts in cultural landscape preservation occurring within the purview of the United States National Park Service. The authors emphasize that sustainable heritage preservation needs to evolve from mere conservation efforts to better integrate the notion of change and progress in commercial terms, and in both cases strive to improve the quality of life of the local communities. They also contend that the cultural landscape paradigm aims to preserve a site's integrity, while at the same time acknowledging its living and dynamic nature. The paper makes reference to a survey on diverse cultural landscapes and heritage parks and delineates the guiding principles that might be helpful in assisting urban planning or preservation projects to simultaneously embrace both heritage and development.

Solmaz Yadollahi's paper, *A Reflection on Methodological Approaches in Assessing and Implementing Social Sustainability in Historical Public Spaces*, is a literature review. Reflecting on the definition of social sustainability and the meaning of public space, the author reviews urban planning approaches which link physical public space and social sustainability. She points out that they are both concerned with concepts such as *communication*, *social cohesion* and *equality*. Reviewing two examples of empirical research in the field, their methodological strengths and weaknesses in assessing social sustainability in public spaces are discussed. The conclusion is an outlook on public space research, suggesting that at the theoretical level, the contribution of physical public space to social sustainability is justifiable. Nevertheless, at the empirical level there is a gap in using qualitative methods and it is therefore that she suggests more empirical methods.

The paper by Juliana Forero, *The Social Function of Cultural Heritage: Conservation Practices on the Basis of Sociocultural Sustainability*, addresses the importance for the improvement of quality of life and well-being as well as the acknowledgement of cultural practices of the local communities where cultural heritage conservation takes place. She identifies and analyses the social function of cultural heritage within the context of sociocultural sustainability principles. Based on critical heritage studies and post-Western perspectives, contemporary patterns of development, sociocultural sustainability and cultural heritage concepts are discussed, to finally introduce the core elements of heritage's social function as an element for the achievement of sustainable development.

Sustainability in Heritage Management Strategies focuses on the role of sustainability on the basis of case studies that shed light on actual practice, beginning with Ron van Oers' paper *Cultural Heritage Management and Sustainability*. The author contends that cultural heritage management has since entered a post-modern phase and is increasingly marked by integration pressures. By outlining a shift towards incorporating culturally contextualized, community-driven and development-oriented approaches, he also argues that because it is a "living entity" cultural heritage holds great potential for sustainable development. The paper addresses real-world applications and contrasts management strategies emanating from two case studies in China: the Historic Centre of Macau and the Sinan Mansions in central Shanghai.

The contribution on *World Heritage and Sustainable Tourism: A Multifaceted Relationship* by Carol Westrik reveals the damaging impacts of tourism on World Heritage properties. Pointing to recent cases in Italy and Croatia, the author advocates the development of a sustainable tourism management approach that is clearly linked to the maintenance of Outstanding Universal Value. A general approach with defined criteria, indicators and tools is needed. She is therefore calling for tourism's firm integration into heritage management procedures, via UNESCO's World Heritage and Sustainable Tourism Programme adopted in 2012, because the programme offers practical hands-on tools, called "How To" Guides, to manage tourism in a sustainable way.

In his paper, *Heritage Impact Assessments as a Tool to Open Up Perspectives for Sustainability: Three Case Studies Related to Discussions Concerning the Visual Integrity of World Heritage Cultural and Urban Landscapes,* Michael Kloos reviews the constructions of the Waldschlösschen bridge in Dresden's Elbe Valley and the Golden Horn metro bridge in Istanbul, in addition to a planned building in Cologne. He recounts three instances where development has posed challenges to preservation, or more specifically to the visual integrity of a heritage site and examples of great controversies arising between local and international bodies. The paper promotes the potential of Heritage Impact Assessment as a powerful instrument that can enable all actors to visualize and evaluate a project's effect on a specific site and facilitate possible mediation options to resolve major disputes.

I Introductory Reflections

Mission and Vision of Sustainability Discourses in Heritage Studies

Marie-Theres Albert

Mission

The world today is undergoing massive changes due to global phenomena: climate change, globalization, economic integration, massive human migration flows, and ongoing developments in information and communication technologies. Given such framework conditions, the notion of sustainable development can be seen as the most important guiding principle for the twenty-first century. Sustainability and sustainable development are indeed the key concepts that are increasingly shaping the worldwide discourse surrounding policy, cultural, social, economic and environmental issues.

With global demands for sustainability come demands to not only better understand the significance of heritage, but also the function of heritage within these transformation processes. The various types of discourse on heritage have also gained prominence in recent years. However, such interchanges often emerge in isolation from each other and, until quite recently, their interrelationships have not been clearly delineated, let alone examined scientifically. As expressed in official discourses and policies, heritage tends to be presented as a key element for the sustainable development of human societies; there is general agreement that heritage should therefore be protected and utilized in a sustainable manner. Accordingly, the concept of sustainability has gradually developed into a paradigm for the conceptualization of heritage and related values. Nevertheless, there is practically no consensus with respect to the implications of this statement in terms how to best to approach and deal with heritage.

On the contrary, the existence of so many different and at times conflicting conceptualizations of sustainability results in heritage-related activities that are anything but sustainable. World Heritage sites are suffering as a result of the immense numbers of visitors and rituals staged for tourists, in turn resulting in the destruction and disappearance of heritage. Rather than being a common good of human societies, heritage becomes nothing more than a highly valuable marketable product. In this context it is imperative to define the concept of sustainability and its implications for heritage. In light of these arguments, the aim of the present volume is to collate and systematically classify a range of disciplinary and interdisciplinary perspectives on heritage and sustainability, and to provide insights on how the paradigm of sustainability can contribute to devising viable lines of action in the context of heritage.

One important aim is to highlight how sustainable development and heritage or World Heritage have mutually enriched each other in the historical process of the emergence and development of these concepts. Much academic discourse is taking place beyond the sphere of the United Nations and related organizations dealing with the issue of heritage, for example the publication by Ernst Ulrich von Weizsäcker et al., *Factor Five: Transforming the Global Economy through 80% Improvements in Resource Productivity* (von Weizsäcker 2009). *Perceptions of Sustainability in Heritage Studies* accordingly begins with a discussion on sustainable development goals directly relating to the World Heritage Convention and for example adopted in the action plan, Future of the World Heritage Convention, by the General Assembly of States Parties 2011 (UNESCO, 2011). Under the heading *Our Vision for 2020*, in reference to the implementation of the action plan by and for the World Heritage Convention it is stated: "International Cooperation and shared responsibility through the World Heritage Convention ensures effective conservation of our common cultural and natural heritage, nurtures respect and understanding among the world's communities and cultures, and contributes to their sustainable development." (UNESCO, 2011, p. 2). It is important to note that while the action plan generally employs terms such as "*visions, missions* and *goals*" the sustainability discourse neglects to mention that the goals and conditions required to sustainably protect World Heritage are not new. They were already formulated in the preamble to the World Heritage Convention and – among other things – stipulate the following:

"Noting that the cultural heritage and the natural heritage are increasingly threatened with destruction not only by the traditional causes of decay, but also by changing social and economic conditions which aggravate the situation with even more formidable phenomena of damage or destruction, Considering that deterioration or disappearance of any item of the cultural or natural heritage constitutes a harmful impoverishment of the heritage of all the nations of the world, ... Considering that the existing international conventions, recommendations and resolutions concerning cultural and natural property demonstrate the importance, for all the peoples of the world, of safeguarding this unique and irreplaceable property, to whatever people it may belong, Considering that parts of the cultural or natural heritage are of outstanding interest and therefore need to be preserved as part of the World Heritage of mankind as a whole, ... Considering that, in view of the magnitude and gravity of the new dangers threatening them, it is incumbent on the international community as a whole to participate in the protection of the cultural and natural heritage of outstanding universal value, by the granting of collective assistance which, although not taking the place of action by the State concerned, will serve as an efficient complement thereto ..." (UNESCO, 1972).

Although these goals and related rationales as formulated in the preamble to the World Heritage Convention are more relevant today than ever, they are rarely explicitly cited in documents when justifying the need for sustainable development. For example they were cited in the final draft document, *World Heritage Convention and*

Sustainable Development, of the World Heritage Centre and Advisory Bodies (UNESCO, 2012) issued during the jubilee year of the World Heritage Convention 2012. In contextual terms they were inextricably linked to the notion of a *global strategy* and further important goals such as *community involvement* and *participation*. The final draft abstained from characterizing World Heritage as a value in and of itself, requiring sustainable protection and utilization guidelines; it rather stated that "preserving heritage and achieving sustainable development – intended as a development that incorporates social and environmental concerns – should not be understood as conflicting goals" (UNESCO, 2012, p. 3, article 16). Another function often attributed to heritage is its role as "driver for sustainable development" (UNESCO, 2011, p. 4; ICOMOS, 2011).

Here, the question needs to be raised, which fundamental societal developments have taken place over the more than forty years of implementing the World Heritage Convention that have on the one hand modified, and on the other hand relativized the immanence of the notion of sustainability as defined in the Convention itself. Has the underlying idea of heritage really changed in the meantime, or rather the concepts associated with sustainable development that have altered? Then, as today, the issue is how to deal with assets that are of the utmost importance for humanity and its future and must therefore be carefully preserved. This approach also served to identify the dangers to which these assets were exposed by the processes of modernization. Nothing has changed in this regard either. Today's threats mainly emanate from the commercial use of these sites for economic gain and related "political, economic, environmental and social pressures on heritage sites" (UNESCO, 2011, p. 4).

If we compare and contrast the significance that cultural heritage holds for mankind today with the rationale for preserving these sites as defined in 1972 in the preamble to the World Heritage Convention, it becomes clear that the reasons for preserving cultural assets have not changed over the past forty years. The 1972 Convention explicitly formulated a vision for the role of sustainability, which even today remains of the utmost significance. The question thus needs to be posed as to why these concerns are not presented in a more forthright fashion nowadays, but rather only indirectly. Why does the mission have to now be redefined using altered terminology, even though the substance of the matter has not changed? In my view, the perceptions of the importance of World Heritage and of sustainable development have changed in association with a wide-ranging paradigm shift within society itself. Heritage is understood less as a natural and cultural asset to be protected, but more and more as a commodity. While the sustainability paradigm is still based on the four cornerstones of social, economic, ecological and cultural development, it nevertheless currently popularizes these development goals as commercial products and brands.

In this publication, my aim is to inject opinions into the debate on sustainability and sustainable development in the context of heritage and World Heritage, and more strongly to link them with how the Convention was originally intended. This includes a look back at the original contexts underpinning the ideas of sustainability and sustainable development. I pose the question whether sustainability and sustainable development and their related concepts can still be reconciled with the originally stated goals. On the topic of how such concepts are employed in ongoing heritage dialogue, I would like to stimulate a return to the fundamental concepts of how to deal with the urgent matter of sustainable implementation of heritage and the methods required to achieve this aim.

This return to the original concepts of the epistemological and practical bases of heritage protection and utilization is already finding expression in our works published by de Gruyter in the series of discussions on Heritage Studies. Although penned by authors from various backgrounds, these discussions, entitled *Understanding Heritage: Perspectives in Heritage Studies* (Albert et al., 2013) provide the reader with a holistic understanding of heritage. Issues relating to heritage are dealt with in a most scientific and interdisciplinary manner; the purely commercial usurpation of the concept of heritage by for-profit interests in the form of labeling and branding is openly criticized. Similar ideas are also expressed in *40 Years World Heritage Convention – Popularizing the Protection of Cultural and Natural Heritage* (Albert and Ringbeck, 2015), in which the authors reflect on the populist implementation of the World Heritage Convention and the preponderance of commercial interests in this undertaking. They reveal how the concrete implementation of the World Heritage Convention has successively contradicted the original precepts of that document and they propose solutions to the problem. I refer to some of these options in my general introduction, as they are explicitly oriented to sustainability.

This publication is the fourth in the Heritage Studies series on the topic *Perceptions of Sustainability in Heritage Studies*. Inspired by the second International Summer Academy Cottbus: Understanding Heritage, held in July 2013 on the topic, The Theoretical Understanding of Sustainability in Heritage Studies and its Corresponding Disciplines, it seeks to theoretically differentiate the interrelated themes of heritage, while underpinning this core issue with important paradigms or documents. The main aim of the event was to give young researchers in Heritage Studies the opportunity to deepen their theoretical understanding of sustainability and to identify effective protection and utilization strategies for the different facets of heritage. This volume therefore includes papers by young researchers and professionals with very good reputations in both the subjects of sustainability and heritage, as well as their interdependence.

Against the backdrop of the political perceptions underlying the Heritage Studies series, in this paper I would like to focus on the key reflections and demands that have been so positively received during the lead-in phase to our discourse on sustainability, although in this case in the context of the "triumph of the term 'sustainable'" (Bauchmüller, 2014, p. 4), which has been "seized" by various interest groups and "abducted to another dimension".

Sustainable development and global policy

The precursors to reflections on sustainability and sustainable development range from Hans Carl von Carlowitz, whose concept of *Sylvicultura oeconomica* was formulated as early as 1713, to Dennis Meadows and the 1973 Club of Rome report on the limits of growth, in addition to the Brundtland Report *Our Common Future* (WCED, 1987). These antecedent concepts persistently championed sustainability by integrating the knowledge and acceptance of the inevitably ensuing "penury of resources" and "restriction of exploitation needs". This pertained to, and today continues to pertain to all kinds of resources, whether forests or the environment, raw materials or soil, water or the heritage of peoples. The various summit conferences elaborating on these fundamental positions, such as the 1992 UN Conference on Environment and Development, the follow-up meeting to the Rio Conference in New York in 2000 (Millennium Summit), and Millennium Development Goals (MDGs), continue to conclude that our living resources are indeed limited. However, these bodies have proffered few recommendations in terms of concrete measures to preserve resources that would impose self-restraint on people when going about their daily lives. Furthermore, the resilience required from both people and the environment to face such stresses is seldom emphasized. In the main, the international community perceives these goals as those of the UN, i. e. goals that still need to be realized in order to overcome the ongoing imbalance between the rich and poor nations. Such demands are completely justified. The question remains, however, whether or not these goals can be reached without restricting the everyday human activities associated with the social, economic, cultural and ecological needs of citizens.

The updating of these goals in terms of engendering a global adjustment of living conditions appears in 2012 on the occasion of the United Nations Conference on Sustainable Development (Rio+20). They also figure in the Post-2015 Development Agenda envisioning a more just world society in the broadest sense. As such, the important international recommendations for sustainable development, insofar as they are laid down in the Agenda, present sustainability as the point of access for all to the available resources. The related limitations pursuant to the exercise of personal or societal-economic and political activities are not explicitly disclosed. Quite rightly, justice here denotes access to all available resources. It remains unclear to what extent the issue of scarcity will have an altogether fatal future impact on the world population, as illustrated in reports published in the *Synthesis* bulletin concerning the fifth report of the Intergovernmental Panel on Climate Change (IPCC), presented on 2 November 2014 in Copenhagen (IPCC, 2014). This report was criticized in the international press as being a "mere" summation and cosmetic refurbishing of already released preliminary reports. Criticism was voiced that new knowledge had not been generated, in particular information on how to motivate societies to better deal with dwindling resources (Bojanowski, 2014). The urgent warning that global temperature increases should be limited to 2° Celsius was not new.

The current goals promoted by the international community can be labelled as "the future we want" (Open Working Group proposal for Sustainable Development Goals, 2014). These goals have crystallized again and again in the context of the sustainability discourse and, in line with these developments, they emphasize the need for more just distribution systems. This understanding that the just distribution of resources requires sacrifices from all users of such resources is only marginally significant in this discussion, or plays no role in it whatsoever. The creation of scientific advisory boards has very little impact here (Federal Ministry of Education and Research, 2014), for example the German federal government's own science advisory board on the topic of Changes in Global Environment with the stated goal of drafting a sustainable protection scheme entailing new responsibilities and outlining new architectures.

If in our perception of these developments we merge them with what is in fact a populist exploitation of the sustainability discourse, we can indeed recognize a change in the real substance of the issue. The term "sustainability can readily prompt accusations of 'false labeling'" (Bauchmüller, 2014, p. 8). It has been re-purposed as a kind of "meaningless advertising cliché" and is now even used as the "PR strategy of numerous companies accused of greenwashing" (ibid., p. 7). Concepts associated with sustainability have also changed. The current interpretations of a sustainable lifestyle are seen to take place in a new world. "It is a world of self-righteousness", where people live "'well' and 'sustainably', but in which no sacrifice is required". "This popular form of sustainability implies that conflicts arising due to finite resources can be solved by good will and a few technical innovations. Such public affirmations of the concept of sustainability are meant to pave the way for further unbridled growth. But that's not the way it works", recounts Michael Bauchmüller in his provocative article published in *Aus Politik und Zeitgeschichte* entitled Schönen Gruß aus der Zukunft *(Greetings from the Future)* (ibid., p. 4).

Bauchmüller further explains that "it lies in the very nature of sustainability ..., that it seeks to economize, and in doing so seeks more a just distribution ... of scarce resources. Inevitably this means that the promised gains for some will entail sacrifices from others over the long term. It is no surprise that the idea of sustainability finds relevancy outside the realm of ecology in those regions of the world where not only lip service is required, but where impending scarcities are indeed the order of the day – for instance in the distribution of contributions paid into the pension system against the backdrop of ongoing demographic change" (Bauchmüller, 2014, p. 4).

In *Think for Yourself: A Handbook for Resistance* (Welzer, 2013), the sociologist Harald Welzer is even more insistent than Bauchmüller, emphasizing how policy-makers still cling to the vision of an even more rosy future in the second half of the twenty-first century by propagating the exploitation of resources without restraints. In a reference to Norbert Elias, he describes how people are still in denial about global changes and about the effects it will have on them personally, rather than getting involved and actively addressing them. According to Welzer, "the people can't keep up" (Welzer, p. 13) which means they recognize the scarcities, but are not willing to change their behaviour in any way.

Visions

If the matter of sustainable development is ever to appropriately address the real existing scarcities, and in doing so to appropriately impact conscientious people on a sustained basis, the overall heritage discourse needs to indeed revive approaches such as these. Various actors have proffered numerous recommendations in this regard. Among the most important and well known are those suggested by Amartya Sen; in *The Idea of Justice* (Sen, 2009) he focuses on people and their existing abilities, which he perceives as a valuable resource in terms of achieving a "good and sustainable life". Sen also directly emphasizes the responsibility we human beings must assume for the world in the future. Based on the concept of empowerment "the capability approach focuses on human lives, and not just on the resources people have, in the form of owning – or having use of – objects of convenience that a person may possess" (ibid., p. 253). The concept of responsibility is a fascinating one, especially when dealing with heritage; it encompasses all actors and not just those who identify with their own humanity and humanity as a whole, but also those actors who exploit the issue for monetary gain.

If in the context of the sustainable development of human heritage we focus on the aspect of scarcity, yet another alternative can be constructed. Common global goods are also a dwindling resource, as identified and established as early as 1990 by Elinor Ostrom in *Governing the Commons: The Evolution of Institutions for Collective Action* (Ostrom, 1990). According to her, the notion of "commons" seeks to convince the public that scarce resources such as air, water and human heritage should be seen as neither private nor public assets, but rather as common resources which need to be handled as such. The community made up of responsible citizens bears the responsibility for such common resources. The sustainability of human heritage is accordingly a reflection of the cultural and natural assets of responsible citizens wishing to maintain such assets in order to preserve their own identity. People seeking to preserve their heritage as an expression of their own identity are willing to assume responsibility in this regard. These are the very framework conditions that can enable people to adjust their needs to ensure the sustainable use of such heritage.

Particularly because Ostrom does not frame her argument in terms of categories, preferring to emphasize common assets rather than assets requiring protection, this paradigm provides new options in terms of strengthening the outreach to civil society. It is therefore not only a question of revising approaches to scarcity or its mitigation, but rather of framing it as a core issue. The aim is to mobilize responsibility for these assets and to create a sense that life without common goods is less worth living. The consequence of this is a concept that promotes sustainability, one that emphasizes knowledge and awareness beyond the constraints of purely morality and politically based arguments.

Once people are empowered with the knowledge they need it will be easier for them to assume direct responsibility and to recognize that "their heritage" is in fact the heritage of all peoples, and thus needs to be protected as a common asset. Empowerment is closely related to calls for broader participation. The notion of empowerment is, however, also based on a multidisciplinary approach that finds expression in societal and democratic commitments in sociocultural and economic contexts, in medicine or active citizenship and can be explained on the basis of political science methodology (Knuf et al., 2007; Herriger, 2002; Choudhury, 2009). Participation and empowerment are important dimensions in achieving sustainable protection and utilization of heritage. These dimensions have yet to undergo real scientific scrutiny in this very context. It is in this light that the dimension of empowerment can also afford new options in terms of implementing the sustainable development and World Heritage concepts.

The discussion on possible approaches or paradigms to achieve a better understanding of sustainability in Heritage Studies has only started. Those offered in this publication are by no means exhaustive. Nevertheless, in line with the objectives of the Heritage Studies series and based on the notion that the sustainable development and heritage need to be perceived as the guiding principles for the twenty-first century, with this publication we are urging our readers to move forward: whether by way of theoretical-abstract reflections or by empowering civil society to accept and implement both the concrete mission and theoretical vision of the sustainable development of heritage.

References

Albert, M.-T., Bernecker, R. and Rudolff, B. 2013. *Understanding Heritage. Perspectives in Heritage Studies.* Berlin, Walter de Gruyter.

Albert, M.-T. and Ringbeck, B. 2015. *40 Years World Heritage Convention – Popularizing the Protection of Cultural and Natural Heritage.* Berlin, Walter de Gruyter.

Bauchmüller, M. 2014. Schönen Gruß aus der Zukunft. In: *Aus Politik und Zeitgeschichte,* 64. Jahrgang 31–32/2014. Bonn, Bundeszentrale für politische Bildung. pp. 3–6.

Bojanowski, A. 2014. *Finaler Report des IPCC: Beim Weltklimarat geht Alarm vor Genauigkeit.* http://www.spiegel.de/wissenschaft/natur/klimawandel-finaler-bericht-des-ipcc-a-1000432.html (Accessed 10 November 2014.)

Choudhury, N. 2009. The question of empowerment: women's perspective on their internet use. *Gender, Technology and Development,* Vol. 13, No. 3, pp. 341–63.

Federal Ministry of Education and Research. 2014. *Wissenschaftlicher Beirat der Bundesregierung Globale Umweltveränderungen (WBGU).* http://www.bmbf.de/de/13296.php (Accessed 10 November 2014.)

Herriger, N. 2002. *Empowerment in der sozialen Arbeit.* Stuttgart, Kohlhammer.

ICOMOS 2011. *Heritage, a Driver of Development. Rising to the Challenge*. Paris, ICOMOS.
IPCC. 2014. *IPCC Fifth Assessment Synthesis Report*. Intergovernmental Panel on Climate Change. http://www.ipcc.ch/pdf/assessment-report/ar5/syr/SYR_AR5_LONGERREPORT.pdf (Accessed 17 November 2014.)
Knuf, A., Osterfeld, M. and Seibert, U. 2007. Selbstbefähigung fördern. *Empowerment und psychiatrische Arbeit*. 5. überarb. Auflage. Bonn, Psychiatrie-Verlag.
Open Working Group proposal for Sustainable Development Goals. 2014. *Sustainable Development Goals*. http://sustainabledevelopment.un.org/focussdgs.html (Accessed 10 November 2014.)
Ostrom, E. 1990. *Governing the Commons: The Evolution of Institutions for Collective Action*. Cambridge, UK, Cambridge University Press.
Sen, A. 2009. *The Idea of Justice*. Cambridge, Mass., Harvard University Press.
UNESCO. 1972. Convention concerning the Protection of the World Cultural and Natural Heritage. Paris. http://whc.unesco.org/archive/convention-en.pdf (Accessed 17 November 2014.)
UNESCO. 2011. *Strategic Action Plan for the Implementation of the World Heritage Convention 2012–2022. Future of the World Heritage Convention*. Document WHC-11/18.GA/11, Paris, 1 August. http://whc.unesco.org/archive/2011/whc11-18ga-11-en.pdf (Accessed 10 November 2014.)
UNESCO. 2012. *World Heritage Convention and Sustainable Development*. Report of the World Heritage Centre and Advisory Bodies. Document WHC-12/36.COM/5C, Paris, 11 May. http://whc.unesco.org/archive/2012/whc12-36com-5C-en.pdf (Accessed 10 November 2014.)
von Weizsäcker, E., Hargroves, K., Smith, M., Desha, C. and Stasinopoulos, P. 2009. *Factor Five: Transforming the Global Economy through 80 % Improvements in Resource Productivity*. London, Earthscan.
WCED. 1987. *Report of the World Commission on Environment and Development: Our Common Future* (Brundtland Report). New York, United Nations. http://www.un-documents.net/wced-ocf.htm
Welzer, H. 2013. *Selbst denken. Eine Anleitung zum Widerstand*. Frankfurt am Main, Germany, Fischer.

Culture in Moving the MDGs to the Post-2015 Development Agenda: Some Reflections on the Role of Living Heritage for Sustainable Development[1]

Minja Yang

Introduction

The role of heritage, or more generally culture, has largely been absent in the mainstream sustainable development debate despite its vital role in the functioning of societies. Reference to cultural heritage, if at all, has been limited as "assets" to generate employment and revenue through tourism, with justification for investments in the conservation of monuments, sites, museums and heritage festivals, primarily measured in terms of the number of tourists, often calculated merely by the rate of occupancy of hotel beds or entry ticket sales to museums and monuments. While cultural tourism is indeed, an increasingly important economic sector with tremendous potential for development based on sustainable low-impact use of resources with high employment-generation possibilities, the "cultural dimension" of development requires recognition that far exceeds the tourism sector. This paper focuses on Agenda 21 for Culture of the United Cities and Local Governments (UCLG) international organization as an operational "charter" for local authorities in integrating culture in the development process, and presents some reflections on the linkages between heritage, culture and sustainable development. Drawn primarily from my personal and professional experience gained from my own multicultural upbringing and thirty-five years of work in "development" as an UN official with the United Nations High Commissioner for Refugees (UNHCR) and the United Nations Educational, Scientific and Cultural Organization (UNESCO), it has no pretension of being an academic paper but is based on my conviction that "culture, as the foundation of the spiritual values, lifestyles and livelihoods of communities worldwide, is vital for social cohesion and peace" (UNESCO, 2001)[2] particularly in increasingly multicultural societies often composed of people of pluricultural identities living simultaneously in different socio-economic stages defined by diverse modes of production and varied means of production in the globalized world of our times.

---

1 This is an adapted version of an article written for United Cities and Local Governments in August 2014.
2 UNESCO Declaration on Cultural Diversity adopted in 2001.

In reflecting on the role of heritage in sustainable development, the starting point is to define what "heritage" is and also clarify the multidimensional notion of "sustainable development". While there are many definitions of "heritage", this paper uses the concept of heritage as defined by UNESCO, notably in the 2001 UNESCO Declaration on Cultural Diversity, "as the set of distinctive spiritual, material, intellectual and emotional features of society or a social group, and that it encompasses, in addition to art and literature, lifestyles, ways of living together, value systems, traditions and beliefs".

Under this broad definition of culture, heritage becomes a repository of knowledge that allows communities and groups to respond to their basic needs, while providing them with a sense of identity and continuity which is also a source of innovation that enables the development of creative approaches to respond to new challenges facing societies.[3] Therefore, culture is fundamental in shaping the attitudes of people and communities in the process of adaptation to access adequate nutrition, clean water, health care, decent work and quality education, as well as in their interaction with the environment, both built and natural, which have been the aims of the Millennium Development Goals (MDGs).

It is regrettable that UNESCO has not been designated a major role or funding for the implementation of the MDGs, when "culture" and "heritage" are of cross-cutting importance in the attainment of all the targets of this international agenda. This can perhaps be attributed to several reasons: (1) that UNESCO's broad intersectoral mandate, from all aspects of education, the sciences, culture and communications, has not permitted the Organization to have the critical mass of personnel or budget in any of its programmes to become operational in the field, especially in developing countries where most of the MDG activities have been concentrated; (2) being more of a normative and standard-setting organization, despite its expertise as a specialized agency of the UN system, it lacks rapid intervention capacity; and (3) in spite of its globally-recognized experience in culture, the international community and the UN lead agencies driving the MDG process have a poor understanding of "culture" and have associated UNESCO's cultural mandate primarily with the safeguarding of monuments and sites.

Since the establishment of UNESCO in 1945 as a specialized agency of the United Nations whose mandate includes culture, the safeguarding of cultural heritage has become one of the Organization's most appreciated and visible activity. Yet this cultural heritage mandate needs to be seen in the context of the UNESCO Constitution, the preamble of which reads *inter alia:*

"That since wars begin in the minds of men, it is in the minds of men that the defenses of peace must be constructed; that ignorance of each other's ways and lives has been a common cause ... of suspicion and mistrust between the peoples of the

3 See UNESCO Convention for the Safeguarding of the Intangible Cultural Heritage adopted in 2003.

world through which their differences have all too often broken into war; that the wide diffusion of culture, and the education of humanity for justice and liberty and peace are indispensable to the dignity of man and constitute a sacred duty which all the nations must fulfill in a spirit of mutual assistance and concern; ... [through] free exchange of ideas and knowledge ... to develop and to increase the means of communication between their peoples and to employ these means for the purposes of mutual understanding and a truer and more perfect knowledge of each other's lives" (UNESCO, 1945).

Thus, from the outset, UNESCO's concern for the conservation of cultural heritage, largely tangible, but also intangible, has been inextricably linked to cultural dialogue for peace through mutual understanding between civilizations.

International solidarity which emerged over the 1959 campaign to save Abu Simbel in Upper Egypt from flooding led to one of UNESCO's most visible programmes, that of the conservation of monuments and sites, focused on international safeguarding campaigns, and subsequently since 1972 in activities for the World Heritage Convention, which is without doubt the most recognized activity of the Organization.

The Universal Declaration on Cultural Diversity released in 2001, however, brought greater visibility to the founding principles of UNESCO's cultural mandate for peace, which had hitherto been treated under the promotion of "cultural pluralism" in a rather theoretical manner little known to the general public. The global signature campaign on the Manifesto 2000 for a Culture for Peace (UNESCO, 1996) launched by the Director-General Federico Mayor in 1996, which led to the UN General Assembly's declaration of the International Year for the Culture of Peace in 1997, brought about a greater focus on UNESCO's peace mandate based on intercultural dialogue. The Universal Declaration on Cultural Diversity further concretized this by noting "that each individual must acknowledge not only otherness in all its forms but also the plurality of his or her own identity, within societies that are themselves plural. Only in this way can cultural diversity be preserved as an adaptive process and as a capacity for expression, creation and innovation. The debate between those countries which defend cultural goods and services 'which, as vectors of identity, values and meaning, must not be treated as mere commodities or consumer goods', and those which would hope to promote cultural rights has thus been surpassed with the two approaches brought together by the Declaration, which has highlighted the causal link uniting two complementary attitudes".[4]

To be sure, this Declaration was timely in view of the new forms of religious and ethnic-based armed conflict and terrorist actions which were engulfing various corners of the world on the one hand, while on the other, free trade agreements on cultural goods and services were also becoming a hotly debated issue in the globalization of

4 See Preface by Director-General Koïchiro Matsuura (2001) in the Universal Declaration on Cultural Diversity.

the knowledge economy. UNESCO's credibility over the Declaration was also heightened by the global interest and recognition of the importance of the World Heritage Convention, particularly with the evolution in the notion of heritage, which had shifted from the monument-centric focus on architectural masterworks to cultural landscapes depicting "combined works of nature and humankind ... [that] express a long and intimate relationship between peoples and their natural environment" (UNESCO, n. d.) which is fundamental to the sustainable development concept. As such, the 2001 Declaration on Cultural Diversity and the 1972 World Heritage Convention, notably through the "site management plan" requisite, were becoming a recognized tool for sustainable development, capable of humanizing globalization through the promotion of new ethics to accompany the development process. The Declaration notes cultural diversity as the common heritage of humanity, and equates its necessity to that of biodiversity for nature. It provides, above all, general guidelines to be turned into policies and operational programmes by Member States in partnership with the private sector and civil society.[5]

Much has been written on the overall concept of sustainable development since the presentation of the concept by the Club of Rome in its 1972 report *The Limits to Growth* (Meadows et al., 1972). Further elaborated in 1987 by the so-called Brundtland Report of the United Nations World Commission on Environment and Development on *Our Common Future* (WCED, 1987), and followed by the 1992 Earth Charter (Earth Charter Commission, 1992) released at the United Nations Conference on Environment and Development held in Rio de Janeiro, when the focus shifted increas-

---

5 The Declaration promotes the principle that "culture takes diverse forms across time and space. This diversity is embodied in the uniqueness and plurality of the identities of the groups and societies making up humankind. As a source of exchange, innovation and creativity, cultural diversity is as necessary for humankind as biodiversity is for nature. In this sense, it is the common heritage of humanity and should be recognized and affirmed for the benefit of present and future generations" (UNESCO, 2001, article 1); emphasizes the understanding of moving from cultural diversity to cultural pluralism. "In our increasingly diverse societies, it is essential to ensure harmonious interaction among people and groups with plural, varied and dynamic cultural identities as well as their willingness to live together. Policies for the inclusion and participation of all citizens are guarantees of social cohesion, the vitality of civil society and peace. Thus defined, cultural pluralism gives policy expression to the reality of cultural diversity. Indissociable from a democratic framework, cultural pluralism is conducive to cultural exchange and to the flourishing of creative capacities that sustain public life" (ibid., article 2); ... delineates cultural diversity as a factor in development. "Cultural diversity widens the range of options open to everyone; it is one of the roots of development, understood not simply in terms of economic growth, but also as a means to achieve a more satisfactory intellectual, emotional, moral and spiritual existence" (ibid., article 3); cultural diversity presupposes the respect for human rights. "The defence of cultural diversity is an ethical imperative, inseparable from respect for human dignity. It implies a commitment to human rights and fundamental freedoms, in particular the rights of persons belonging to minorities and those of indigenous peoples. No one may invoke cultural diversity to infringe upon human rights guaranteed by international law, nor to limit their scope" (ibid., article 4).

ingly to poverty alleviation and on the multifaceted dimension of development with interdependent pillars of the economic, environmental and social aspects of human development. The action plan Agenda 21 (UN, 1992), which sets targets for the UN, other multilateral organizations, and individual governments around the world that can be executed at local, national and global levels, launched at the Rio Conference, has subsequently become an important operational tool for implementation of sustainable development objectives. It identified information, integration and participation as key building blocks to help countries achieve development that recognizes these interdependent pillars and stressed the need for new approaches that involve cross-sectoral coordination and the integration of environmental and social concerns into all development processes (UN, 1992).

UNESCO, among a few other institutions, has subsequently pointed out that a fourth dimension, that of culture, should be added to the three dimensions of sustainable development (economic, environmental and social) in order to reflect better on the complexity of contemporary society. In recognizing the process of growing political decentralization and the vital role of local authorities in the implementation of policies and programmes in an intersectoral framework, UCLG took the lead in the preparation of Agenda 21 for Culture (UCLG, 2008) which was adopted by cities and local governments from around the world on 8 May 2004 at a forum held in Barcelona (Spain). It was further developed as a policy statement, Culture: Fourth Pillar of Sustainable Development (UCLG, 2010) and officially adopted on 17 November 2010, at the World Summit of Local and Regional Leaders – 3rd World Congress of UCLG, held in Mexico City.

Within ten years, since 2004, Agenda 21 for Culture has succeeded in being endorsed by some 500 cities and local authorities. Being more of a charter, setting out a series of principles, rather than a Plan of Action, Agenda 21 for Culture has necessarily been left for UCLG-member cities and governments to implement in accordance with their local conditions. Given the specificities of the national and local contexts and the diversity in sociocultural, economic, legal and fiscal systems, and moreover, in the degree of decentralization attained, any international agenda, particularly on the cultural dimension of development, can only serve as a guideline. Case studies on cultural policies, programmes and projects are however now emerging as local authorities volunteer to showcase their actions as pilot cities of UCLG. It is clear that the difference in the realities of North and South (to use these terms for the sake of convenience), and even within these broad groupings of nations, require each city and local authority to establish its own plan of action. In offering a few suggestions on how to proceed in turning theory into practice, and in linking these to the ongoing global discussions on the Post-2015 Development Agenda, let me start by repeating the principles for the benefit of the uninitiated.

The principles of Agenda 21 for Culture are intertwined with those enunciated in the global call for sustainable development, notably with regard to human rights – social, economic and cultural rights of groups as well as of individuals, which cover concerns over issues as wide as environment protection, climate change, risk mitigation, equitable access to basic utilities particularly to water, and services – ranging from education, housing and healthcare to the more specific access relating to employable skills, creative cultural and artistic expressions, and all that can be qualified as impacting on the quality of life. In this regard, Agenda 21 for Culture, prepared in cooperation with international and regional normative and standard-setting entities, notably of the United Nations system, adopted the UNESCO (2001) definition of "culture". Article 3 of Agenda 21 for Culture reaffirms that cultural rights are an integral part of human rights, taking as their reference, the Universal Declaration of Human Rights (1948), The International Covenant on Economic, Social and Cultural Rights (1966) and the UNESCO Universal Declaration on Cultural Diversity (2001), noting that cultural freedom of individuals and communities is an essential condition for democracy. The necessity of local governments to adopt and act on this Agenda was stressed in view of the current economic development models that prey on natural resources and common goods of humanity causing increasing concern for the environment, and of establishing political analogies that exist between cultural and ecological questions, with both culture and the environment being common assets of humanity (article 2).

Further links were made between Agenda 21 for Culture and the Millennium Development Goals (MDGs) and other internationally agreed development goals, the attainment of which was pledged by local governments, both through their national governments and collectively through UCLG. It is in this regard that UCLG has been involved in the international process over the past four years in evaluating the achievements of the MDGs and in framing the Post-2015 Development Agenda. Some of the most important post-2015 policy documents have underscored the importance of culture for sustainable development, including UN General Assembly Resolutions N. 65/1 (Keeping the Promise: United to Achieve the Millennium Development Goals, 2010), N. 65/166 (2011) and N. 66/208 (2012) on Culture and Development, as well as a number of other relevant declarations, statements and normative instruments adopted at international, regional and national levels. The outcome document of the UN Conference on Sustainable Development, *The Future We Want* (Rio de Janeiro, June 2012) highlighted the importance of cultural diversity and the need for a more holistic and integrated approach to sustainable development.

The Hangzhou Declaration, Placing Culture at the Heart of Sustainable Development Policies, of 17 May 2013, resulting from the UNESCO International Congress on Culture: Key to Sustainable Development, reaffirms the "urgent need for new approaches" that "account for a broader picture of human progress", such as "harmony among peoples and between humans and nature, equity" (UNESCO, 2013, p. 2) and calls for the acknowledgement of "culture" as a system of values and knowledge capital, and as an enabler of sustainability as a source of meaning, creativity and innovation and a resource to address challenges in order to find appropriate solutions through people-centred and place-based approaches. It stresses, above all, that different cultural perspectives will result in different paths to development, noting that "one size fits all" policies cannot work.

How exactly can these rather theoretical "wish all" principles be turned into action? In what way can governments respond to such calls to put culture at the heart of future policies for sustainable development? Let us look at how culture can be an enabler in the achievement of the eight international development goals established in 2000 following the adoption of the United Nations Millennium Declaration.[6]

The MDGs were targeted primarily for the nations of the South, but they have also served in addressing issues of poverty in those of the North, just as the rights-based approach of Agenda 21 for Culture transcends the divide between North and South. In reviewing the eight MDGs from the perspective of how success could have been better achieved with greater understanding of the role of culture in the development process, and of the role local governments could have or should have been enabled to play, the limitation of a sectorial approach in gauging the attainment of these goals must be stressed. While "quantifiable" targets are necessary, especially to justify the investment of development aid funds and of course, national and local government expenditures, the interlinkages between these eight goals make "measurable results" very difficult, if not impossible for some of the individual goals. Numerous studies carried out primarily from the sectorial approach generally conclude with criticism of the "top-down" approach and the lack of local participation. Over-emphasis on the macro-economic aspects as well as the purely economic approach in gauging success has also been raised as a concern. The fact that more than half of the aid from developed countries goes to debt relief and an important proportion of the remaining funds is used for disaster relief and military aid perhaps explains the reason for the top-down approach and the almost exclusive dependence on the national state mechanism, with all its known limitations (UN, 2006).

The High Level Panel on the Post-2015 Development Agenda noted that "economic growth alone is not sufficient to ensure social justice, equity and sustained prosperity for all people ... protection and empowerment of people is crucial" (UN, 2012*b*).[7]

6 All 189 United Nations Member States at the time (currently 193) and at least 23 international organizations committed to help achieve the Millennium Development Goals by 2015:
1. eradicate extreme poverty and hunger; 2. achieve universal primary education; 3. promote gender equality and empowering women; 4. reduce child mortality rates; 5. improve maternal health; 6. combat HIV/AIDS, malaria, and other diseases; 7. ensure environmental sustainability; 8. develop a global partnership for development (UN, 2000).

7 The High Level Panel on the Post-2015 Development Agenda, appointed by United Nations Secretary-General Ban Ki-moon in July 2012, was co-chaired by President Susilo Bambang Yudhoyono of Indonesia; President Ellen Johnson Sirleaf of Liberia; and Prime Minister David Cameron of the United Kingdom.

It is hard to imagine how the cultural dimension in poverty eradication, hunger relief, education, gender equity, child and maternal health, or the combat against HIV/AIDS, or the protection of the environment can be ignored. Yet it has been. Despite the growing proportion of the world population now living in urban settlements where adherence to "tradition" may be less pronounced than in the rural area of their origin, the strong social and economic ties that the recent migrants have to their ethnic and religious group or to their clan, especially in the alien land of the city, cannot be ignored. Poverty may be even more pronounced in the city, hence create greater dependence on the sociocultural network to survive. Particularly in the cities of many developing countries where governance and the rule of law are weak, if not altogether absent, community control takes over. This self-help type of community welfare can be excellent, also in the delivery of development aid to the poor, but requires oversight by public authorities to ensure that community traditions are not oppressive and undemocratic. Social welfare policies and programmes, whether for health care or education, as well as access to basic survival needs such as drinking water and its distribution, have extremely important culture-based practices that must be understood by the local authorities responsible for the delivery of services.

As a follow-up to the MDGs, on 30 May 2013 the UN unveiled a new report, *A New Global Partnership: Eradicate Poverty and Transform Economies through Sustainable Development* (UN, 2013), prepared by the High Level Panel on the Post-2015 Development Agenda, setting out a universal agenda up to 2030. The non-sectoral, or more positively intersectoral, approach of this call stresses social inclusion and employment creation through partnerships at all levels, and good governance through transparency can perhaps be translated more aptly into action by local governments and civil society around the world than the MDGs, which primarily target governments to introduce local change through external innovations supported by external financing. The Post-2015 Agenda lays great emphasis on community initiative, building from resources of solidarity and local growth within existing sociocultural and government structures.

The following are a few examples of concrete actions that can be undertaken by municipal and local governments to translate the global and theoretical principles referred to above into local policies, programmes and projects.

1.) *Leave no one behind:* It is clear that authorities at the lowest administrative level of the governance structure – be they village councils or wards in a city council, are better placed to identify the different forms of extreme poverty. Hence any form of financial or food subsidies for the poor can best be distributed at this level. In countries where no form of public subsidies can be expected, the local government could establish an anti-poverty unit or at least assign an officer to look into local support mechanisms, by soliciting the support of local NGOs and CBOs. Entrepreneurs can also be solicited more effectively by local authorities to offer jobs to local residents and participate in social welfare actions. Despite the different nature and degree of poverty, application of the notion of "shared poverty"[8] can be studied to see how local wealth and resources can be better distributed, without resorting to excessive taxation that would only cripple the local economy. In order not to create dependency on free provision of food and shelter, local governments should ensure that the recipients of such aid participate in public or private work. Food-for-work projects implemented in the South can also be applied to promote urban agriculture in the cities of the South as well as the North so that citizens can participate in the local production of food, even if it may only provide a small proportion of local food needs.[9] Urban agriculture permits citizens, especially youth, to stay in touch with the fundamental importance of nature. To study the causes of poverty and to adopt equitable measures in the fight against it, public authorities should solicit the support of universities and research institutions to carry out socio-economic surveys as well as scientific research with the view of finding appropriate solutions to local problems. The optimization of the sociocultural capital, including traditional practices, which can be considered as "intangible heritage", are more important foundations of a society from which innovations can be made than the importation of management practices which may be alien to the local communities.

2.) *Put sustainable development at the core:* If the all-encompassing notion of "sustainable development" (UCLG, 2010) is defined to cover economic, ecological, political and cultural[10] sustainability, and as "development that meets the needs of the present without compromising the ability of future generations to meet their own needs"[11] (WCED, 1987) local governments must start by taking stock of local assets, including the natural and built heritage to understand the "what, why and how" of the existing physical, economic and social infrastructure came into being. Analyses of locally based companies and factories are crucial to determine public policies and programmes that can support the business sector to maintain employment of the local population, to adopt anti-pollution and energy-efficient measures. When upgrading of skills for jobs or new technological advancements for industries are necessary, local authorities can foster partnerships with education and skills training institutions as well as with scientific research bodies. The growth of cities should be anticipated and territorial extensions avoided as much as possible in favour of densification to prevent urban sprawl that places further stress on public utility systems and services. Existing housing

8 This term, initially coined by Clifford Geertz for his study on Javanese rural societies, has evolved over the years to mean the sharing of scarce resources for the survival of a community.

9 Interesting programmes on urban agriculture exist in the North as well as the South, e.g. Strasbourg (France), Luang Prabang (Lao PDR).

10 UCLG puts "culture" as the fourth pillar of sustainable development (UCLG, 2010).

11 Definition as per Brundtland Commission in its 1987 report, *Our Common Future* (WCED, 1987).

stock, especially in the historic centres, should be maintained through adaptive reuse of historic buildings, not only for the conservation of the built heritage but for the historic centre to be inhabited and integrated into the larger city, rather than allowing it to degrade as a settlement for the poor or become gentrified as an oasis for tourists. Moreover, a new paradigm of urban growth needs to be promoted through adoption of urban design, building standards and regulations that favour compact cities and the retrofitting of existing buildings, which cause fewer environmental impacts than demolition and new construction as in the recent past. Historic cities can offer examples of density, mixed use, mixed tenure, energy efficiency and reduced vehicular circulation, with greater harmony between the natural and built environments. Local governments, in this regard, must make available mass public transport systems to provide an alternative to individual vehicles and preserve public space for the residents instead of individual cars. To finance such public transport systems, participation by companies employing more than a given number of staff (to be determined case by case) and schools for the transport of pupils should be sought either through taxes or through financial or in-kind contributions, depending on the local situation. Whereas mobility is indeed a service that should be provided, or at least facilitated, by the public authority, innovative public-private partnerships and even voluntarism should be sought if public funds are insufficient. The system of car-sharing between private individuals should also be promoted and facilitated through government policies, taking into consideration the cultural sensitivities of the target population. The principle of "polluters pay" should be applied for both the trucking of goods and passenger vehicles. The overarching idea of soft urban transport is to reduce vehicular congestion and pollution in the process of "humanizing" the city.

In finding measures to combat environmental degradation – whether of air, water, solid waste or other – local authorities should seek the engagement of all stakeholders with a view to reducing the cause of pollution as well as treating the waste. Public awareness-raising being the key to reducing environmental degradation, local authorities should prompt the preparation and diffusion of culturally adapted didactic public information material, jointly with the communities concerned, supported by educators and communication professionals on all aspects of environmental protection relating to their locality. In all these sectors concerned with sustainable development, local governments can make better use of "heritage" defined as the sum of existing assets, and "culture" defined as the dynamics of social relations, by mobilizing socio-cultural networks that constitute the basis for positive community resilience and action including the introduction of innovations.

3.) *Transform economies for jobs and inclusive growth:* While noting the importance of profit-based economic growth, the recent economic crises have shown that the global economy must be geared for the creation of local employment and sustained local economic growth to ensure citizens' livelihood and social development. Without this, progress in human and social development would depend on external and domestic transfer mechanisms of aid and redistribution of public spending, with their inherent limitations. Local authorities need to adopt policies to secure productive job opportunities and translate growth to social development. Local governments all over the world have shown the importance of their role in soliciting private sector investments in their territory. Concessionary lease of public land or tax benefits under transparent procedures to solicit the implantation of private companies to create employment opportunities is now current practice everywhere in the world. As land-ownership has strong cultural roots, it is vital that all communities be fairly treated, as many cases exist of certain ethnic groups being dispossessed of their traditional right to property. While noting the principles of fair competition, local governments when issuing public contracts are increasingly including in their selection criteria aspects such as employment or training benefits for local residents, particularly of marginalized groups, so that employment becomes a means of social integration. More diversified economies can be promoted by capitalizing on the cultural diversity of the citizens with the valorization of their cultural assets, both tangible and intangible, in order to promote the creative cultural industries, going beyond that of tourism. Local governments can thus foster socially inclusive and environmentally friendly policies. There are interesting examples of local government support for cultural business incubators, notably for young designers, crafters, artists and IT start-ups who have succeeded thanks to municipal government provision of low-rent or rent-free shops and offices for an initial period of two to three years, or soft loans from a revolving micro-credit system for cultural industries.[12] In the selection of places to invest companies give importance to the city's attractiveness, which is greatly valorized by its cultural heritage and natural setting forming important public spaces, in addition of course to security and good educational facilities. Urban heritage is also a valuable endowment with vast non-economic development potential to strengthen social ties through identity and improved livability of the city.

4.) *Build peace and effective, open and accountable institutions for all:* If decentralization is considered the best mechanism for democratic participatory governance, it must come together with the decentralization of technical competence and financial means. Despite a third of the Official Development Assistance (ODA) channelled to the fifty Least Developed Countries, the lack of funds trickling down to local level has not proved effective in promoting local development. The

12 Among the many examples are success stories in Lyon and Strasbourg (France), as well as in Saint-Louis (Senegal) and Porto Novo (Benin) on business incubators of cultural industries.

tasks of local authorities multiply in facing the multifarious challenges of governance with limited funds and personnel. With multi-ethnicity being a reality in almost every city today, the management of cultural diversity to avoid ethnic-based conflict is becoming an important task for local governments, which can be close enough to the different communities to foster tolerance and pre-empt tension, and above all to promote equity among communities through socially inclusive policies. Honest and accountable governance being a precondition of successful decentralization, local governments can hardly exercise good governance if the national government is dishonest and undemocratic in the distribution of budgetary resources. Local governments can nonetheless foster cooperation among community-based associations and seek their support in grass-roots governance through equitable and transparent distribution of resources, even if they may only amount to seed funds to generate partnerships and co-finance necessary services. Even if the local authority is not able to provide financial subsidies, an inclusive approach by creating a platform for civil society involvement in urban projects has proven effective in many countries.

5.) *Forge a new global partnership:* This fifth point on solidarity, cooperation and mutual accountability calls for new forms of people-focused partnership for inclusive development, linking national and local governments, multilateral institutions, civil society organizations, and the scientific and academic community, businesses and private philanthropy. This arises from the recognition that public authorities cannot on their own deliver social programmes to reach the people, particularly vulnerable groups. While no specific mention is made of the importance of culture, it is again clear that greater understanding of the sociocultural specificities of vulnerable groups is required as well as the participation of civil society groups, particularly CBOs and other associations that are culturally linked to the target beneficiaries. As referred to above, forging alliance with universities and research entities is vital to develop sustainable development actions adapted for the local situation.

UNESCO World Heritage Centre's involvement in the promotion of the Outstanding Universal Value of sites such as Luang Prabang (Lao PDR), the Grande Ile de Strasbourg (France), or Saint-Louis (Senegal) as a tool for sustainable urban and territorial development beyond the core protected area can have demonstration value. Reinforcing the strong "nature-culture links" between the river and built environment in these three cities and the convivial historic urban pattern replicated in the new town extension area, as well as the soft transport mode, and promoting mixed-use, mixed-tenure policies throughout the greater city based on principles of socio-equity and valorization of living heritage founded on the strength of local cultural identity for the promotion of creative industries, can serve as examples of cultural and natural heritage-sensitive development in the new globally connected knowledge-based economy.

In conclusion, culture being omnipresent in all aspects of social dynamics, knowledge and management of cultural diversity in the promotion of development goals are of vital importance. If harnessed positively, and with democratic principles of equity and transparency, differences between communities can be worked out through consultations to reach the necessary compromises required for collective interest, as long as governments, particularly local authorities, provide the enabling environment to play its role as mediator with fairness and direction. With regard to the built environment, especially of the city, its heritage represents an important physical and socio-economic capital accumulated by the local residents and the city government through investments of knowledge and labour over long periods, giving character to the city's identity and wealth to be optimized for the present and the future with public education for sustainable practices. Sustainable development is not the sum total of the Post-2015 Development Agenda nor of the MDGs, as it is a "humanization process" where success can only be attained when the common interest of "civilization" of all nations and peoples is understood and pursued. In this regard, Agenda 21 for Culture is not only the fourth pillar of development but a transversal principle that needs to be integrated in good governance.

References

Earth Charter Commission. 1992. *The Earth Charter.* http://www.earthcharterinaction.org/invent/images/uploads/echarter_english.pdf (Accessed 18 November 2014.)

Matsuura, K. 2001. Universal Declaration on Cultural Diversity. Paris, UNESCO, p. 11. http://unesdoc.unesco.org/images/0012/001271/127160m.pdf (Accessed 18 November 2014.)

Meadows, D. H., Meadows, D. L., Randers, J. and Behrens III, W. W. 1972. *The Limits to Growth – a report for the Club of Rome's project on the predicament of mankind.* New York, New American Library.

UNESCO. n. d. Website on Cultural Landscapes. Paris, UNESCO. http://whc.unesco.org/en/culturallandscape/ (Accessed 18 November 2014.)

UNESCO. 1945. UNESCO Constitution. In: *Basic Texts – 2014 edition.* Paris, UNESCO. pp. 5–18.

UNESCO. 1996. *Manifesto 2000 for a Culture of Peace and Non-Violence.* Paris, UNESCO. http://www3.unesco.org/manifesto2000/uk/uk_manifeste.htm (Accessed 18 November 2014.)

UNESCO. 2001. Universal Declaration on Cultural Diversity. Paris, UNESCO. http://unesdoc.unesco.org/images/0012/001271/127160m.pdf (Accessed 18 November 2014.)

UNESCO. 2013. The Hangzhou Declaration – Placing Culture at the Heart of Sustainable Development Policies. Paris, UNESCO. http://www.unesco.org/new/fileadmin/MULTIMEDIA/HQ/CLT/images/FinalHangzhouDeclaration20130517.pdf (Accessed 18 November 2014.)

UCLG. 2008. Agenda 21 for Culture. Barcelona, United Cities and Local Governments/Institut de Cultura.

UCLG. 2010. Culture: Fourth Pillar of Sustainable Development. Barcelona, United Cities and Local Governments/Institut de Cultura.

UN. n. d. Millennium Development Goals. New York, United Nations. http://www.un.org/millenniumgoals/ (Accessed 18 November 2014.)

UN. 1945. Universal Declaration of Human Rights. New York, United Nations. http://www.un.org/en/documents/udhr/ (Accessed 18 November 2014.)
UN. 1966. International Covenant on Economic, Social and Cultural Rights. Adopted and opened for signature, ratification and accession by General Assembly Resolution 2200 A (XXI) of 16 December 1966, entry into force 3 January 1976, in accordance with article 27. New York, United Nations. http://www.ohchr.org/Documents/ProfessionalInterest/cescr.pdf (Accessed 18 November 2014.)
UN. 1992. *Agenda 21, United Nations Conference on Environment and Development in Rio de Janerio, Brazil, 3 to 14 June 1992.* New York, United Nations. http://sustainabledevelopment.un.org/content/documents/Agenda21.pdf (Accessed 18 November 2014.)
UN. 2000. *Resolution 55/2. United Nations Millennium Declaration.* New York, United Nations. http://www.un.org/millennium/declaration/ares552e.htm (Accessed 18 November 2014.)
UN. 2006. *High Level Dialogue on International Migration and Development.* http://www.un.org/esa/population/migration/hld/index.html (Accessed 18 November 2014.)
UN. 2010. *Resolution 65/1. Keeping the promise: united to achieve the Millennium Development Goals.* New York, United Nations. http://www.un.org/en/mdg/summit2010/pdf/outcome_documentN1051260.pdf (Accessed: 18 November 2014.)
UN. 2011. *Resolution 65/166. Culture and development.* New York, United Nations. http://whc.unesco.org/document/115934 (Accessed 18 November 2014.)
UN. 2012*a*. *Resolution 66/208. Culture and development.* New York, United Nations. http://www.un.org/en/ga/search/view_doc.asp?symbol=20A/RES/66/208 (Accessed 18 November 2014.)
UN. 2012*b*. *Communiqué from the Meeting of the High-level Panel of Eminent Persons on the Post-2015 Development Agenda in Monrovia, Liberia.* New York, United Nations. http://www.un.org/sg/management/pdf/Monrovia_Communique_1_Feb_2013.pdf (Accessed 18 November 2014.)
UN. 2013. *A New Global Partnership: Eradicate Poverty and Transform Economies through Sustainable Development,* The Report of the High-Level Panel of Eminent Persons on the Post-2015 Development Agenda. New York, United Nations. http://www.post2015hlp.org/wp-content/uploads/2013/05/UN-Report.pdf (Accessed 18 November 2014.)
WCED. 1987. *Report of the World Commission on Environment and Development. Our Common Future.* (Brundtland Report). New York, United Nations. http://www.un-documents.net/wced-ocf.htm (Accessed 18 November 2014.)

Sustainability in the World Heritage Convention: The Making of a Policy Framework

Francesco Bandarin

Introduction

In 2012, the 40th anniversary of the World Heritage Convention was celebrated by UNESCO and the States Parties that have ratified this flagship international instrument for the conservation of cultural and natural heritage. In 2014 the World Heritage List passed the threshold of 1,000 sites inscribed, as shown in the following table of the distribution of World Heritage sites by region and type, and the Convention had been ratified by 193 Member States. The Convention can certainly be considered a global success. In forty years it has achieved a record number of ratifications and a strong commitment of States Parties for its implementation.

Table: Distribution of World Heritage Sites by region and type (UNESCO World Heritage Centre (2014))

	CULTURAL	NATURAL	MIXED	Total	%
Africa	48	37	4	89	9%
Arab States	71	4	2	77	8%
Asia & Pacific	161	59	11	231	23%
Europe & North America	408	61	10	479	48%
Latin America & Caribbean	91	36	4	131	13%
Total	779	197	31	1007	

Throughout the world, the Convention has driven change in national institutions, promoted the improvement of heritage conservation policies and the building of national capacities, fostered the participation and involvement of a wide range of stakeholders, and generated great opportunities for partnerships and the development of innovative financial mechanisms.

As the Convention has contributed considerably to conserving our planet and our built heritage, it can claim to be one of the most effective international instruments and a milestone in the conservation world.

Forty years on, the Convention faces new challenges brought about by the changes that have characterized the economic, social and environmental scene on a global scale. Globalization, with its ever-increasing social and economic interdependencies, provides opportunities for development, while also presenting enormous challenges to local communities, livelihoods and identities. Global challenges such as climate change, conflicts and wars, endemic poverty, the financial crisis, rapid urbanization and environmental degradation have rendered people all the more vulnerable to change and to the impacts of natural disasters, and have led to the progressive loss of local cultures. It is increasingly evident that the future challenges of heritage conservation will be linked to sustainability and to the integration of heritage in the life of the communities within a development framework.

The decision of the World Heritage Committee to link the 40th anniversary celebrations to the theme of development[1] is therefore of great importance because it links the effective and long-term conservation of sites to a sustainable development process that benefits local communities. In so doing, the Convention joins the policy promoted by UNESCO, aiming to have culture recognized as an important dimension in international development policies.

Furthermore, this decision strengthens the positions adopted by several international organizations involved in heritage conservation and management,[2] and the positions expressed by two of the Advisory Bodies of the Convention, the International Council on Monuments and Sites (ICOMOS) and the International Union for Conservation of Nature (IUCN).[3]

Culture in the international development agenda

As demonstrated by the failure of many projects under way since the 1970s, development is not synonymous with economic growth alone. It is a means of achieving a more satisfactory intellectual, emotional, moral and spiritual existence.

Since the 1980s, UNESCO has supported the role of culture in social and economic development.[4]

---

1 The theme selected by the World Heritage Committee was World Heritage and Sustainable Development: the Role of Local Communities.

2 In particular, the most active organization in this area has been United Cities and Local Governments, which promoted Agenda 21 for Culture (UCLG, 2008). The Agenda and the Declaration on Culture: Fourth Pillar of Sustainable Development (UCLG, 2010) explicitly includes culture in the development model that "meets the needs of the present without compromising the ability of future generations to meet their own needs". See in particular the document Culture as a Goal in the Post-2015 Development Agenda at http://www.agenda21culture.net/index.php.

3 ICOMOS expressed its position at its 17th General Assembly in 2011, with the Paris Declaration on Heritage as a Driver of Development, (ICOMOS, 2011). IUCN is discussing the issue at the World Parks Congress in November 2014.

4 The first document issued on this matter was the Mexico City Declaration on Cultural Policy (1982), which highlights the role of culture as a vector of identity, value systems, traditions and cohesion, and as an engine for creativity, and recognizes that culture constitutes a fundamental dimension of the development process. World Conference on Cultural Policies, Mexico City, 26 July-6 August 1982.

This goal was defined in connection with the World Decade for Cultural Development[5] (1988–1997). Ever since, an important range of standard-setting instruments[6] and demonstration tools such as cultural statistics, inventories, regional and national mapping of cultural resources have been developed within UNESCO and by a large group of intellectuals, academics and practitioners (see e. g. UNESCO, 2010).

Among the most significant activities promoted during the Cultural Development Decade was the work of the World Commission on Culture and Development, led by former UN Secretary-General Javier Pérez de Cuéllar, which issued the report *Our Creative Diversity* (UNESCO, 1996).

In 1998 these ideas were discussed during an important international meeting held in Stockholm (Sweden), whose purpose was to contribute to the integration of cultural policies in human development strategies at international and national levels, and to help strengthen UNESCO's contributions to cultural policy formulation and international cultural cooperation.[7] The Action Plan issued by the Conference represented a major policy guidance document for over a decade (UNESCO, 1998*a*).

The efforts of UNESCO were at that time matched by an important initiative launched by the World Bank, which culminated in the international conference "Culture Counts" held in Florence in 1999 (World Bank, 2000). This conference addressed the importance of financing, resources, and the economics of culture in sustainable development, and offered methods for integrating culture more fully into the development process.

However, the Millennium Development Goals (MDGs), launched in 2000, did not include culture as a dimension of development. They neither recognized, nor capitalized on, the intrinsic links between cultural diversity and biodiversity, or the links

---

5 The decade was proclaimed by the UNESCO General Assembly (A/RES/41/187, 8 December 1986) following Recommendation 27 of the Mexico Declaration. See in particular the Plan of Action for the decade (UNESCO, 1990). Four concepts were at the core of the activities promoted during the decade: 1. acknowledging the cultural dimension in development; 2. asserting and enhancing cultural identities; 3. broadening participation in cultural life; 4. promoting international cultural cooperation.

6 In particular, the links between culture and development are very explicit in the Universal Declaration on Cultural Diversity (2001) and in the two conventions approved after the decade, the Convention for the Safeguarding of the Intangible Cultural Heritage (2003) and the Convention for the Protection and Promotion of the Diversity of Cultural Expressions (2005).

7 The two main themes which served as the basic framework for the conference were: (1) the challenges of cultural diversity; (2) the challenges of recasting cultural policies.

Under the first theme, the challenges of cultural diversity, the following issues were discussed: (1.1) a commitment to pluralism; (1.2) cultural rights; (1.3*a*) cultural heritage for development; (1.3*b*) cultural creativity and cultural industries; (1.4) culture for children and young people.

Under the second theme, the challenges of recasting cultural policies, the following issues were discussed: (2.1) improving research and international cooperation for cultural policy; (2.2) mobilizing resources for cultural activities; (2.3) the media in cultural policy; (2.4) culture and the new media technologies.

between natural and cultural heritage conservation on the one hand, and environmental sustainability on the other, links that lie at the heart of the World Heritage Convention.

Clearly, the MDGs are still a reflection of a traditional vision of the development process, addressing economic and humanitarian issues as isolated processes to be dealt with through the transfer of resources from developed to underdeveloped societies.[8]

Reassessment of the MDGs: A new opportunity

In view of the reassessment of the MDGs, scheduled for 2015, the international community embarked on an important discussion on the future Development Agenda, with the aim of defining a new system of objectives in line with current strategic orientations.

The Outcome Document of the 2010 MDG Summit (UN General Assembly, 2010), published ten years after the Millennium Declaration, emphasized the importance of culture for development and its contribution to the achievement of the Millennium Development Goals.

The discussion on the Post-2015 Development Agenda found a first important moment at the Rio+20 United Nations Conference on Sustainable Development that took place in Rio de Janeiro in June 2012 where the global community recognized the relationship between people, their ecosystems and their cultural heritage, the value of sustainable uses of resources by indigenous peoples and local communities, the need for conservation of the natural and cultural heritage, the need to revitalize historic districts and rehabilitate city centers, as well as the importance of investing in cultural tourism.

The Outcome Document of the Rio+20[9] demonstrated much positive advancement in the international community's understanding of sustainable development. In recognizing that "people are at the centre of sustainable development" (para. 6) and that there is a need for "holistic and integrated approaches to sustainable develop-

---

8 The eight MDGs are: (1) to halve the number of undernourished people; (2) to achieve universal primary education; (3) to promote gender equality and empower women; (4) to reduce child mortality; (5) to improve maternal health; (6) to combat HIV/AIDS, malaria, and other diseases; (7) to ensure environmental sustainability; (8) to develop a global partnership for development.

9 The United Nations Conference on Sustainable Development (Rio+20) took place in Rio de Janeiro (Brazil) on 20–22 June 2012. It resulted in a focused political Outcome Document, *The Future We Want* (UNCSD, 2012), which contains clear and practical measures for implementing sustainable development. In Rio, Member States decided to launch a process to develop a set of Sustainable Development Goals (SDGs), which will build upon the Millennium Development Goals and converge with the Post-2015 Development Agenda.

ment" (para. 40), focus is put on human development. The very recognition "that there are different approaches, visions, models and tools available to each country" (para. 56) represents positive steps being taken towards a more humanistic, flexible approach to development and helps to pave the way for the recognition of culture as an important factor in creating appropriate, and therefore effective, development programmes.

The Outcome Document itself mentions culture in a number of paragraphs. The most significant reference to culture is in support of the importance of cultural diversity: "We acknowledge the natural and cultural diversity of the world and recognize that all cultures and civilizations can contribute to sustainable development" (para. 41). But there is also recognition of the relationship between people, their ecosystems and their cultural heritage (para. 30); the importance of investing in cultural tourism (paras 130, 131); "the need for conservation, as appropriate, of the natural and cultural heritage of human settlements, the revitalization of historic districts and the rehabilitation of city centres" (para. 134); the important relationship between culture and biodiversity was also affirmed (para. 197).

In addition, Rio+20 recognized that "indigenous peoples and local communities, ... have developed sustainable uses of ... resources" (paras 211, 109, 197), as well as the importance of "avoiding endangering their [indigenous peoples'] cultural heritage" (para. 58j).

Although the conclusions of the Rio+20 still do not fully recognize the need to integrate culture in international development policies, the Conference has been an important step in mainstreaming the role of culture.

These crucial messages were reiterated in two consecutive Resolutions of the UN General Assembly on Culture and Development in 2010[10] and 2011,[11] which called for the mainstreaming of culture into development policies and strategies, underscored culture's intrinsic contribution to sustainable development, and invited Member States to "support national legal frameworks and policies for the protection and preservation of cultural heritage".

In December 2013, the UN General Assembly issued a third Resolution on this matter, clearly positioning culture in the Post-2015 Development Agenda.[12] Building on the recognition of the role of culture for development acknowledged in the previous Resolutions, the new Resolution represents an important breakthrough in the development agenda as it explicitly recognizes the direct links between culture and the three pillars of sustainable development (economic, social and environmental) as well

---

10 UN General Assembly Resolution 65/166. (A/65/438) adopted on the Report of the Second Committee, 65th plenary meeting, 20 December 2010.

11 UN General Assembly Resolution 66/208 (a/66/187) adopted at the 66th plenary meeting, 22 December 2011.

12 UN General Assembly 68th Session, 5 December 2013, Document A/C.2/68/L.69N.

as peace and security. The text clearly states that culture is both an enabler and driver of sustainable development and further spells out culture's potential contribution to sustainable production and consumption patterns. Finally, the Resolution highlights the importance of giving due consideration to culture and sustainable development in the elaboration of the Post-2015 Development Agenda.

UNESCO policy for the inclusion of culture in the Post-2015 Development Agenda

Most of the positive results obtained during the reassessment of the Millennium Development Goals are linked to an intensive campaign launched by UNESCO in 2010. This campaign, supported by other governmental and non-governmental partners, aimed first of all to give an operational dimension to the main message on the role of culture in development, that had been elaborated in previous decades from different angles and perspectives. Secondly, it aimed to present to the international community a broad range of concrete demonstrations and assessments of the role of culture in development. And finally, it aimed to pay greater attention to the political processes in international fora and in particular within the UN General Assembly, in charge of the formulation of the new Sustainable Development Goals.

The first objective was attained through an internal process of reflection, which culminated in the drafting of a "think piece" (UNESCO, 2012) that offered a re-examination of the issue and particularly stressed two aspects to be considered in the Sustainable Development Goals: (1) culture as an enabler of sustainable and community-oriented development processes; (2) culture as a driver of economic development, employment generation and investment processes.

Furthermore, and in order to strengthen this policy position, UNESCO defined a comprehensive "umbrella" strategy, involving all its activities, programmes and international normative instruments in the field of culture within a common policy drive, framed by the Culture and Development policy.

This approach allowed the World Heritage Convention to rejoin the orientations of the other UNESCO conventions, in particular the 2003 Convention for the Safeguarding of the Intangible Cultural Heritage and the 2005 Convention on the Protection and Promotion of the Diversity of Cultural Expressions, that – as outcomes of the World Decade for Cultural Development – already included in their Strategic Objectives the promotion of culture in sustainable development.

The six international cultural conventions managed by UNESCO offered a broad spectrum of demonstrations of the power of culture in the development process. In addition, UNESCO had the chance to expand its demonstration strategy through two major activities linked to the Culture and Development policy.

The first activity was the implementation of the Culture and Development thematic window of the MDG Achievement Fund. Within this programme, UNESCO was asked to play a leading role in the UN system for the implementation of the US$ 95 million fund made available by the government of Spain (UNESCO/MDG-F, 2012).

A total of eighteen projects dealing with different types of culture and heritage were developed and implemented,[13] thus allowing an important demonstration of the role of heritage and culture in local development (MDG-F, 2013).

The second activity was the development of specific indicators on the impact of culture on development, aiming to demonstrate the quantitative and qualitative role played by culture in sustainable development. This initiative allowed data and figures to be gathered on culture's contribution to the economy, and a specific case to be presented for culture and development in international fora.

The results of all these activities were discussed in several major international conferences. In 2013 alone, three significant international events stressed the relevance of culture in the development process: the Expert Conference held in Hangzhou (China) in May 2013; the UN Economic and Social Council (ECOSOC) Annual Ministerial Review in July 2013 in Geneva (Switzerland); and the Culture for Development World Forum, in Bali (Indonesia), in November 2013.

The Hangzhou Conference was the culmination of the efforts promoted by UNESCO since 2010 to assert the role of culture in development. The Conference issued a Declaration on Placing Culture at the Heart of Sustainable Development Policies. The Declaration proposed a nine-point Agenda[14] dealing with the role of culture in the development process and was considered the main platform to set the terms for that debate and push for the integration of culture into the Post-2015 Development Agenda.

Organized in Geneva in July 2013, the ECOSOC Annual Ministerial Review examined a Report of the UN Secretary-General on the role of science, technology and

---

13 The countries involved were Albania, Bosnia & Herzegovina, Cambodia, China, Costa Rica, Ecuador, Egypt, Ethiopia, Honduras, Mauritania, Morocco, Mozambique, Namibia, Nicaragua, Palestine, Senegal, Turkey, Uruguay. The programmes under the Culture and Development thematic window followed a wide range of approaches, due in part to the different contexts in which activities have been implemented (e. g. regional diversity, income diversity), and the range of needs and priorities identified.

14 The nine points of the Hangzhou Agenda are the following:
- Integrate culture within all development policies and programmes, as equal measure with human rights, equality and sustainability.
- Mobilize culture and mutual understanding to foster peace and reconciliation.
- Ensure cultural rights for all to promote inclusive social development.
- Leverage culture for poverty reduction and inclusive economic development.
- Build on culture to promote environmental sustainability.
- Use culture to strengthen resilience to disasters and combat climate change through mitigation and adaptation.
- Value, safeguard and transmit culture to future generations.
- Harness culture as a resource for achieving sustainable urban development and management.
- Capitalize on culture to foster innovative and sustainable models of cooperation.

innovation, and the potential of culture for promoting sustainable development and achieving the Millennium Development Goals (ECOSOC, 2013). The Report included an important statement on the role of Culture in Development, concluding: “It is critical that a post-2015 framework should integrate culture as a key element. Supporting evidence-based policy making in the field of culture, and informing government policies on trade, industry practices, systems of incentives and the rights of creators should be part of this framework”.[15]

The Culture and Development World Forum, promoted by the Government of Indonesia in November 2013 issued the Bali Promise, a document supporting the inclusion of Culture in the Post-2015 Agenda.[16]

In May 2014, the results of these international fora were again brought to the attention of the UN General Assembly during a Thematic Debate on Culture and Sustainable Development in the Post-2015 Development Agenda.[17]

This long process is currently being finalized: in 2014 and 2015, the UN General Assembly will examine the documents issued by the Open Working Group created by the Member States to prepare the discussion, and will establish the new Sustainable Development Goals. Whatever the final result and wording chosen, the effort deployed by UNESCO during these years has brought significant results: culture and heritage are now perceived as fundamental components of the development process by an increasing number of countries,[18] and are present in national policies both in the developed and the emerging world (see e. g. DANIDA, 2013). Furthermore, the main international development agencies such as the UN Development Programme (UNDP) or the World Bank[19] have now incorporated the cultural dimension in their investment programmes, recognizing its role in the development of creative industries, heritage tourism and in promoting education and social stability.

A key demonstration of the role of culture in economic and social development was provided by the *Creative Economy Report* issued in 2013 (UNESCO-UNDP, 2013).

---

15 ECOSOC (2013, para. 56). The Report provides a detailed assessment of the role of Culture in Development, stating that “... (7) Culture is also a powerful global economic engine generating jobs and income. Cultural goods and services often need low capital investment by building on practices, materials and skills available within the community. Furthermore, the creative and cultural industries represent some of the most dynamic sectors in the global economy, with rapidly expanding growth in Africa and the Middle East in particular.”

16 The Bali Promise also includes ten recommendations on explicitly integrating the cultural dimension of development throughout the Sustainable Development Goals.

17 The debate was held on 5 May 2014. See: http://www.un.org/en/ga/president/68/events/culture_sd.shtml

18 The survey conducted by UNESCO during the implementation of the MDG-F Culture and Development window indicated that over 70 per cent of the worldwide UN Development Assistance Framework programmes included elements of culture (UNESCO, 2013).

19 See, for example, the strong cultural orientation of the World Bank’s *World Development Report 2015, Mind, Society and Behavior.*

This document analyses the rise of the creative economy as one of the fastest growing sectors in the world economy and shows how the cultural and creative industries can support new development pathways aligned with the principles of equity and sustainability promoted by the UN Post-2015 Development Agenda.

The World Heritage Convention in the Post-2015 Development Agenda

As can be concluded from the above analysis, the decision of the World Heritage Committee to promote sustainable development within the World Heritage sites management and conservation processes is aligned with the policies developed by UNESCO and other international agencies within the post-2015 framework.

Undoubtedly, the World Heritage Convention can play an important role in demonstrating the importance of heritage in support of sustainable development processes and community empowerment.

The main development objectives supported by the World Heritage Convention are related to the goals of strengthening the community and the local identity, promoting the growth of sustainable tourism activities with related investments and services, fostering local craft and creative industries, and enhancing the local quality of life and environmental sustainability.

As the text of the Convention, adopted long before the emergence of the Culture and Development policy, does not make any specific mention of the term "sustainable development", the Convention needs to better define its own approach, based specifically on its Articles 4 and 5, which recognize that Member States have the duty "of ensuring the identification, protection, conservation, presentation and transmission to future generations of the cultural and natural heritage", as well as "to adopt a general policy which aims to give the cultural and natural heritage a function in the life of the community and to integrate the protection of that heritage into comprehensive planning programmes".

A turning point in the development of this new approach was the adoption of the "4Cs"[20] on the occasion of the 30th anniversary of the Convention in Budapest (Hungary) in 2002. The Budapest Declaration stressed the need to "ensure an appropriate and equitable balance between conservation, sustainability and development, so that World Heritage properties can be protected through appropriate activities contributing to the social and economic development and the quality of life of our communities". The inclusion of a 5th "C" (Communities) in the Strategic Objectives of

---

20 The Strategic Objectives of the World Heritage Convention, i.e. the 4Cs approved in Budapest, are: Credibility, Conservation, Capacity-building, Communication.

the Convention in 2007 in Christchurch (New Zealand), further advanced this orientation.[21]

Since then, the World Heritage Committee has consistently promoted the notion of sustainable development in the *Operational Guidelines* for the implementation of the Convention, while obviously linking it to the primary scope of the Convention, i. e. heritage conservation.[22]

The Strategic Action Plan for the implementation of the Convention, 2012–2022[23] also considered sustainable development, and called the Convention to "contribute to the sustainable development of the world's communities and cultures".

The culmination of this policy development process was the 40th anniversary event that took place in Kyoto (Japan) in November 2012. On that occasion, besides a major publication presenting a variety of case studies on the impact of heritage conservation on community development (UNESCO World Heritage Centre, 2012), a document was issued, the *Kyoto Vision*, highlighting the strategic link between conservation and communities as a tool to fulfill the mission of the World Heritage Convention. In particular, the document stresses the need to strengthen the relationship between people and heritage, and to integrate tangible and intangible heritage policies within a common goal of sustainable development, as the only condition to ensure long-term conservation and the preservation of the Outstanding Universal Value of the sites.[24]

With the Kyoto Vision, the World Heritage Convention has marked a significant reformulation of its own objectives. Can this be considered a full-fledged policy?

In spite of these advancements and the alignment of the World Heritage Convention with the Culture and Development policy promoted internationally, there obviously

21 Decision 31 COM 13B.

22 Several expert meetings have been dedicated to the inclusion of development in the framework of the World Heritage Convention. Note, in particular, the Paraty Meeting on the Relationship between the World Heritage Convention, Conservation and Sustainable Development '(29–31 March 2010); the Ouro Preto Meeting on World Heritage and Sustainable Development (5–8 February 2012); the Toyama Meeting on World Heritage and Sustainable Development: from principles to Practice (3–5 November 2012).

23 The Strategic Action Plan was adopted by the 18th General Assembly, Paris, 2011. See in particular the Vision for 2022.

24 The *Kyoto Vision* states the following:

The Importance of the Role of Community

We reiterate the important role of communities, including local communities and indigenous peoples, in the implementation of the World Heritage Convention, in accordance with one of its five Strategic Objectives, the fifth "C" adopted in 2007, and the Strategic Action Plan 2012–2022 [...] Only through strengthened relationships between people and heritage, based on respect for cultural and biological diversity as a whole, integrating both tangible and intangible aspects and geared toward sustainable development, will the "future we want" become attainable.

are still several missing elements that will require discussions and decisions by the World Heritage Committee in the near future.

In particular, there is a need for better specification, within the *Operational Guidelines,* of the mechanisms that governments should adopt and incorporate within the different stages of implementation of their conservation strategies, from the moment of the preparation of the nomination to the implementation and evaluation of the management practices.

A proper answer to these challenges will constitute a major contribution to a strategy of long-term site conservation as well as to the promotion and implementation of the UNESCO Culture and Development policy.

References

Bandarin, F., Hosagrahar, J. and Albernaz, F. 2011. Why development needs culture. *Journal of Cultural Heritage Management and Sustainable Development,* Vol. 1, No. 1, pp. 15–25.

DANIDA. 2013. *The Right to Art and Culture. Strategic Framework for Culture and Development.* Copenhagen, Ministry of Foreign Affairs of Denmark.

ECOSOC. 2013. *Report of the Secretary-General on "Science, technology and innovation, and the potential of culture, for promoting sustainable development and achieving the Millennium Development Goals",* for the 2013 Annual Ministerial Review. Geneva, UN Economic and Social Council, Substantive session of 2013, Geneva, 1–26 July 2013.

Galla, A. (ed.). 2012. *World Heritage: Benefits Beyond Borders.* Paris/Cambridge, UK, UNESCO Publishing/Cambridge University Press.

ICOMOS. 2011. The Paris Declaration on Heritage as a Driver of Development. Adopted at the ICOMOS 17th General Assembly, UNESCO Headquarters, Paris, on 1 December 2011.

MDG-F. 2013. *Culture and Development. Thematic Window Development Results Report.* New York, United Nations.

UCLG. 2008. Agenda 21 for Culture. Barcelona, United Cities and Local Governments/Institut de Cultura.

UCLG. 2010. Culture: Fourth Pillar of Sustainable Development. Barcelona, United Cities and Local Governments/Institut de Cultura.

UNCSD. 2012. *The Future We Want.* Outcome Document adopted at Rio+20 Conference, Rio de Janeiro, Brazil, 20–22 June. New York, United Nations Commission on Sustainable Development. http://www.uncsd2012.org

UNESCO. 1990. *World Decade for Cultural Development, 1988–1997. Plan of Action.* Paris, UNESCO.

UNESCO. 1996. *Our Creative Diversity.* Report of the World Commission on Culture and Development. Paris, UNESCO.

UNESCO. 1998*a*. *Intergovernmental Conference on Cultural Policies for Development. Final Report.* Stockholm, Sweden, 30 March-2 April 1998.

UNESCO. 1998*b*. *Linking Nature and Culture.* Global Strategy Natural and Cultural Heritage Expert Meeting. Amsterdam, Netherlands Ministry of Education, Culture and Science.

UNESCO. 1998*c*. *World Culture Report: Culture, Creativity and Markets.* Paris, UNESCO.

UNESCO. 2000. *World Culture Report: Cultural Diversity, Conflict and Pluralism.* Paris, UNESCO.

UNESCO. 2003. *Shared Legacy, Common Responsibility.* Proceedings of the International Congress organized by UNESCO's World Heritage Centre with the support of the Italian Government on the occasion of the 30th anniversary of the World Heritage Convention. Cini Foundation, Island of San Giorgio Maggiore, Venice, Italy, 14–16 November 2002. Paris, UNESCO.

UNESCO. 2004. *Partnerships for World Heritage Cities: Culture as a Vector for Sustainable Urban Development*. Paris, UNESCO. (World Heritage Papers No. 9.)

UNESCO. 2007. *World Heritage. Challenges for the Millennium*. Paris, UNESCO World Heritage Centre.

UNESCO. 2009. *Preliminary study on the technical and legal aspects relating to the desirability of a standard-setting instrument on the conservation of the Historic Urban Landscape*. Paris, UNESCO. (181 Executive Board Session Doc. 29.)

UNESCO. 2010. *World Report N.2. Investing in Cultural Diversity and Intercultural Dialogue*. Paris, UNESCO Publishing.

UNESCO. 2012. *UN Task Team on the Post-2015 Development Agenda. Culture, an enabler and driver of sustainable development. Thematic think piece*. Paris, UNESCO.

UNESCO. 2013. *Analytical Survey of the Inclusion of Culture in the United Nations Development Assistance Framework (UNDAF)*. Paris, UNESCO. (CLT-2012/WS/17.)

UNESCO/MDG-F. 2012. *Knowledge Management for Culture and Development*. Paris, UNESCO.

UNESCO/UNDP. 2013. *Creative Economy Report, 2013 Special Edition. Widening Local Development Pathways*. New York/Paris, UNDP/UNESCO.

UN General Assembly. 2010. *Keeping the Promise: United to Achieve the Millennium Development Goals*. 65th session. New York, United Nations. (Document A/65/L.1.)

World Bank. 2000. *Culture Counts. Financing, Resources and the Economics of Culture Sustainable Development*. Proceedings of the Conference held in Florence, Italy, 4–7 October 1999, cosponsored by the Government of Italy and the World Bank in cooperation with UNESCO. Washington DC, World Bank.

World Bank. 2015. *World Development Report: Mind, Society and Behavior*. Washington DC, World Bank.

II History and Documents

Natural Heritage and Sustainable Development – A Realistic Option or Wishful Thinking?

Barbara Engels

Introduction

Although the UNESCO World Heritage Convention speaks about safeguarding heritage and values and not about sustainable use, the discussion on sustainable development has gained importance in World Heritage-related discussions. Culminating in the 40th anniversary of the Convention celebrations' theme, World Heritage and Sustainable Development: the Role of Local Communities, the focus in World Heritage discussions – especially those relating to planned developments in and around World Heritage sites – seems to have shifted from conservation to development.

This paper looks into linkages between natural World Heritage and sustainable development on the basis of the Convention text and the *Operational Guidelines* for its implementation, as well as some strategic documents adopted by the Committee during recent years.

It explores linkages to other international biodiversity-related conventions and programmes (notably the Convention on Biological Diversity, RAMSAR and the Man and the Biosphere programme) and analyses how sustainable use is positioned in these instruments.

Looking into selected examples and case studies, I seek to prove the thesis that there will be no future for natural World Heritage sites without sustainable development: sustainable development is to be realized preferably not in the perimeter of the World Heritage site as such but rather in its immediate and/or wider surroundings. The conclusion is an urgent call for refocusing on conservation and management of natural World Heritage sites, taking into account the wider context of the sites and the options for sustainable use.

Sustainability in the international conservation context

Sustainability was first used as a notion in the sense of responsible long-term use of resources in 1713 by Hans Carl von Carlowitz in his *Silvicultura oeconomica* (von Carlowitz, 1732), asking how sylviculture could be best done to achieve a continuous sustainable use because it was indispensable and without it the country would have nothing to eat (Grober, 2013).

Since the 1980s, sustainability has been used more in the sense of human sustainability on planet Earth and this has resulted in the most widely quoted definition of sustainability of the United Nations Brundtland Commission in its report *Our Common Future* defining the concept of sustainable development as "development that meets the needs of the present without compromising the ability of future generations to meet their own needs" (WCED, 1987).

In the 1990s, sustainable development found its way into the UNESCO World Heritage Convention as well as into a series of natural heritage and biodiversity-related conventions and programmes, such as the Convention on Biological Diversity (CBD), the Convention on Wetlands of International Importance (RAMSAR Convention) and especially the UNESCO Man and the Biosphere (MAB) programme.

Whereas the CBD from the outset puts the sustainable use of biological diversity in its three main objectives on the same level as conservation of biodiversity and the equitable sharing of benefits derived from its use (CBD, 1992), the RAMSAR Convention uses a different terminology and promotes the "wise use" of wetlands as follows:

"The Contracting Parties shall formulate and implement their planning so as to promote the conservation of the wetlands included in the List, and as far as possible the wise use of wetlands in their territory" (RAMSAR, 1971, article 3).

The UNESCO MAB programme, when established in 1976, focused on a more scientific approach on the linkages between people and the environment, but in 1995 in its Seville Strategy for Biosphere Reserves promotes a systematic approach to develop UNESCO biosphere reserves as models for sustainable development, effectively reconciling the protection and use of biodiversity and ecosystems (UNESCO, 1995).

Role of natural and cultural heritage in the international sustainability context

Following the Rio Summit in 1992, the UN Millennium Summit set goals for the international development agenda. While the Millennium Development Goals include an ecological perspective as Goal 7 "to ensure environmental sustainability" (UN, 2000), a specific heritage perspective is missing. This changed considerably in the following decade. The outcome document of the UN Rio+20 Summit in 2012, *The Future We Want* (UNCSD, 2012) includes several references to natural and cultural heritage in different contexts, *inter alia:*

- recognizes the importance of intact ecosystems for human well-being and cultural heritage and the need for sustainable use of natural resources and ecosystems (para. 30);
- affirms the need for a green economy to avoid endangering cultural heritage (para 58j);
- recognizes "the need for conservation, as appropriate, of the natural and cultural heritage of human settlements" (para. 134).

This clearly demonstrates that a heritage perspective has penetrated the international sustainability discussions, certainly influenced by the growing interconnectivity of the various international conventions and organizations.

Sustainability in the UNESCO World Heritage Convention

The Convention concerning the Protection of the World Cultural and Natural Heritage (World Heritage Convention) was adopted in 1972 following an international campaign to safeguard the Abu Simbel temples in Upper Egypt, together with an international movement to preserve natural heritage (UNESCO, 2014*a*).

The aim of the Convention is to ensure the "identification, protection, conservation, presentation and transmission to future generations of the cultural and natural heritage" (UNESCO, 1972, article 4). It is the first (and still the only) international convention that links together in a single document the concepts of nature conservation and the preservation of cultural properties.

It is important to note that the World Heritage Convention itself does not include any direct reference to sustainability or sustainable development. This is no surprise, as the Convention has never been amended since its adoption in 1972. However it has been argued that the Convention itself carries the spirit of sustainability by calling for the safeguard of natural and cultural heritage (UNESCO, 2014*b*).

The topic of sustainable development has gained importance in World Heritage-related discussions in recent years. It is especially in the context of planned developments in and around World Heritage sites where the discussion seems to have shifted from conservation to development.

The World Heritage Committee, the Convention's decision-making body, first discussed sustainable development in 1991, when taking note in its decisions of the results of an international workshop on sustainable development of tourism in the natural World Heritage site of Mount Huangshan, China (WHC, 1991). Then in 1993, during its deliberations the Committee expressed the explicit need to take the Rio Summit negotiations into account (WHC, 1993).

However, it was only in 1994 that the term "sustainable land-use" was first used in the *Operational Guidelines*, the Convention's main guiding instrument that has – in contrast to the Convention text itself – undergone several revisions since its first edition in 1977. The first reference to sustainable use was in the context of cultural landscapes, a category of World Heritage sites introduced in 1992. Para. 38 of the *Operational Guidelines* acknowledged that protection of cultural landscapes can contribute to sustainable land-use[1] (UNESCO, 1994).

---

1 Para. 38 of the *Operational Guidelines:* "Cultural landscapes often reflect specific techniques of sustainable land-use, considering the characteristics and limits of the natural environment they are

Since 2002 the *Operational Guidelines* include the notion of sustainable use/ development in various paragraphs. Para. 6 importantly notes: "The protection and conservation of the natural and cultural heritage are a significant contribution to sustainable development". By embracing the notion of sustainable development in one of the first leading paragraphs, the World Heritage Committee has (a) taken into account that sustainable development had gained importance in discussions of the international community since the 1992 Rio Summit and (b) clearly integrated a sustainability approach in the Convention's aims.

Furthermore, a section of the *Operational Guidelines* deals specifically with "sustainable use" of natural and cultural heritage as a potential contribution to the quality of life of communities: "World Heritage properties may support a variety of ongoing and proposed uses that are ecologically and culturally sustainable and which may contribute to the quality of life of communities concerned. The State Party and its partners must ensure that such sustainable use or any other change does not impact adversely on the Outstanding Universal Value of the property. For some properties, human use would not be appropriate. Legislations, policies and strategies affecting World Heritage properties should ensure the protection of the Outstanding Universal Value, support the wider conservation of natural and cultural heritage, and promote and encourage the active participation of the communities and stakeholders concerned with the property as necessary conditions to its sustainable protection, conservation, management and presentation" (UNESCO, 2013, para. 119).

Research in the World Heritage Centre's database on Committee decisions[2] reveals that since 1999 the Committee in its decisions more regularly referred to sustainable development (between 3 and 11 findings/year; 116 findings in total; own research) or sustainable use (27 findings in total). While most of the decisions relate to individual sites and their state of conservation, only a few are of more strategic character.

In 2002 the Committee in its Budapest Declaration on World Heritage recognizes "the universality of the 1972 UNESCO World Heritage Convention and the consequent need to ensure that it applies to heritage in all its diversity, as an instrument for the sustainable development of all societies through dialogue and mutual understanding" (WHC, 2002, article 1) and furthermore "seek(s) to ensure an appropriate and equitable balance between conservation, sustainability and development, so that World Heritage properties can be protected through appropriate activities contributing to

established in, and a specific spiritual relation to nature. Protection of cultural landscapes can contribute to modern techniques of sustainable land-use and can maintain or enhance natural values in the landscape. The continued existence of traditional forms of land-use supports biological diversity in many regions of the world. The protection of traditional cultural landscapes is therefore helpful in maintaining biological diversity."

2 http://whc.unesco.org/en/decisions allows for keyword search.

the social and economic development and the quality of life of our communities" (WHC, 2002, article 3c).

With this decision a general contribution of World Heritage to sustainable development is acknowledged.

At its 31st session in 2007, the World Heritage Committee decided to add "communities" to the previous four Strategic Objectives "to enhance the role of communities in the implementation of the World Heritage Convention" (Decision 31 COM 13B, 2007) again introducing a development approach to the Convention.

The Strategic Action Plan for the Implementation of the Convention, 2012–2022, adopted by the 18th General Assembly (Paris, 2011), also integrates a concern for sustainable development, notably in its *Vision for 2022*, which calls for the World Heritage Convention to "contribute to the sustainable development of the world's communities and cultures" (WHC, 2011). Subsequently, the Committee in its decisions at its 36th session in 2012 called for the development of policy guidance on the integration of sustainable development in the Convention's processes (WHC, 2012a). However, this development has not yet happened as it depends on extrabudgetary funding (WHC, 2014).

In conclusion, although the high-level discussions as well as some strategic documents adopted by the Committee during the last years regularly seem to focus on sustainable development, a more systematic approach and clear guidance documents are still missing.

Sustainable use vs. protection of natural World Heritage

In October 2006, the UNESCO World Heritage Centre published the Natural Heritage Strategy,[3] which was endorsed by the World Heritage Committee. This Strategy refers directly to sustainable development in its mission statement[4] (UNESCO, 2006).

Natural World Heritage properties worldwide provide a wealth of ecosystem services from which people and local communities in and around the surroundings of the properties directly and indirectly benefit (IUCN, 2014). In many cases local communities directly depend on these intact ecosystems and use the natural resources the natural heritage sites provide, for example by subsistence fishing or hunting, collection of firewood or use of drinking water. Where indigenous communities have for a long time lived off and with their natural environment, sustainability is inherent

3 http://whc.unesco.org/uploads/activities/documents/activity-398-1.pdf

4 "To promote the fullest and broadest application of the World Heritage Convention by all relevant stakeholders, from site level individuals to global organizations, in the pursuit of long-term conservation of biodiversity and sustainable development."

to their way of using natural resources. However, the use of natural resources may threaten the natural values.

For natural heritage sites to be inscribed on the World Heritage List their "bio-physical processes and landform features should be relatively intact" in order to meet the condition of integrity (UNESCO, 2013, para. 90). In this context the *Operational Guidelines* also acknowledge "that no area is totally pristine and that all natural areas are in a dynamic state, and to some extent involve contact with people". The paragraph continues as follows: "Human activities, including those of traditional societies and local communities, often occur in natural areas. These activities may be consistent with the Outstanding Universal Value of the area where they are ecologically sustainable" (UNESCO, 2013, para. 90). This paragraph already signals that human activities may present a conflict to natural heritage values and suggests sustainability as a potential solution. Inherent in this is the ongoing discussion on the compatibility of different land-use options such as mining, agriculture or tourism with the integrity of natural World Heritage sites.

As of today, 19 of the 197 listed Natural World Heritage properties are listed as World Heritage in Danger as their values are severely threatened (UNESCO, 2014*c*). These dangers include:

- encroachment (Simien National Park, Ethiopia, WHC 38 COM 7a.38, Rainforests of the Atsinanana, Madagascar, WHC 38 COM 7 A. 44);
- poaching (Tropical Rainforest Heritage of Sumatra, Indonesia, WHC 38 COM 7 A.28, Virunga National Park, Democratic Republic of the Congo, 38 COM 7 A.28, Selous Game Reserve, United Republic of Tanzania, WHC 38 COM 7B.85);
- illegal logging (Río Plátano Biosphere Reserve, Honduras, WHC 38 COM 7 A.33; Tropical Rainforest Heritage of Sumatra, Indonesia, WHC 38 COM 7 A.28);
- over-exploitation of marine resources (East Rennell, Solomon Islands, WHC 38 COM 7 A.29);
- mining (Virunga National Park, Democratic Republic of the Congo, 38 COM 7 A.28);
- sale and lease of public lands for the purposes of development (Belize Barrier Reef Reserve System, Belize, WHC 38.COM 7 A.31); or
- road infrastructure development (Belize Barrier Reef Reserve System, Belize, WHC 38.COM 7 A.31).

In 2010 a broader analysis on threats to World Heritage properties resulted in "development and infrastructure" (including buildings and development, transportation infrastructure, utilities or service infrastructure, physical resource extraction) and "other human activities" (including biological resource use/modification and social/cultural uses of heritage) being the main threat to natural heritage sites (WHC, 2010). These examples illustrate forms of unsustainable use of natural resources, which are not in line with the World Heritage Convention and thus confirm that "Sustainable development is really a prerequisite for conservation; with unsustainable development and in particular unsustainable resource use being among the most significant threats to conservation" (UNESCO, 2012, p. 57). In many cases the unsustainable resource use is less a problem of adequate legal protection but rather due to insufficient management effectiveness (see also a more detailed analysis in WHC 34.COM 7C, 2010). This leads to the conclusion that more detailed guidance on sustainable use of natural resources in heritage sites is needed.

On the other hand, a number of case studies prove that natural World Heritage sites can act as a motor for sustainable development (see Galla, 2012). A successful example is the sustainable tourism development in the transnational Dutch-German natural site The Wadden Sea (Engels and Westrik, 2012).

It should be noted that in most cases natural World Heritage sites benefit from a high protection status (often as strict reserves or national parks) where resource use inside the property is normally restricted and limited to non-consumptive uses (such as tourism). Sustainable development therefore mostly takes place outside the World Heritage site (UNESCO, 2012).

Looking for guidance: Linkages between natural World Heritage and other biodiversity-related conventions

The UNESCO Resource Manual on managing natural World Heritage poses the crucial question: "Are effective mechanisms in place to ensure that resource use permitted in and around the World Heritage site is sustainable and does not impact negatively on its OUV?" (UNESCO, 2012).

As demonstrated above, the World Heritage Convention and its *Operational Guidelines* fail to give much guidance on how to ensure sustainable use in natural World Heritage sites. It is therefore worth referring back to other biodiversity-related conventions and programmes. The Convention on Biological Diversity defines sustainable use as: "The use of components of biological diversity in a way and at a rate that does not lead to the long-term decline of biological diversity, thereby maintaining its potential to meet the needs and aspirations of present and future generations" (CBD, 1992). Furthermore the CBD has developed a set of principles for sustainable use of biodiversity, the Addis Ababa Principles (CBD, 2004), which can serve as a guiding model for management of natural World Heritage sites (UNESCO, 2012). These guidelines call *inter alia* for a participatory approach to biodiversity management. This can be seen as a key for successful management in line with sustainable development as this enables World Heritage sites to engage with a broad range of stakeholders. For example in Niokolo-Koba National Park (Senegal) a main issue is encroachment in the park by local cattle for water resources. Realizing alternative water sources and the creation of alternative income options for local communities outside the park boundaries has proven an essential step to reduce pressure on the park (own research). Therefore, systematic integration of sustainable use into management planning is an essential tool (Galla, 2012). The World Heritage and Sustainable

Tourism Programme was adopted in 2012 by the World Heritage Committee (WHC, 2012*b*) and aims at achieving sustainable tourism more widely in World Heritage sites.

As stated earlier, sustainable development issues will usually need to consider activities not only in the site itself, but rather in its broader surroundings. The UNESCO Resource Manual on managing natural World Heritage sites states in this regard: "This implies working with other stakeholders and institutions both within the site and in the surrounding area, and might require innovative approaches to governance or the development of partnerships and use agreements" (UNESCO, 2012).

Zoning is therefore an essential management instrument. When properly designed and given an adequate legal status (e. g. providing for sustainable use) the World Heritage site's buffer zone can be the ideal place for putting sustainable development into practice.

This suggests a more detailed look at the concept of UNESCO biosphere reserves, which are designed to serve as models for sustainable development. Biosphere reserves are meant to fulfil three main functions: conservation, logistic support for science and education and sustainable development (Batisse, 2001). The biosphere reserve concept includes a detailed zoning approach with (1) core zones, (2) buffer zones[5] and (3) development zones which provide the territory for testing sustainable development approaches (UNESCO, 1995).

Several natural World Heritage sites are embedded in much larger biosphere reserves where the core area of the biosphere reserve equals the World Heritage property, and the biosphere reserve's buffer and development zone enable proper sustainable management of the wider surroundings. Examples can be found at the Monarch Butterfly Reserve (Mexico), Tubbataha Reef Biosphere Reserve (Philippines) or the Maya Biosphere Reserve comprising Guatemala's Tikal National Park World Heritage site (Batisse, 2001). These management models have been hardely researched so far and clearly need more in-depth consideration.

Biosphere reserves can furthermore present an alternative international designation for sites where sustainable practices (e. g. in agriculture or forestry) are essential to maintain the sites' future biodiversity. World Heritage and biosphere reserves have fundamentally different purposes, objectives and management principles and should therefore not be confused (Batisse, 2001). As biosphere reserves do not require to be of Outstanding Universal Value but focus on sustainable development, this instrument should been seen as a complementary instrument to World Heritage rather than as a competitor.

5 The biosphere reserve buffer zone differs from the concept of a buffer zone given by the World Heritage Convention.

The future of natural World Heritage: With or without development?

The recently published IUCN study on the benefits of natural World Heritage sites confirms that these sites provide a broad range of benefits to both local communities and a wider population. However, these benefits can only be guaranteed in a long-term perspective when the sites are properly managed (IUCN, 2014). The key to long-term conservation is sustainable use of natural resources along with sustainable development of the site and its broader surroundings. It is therefore essential to refocus the discussions and deliberations in the Convention's processes on conservation and management, taking into account the wider context of the sites. More specific guidance needs to be developed for helping site managers and States Parties to integrate sustainable use in their current management practices.

References

Batisse, M. 2001. World Heritage and biosphere reserves: complementary instruments. *Parks,* Vol. 11, No. 1, pp. 38–44.

CBD. 1992. Convention on Biological Diversity. http://www.cbd.int/convention/text/

CBD. 2004. Addis Ababa Principles and Guidelines. http://www.cbd.int/sustainable/addis.shtml

Engels, B. and Westrik, C. 2012. Sustainable development in a Dutch-German World Heritage site: The Wadden Sea, Germany and the Netherlands. In: Galla, op. cit., pp. 279–89.

Galla, A. (ed.). 2012. *World Heritage: Benefits Beyond Borders.* Paris/Cambridge, UK, UNESCO Publishing/Cambridge University Press.

Grober, U. 2013. Urtexte – Carlowitz und die Quellen unseres Nachhaltigkeitsbegriffs. *Natur und Landschaft,* Vol. 2, p. 46.

IUCN. 2014. *The Benefits of Natural World Heritage: identifying and assessing ecosystem services and benefits provided by the world's most iconic natural places.* Gland, Switzerland, IUCN. https://portals.iucn.org/library/sites/library/files/documents/2014-045.pdf

RAMSAR. 1971. Convention on Wetlands of International Importance. Text adopted by the International Conference on the Wetlands and Waterfowl at Ramsar, Iran, 2 February 1971. http://www.ramsar.org/cda/en/ramsar-documents-texts-convention-on-20708/main/ramsar/1-31-38^20708_4000_0__

UNCSD. 2012. *The Future We Want.* Outcome Document adopted at Rio+20 Conference, Rio de Janeiro, Brazil, 20–22 June. New York, United Nations Commission on Sustainable Development. http://www.uncsd2012.org

UNESCO. 1972. Convention concerning the Protection of the World Cultural and Natural Heritage. Paris, UNESCO World Heritage Centre.

UNESCO. 1994, rev. edn. 2013. *Operational Guidelines for the Implementation of the World Heritage Convention.* Paris, UNESCO World Heritage Centre.

UNESCO. 1995. Seville Strategy for Biosphere Reserves. Paris, UNESCO World Heritage Centre.

UNESCO. 2006. The UNESCO World Heritage Centre's Natural Heritage Strategy. Paris, UNESCO World Heritage Centre. http://whc.unesco.org/uploads/activities/documents/activity-398-1.pdf

UNESCO. 2012. *Managing Natural World Heritage.* Resource Manual. Paris, UNESCO World Heritage Centre.

UNESCO. 2014*a*. The World Heritage Convention. http://whc.unesco.org/en/convention/ (Accessed 10 October 2014.)
UNESCO. 2014*b*. World Heritage and Sustainable Development. http://whc.unesco.org/en/sustainabledevelopment/ (Accessed 10 October 2014.)
UNESCO. 2014*c*. List of World Heritage in Danger. http://whc.unesco.org/en/danger/ (Accessed 10 October 2014.)
UN. 2000. United Nations Millennium Development Goals. New York, United Nations. http://www.un.org/millenniumgoals/bkgd.shtml (Accessed 10 October 2014.)
von Carlowitz, C. 1732. *Sylvicultura oeconomica*. Leipzig 1732, Braun, p. 105.
WCED. 1987. *Report of the World Commission on Environment and Development. Our Common Future*. (Brundtland Report). New York, United Nations. http://www.un-documents.net/wced-ocf.htm

Decisions of the UNESCO World Heritage Committee:
WHC. 1991. Committee Decision CONF 0002 VIII.
WHC. 1993. Committee Decision CONF 002 VIII 1–6.
WHC. 2002. Budapest Declaration on World Heritage.
WHC. 2007. Committee Decision 31 COM 13B.
WHC. 2010. Committee Decision Document 34.COM 7C.
WHC. 2011. Committee Decision 11/18.GA/11.
WHC. 2012*a*. Committee Decision WHC 36 COM 5C.
WHC. 2012*b*. Committee Decision WHC 36 COM 5E.
WHC. 2014. Committee Decision WHC 36 COM 5D.

The Landscape Approach – A Global Context for Sustainability

Mechtild Rössler[1]

Introduction

There is continuous and ever growing interest in "landscape" in the twenty-first century. This is most evident with attempts to create new international legal instruments, but also through numerous international conferences on the topic of landscape, cultural landscapes or specific types such as urban or rural landscapes. It is also clearly in the forefront with the key themes of general assemblies of professional organizations such as ICOMOS' Heritage and Landscape as Human Values in 2014 or ICOM's Museums and Cultural Landscapes in 2016.

UNESCO, as the main United Nations organization dealing with this topic, has included it in its heritage conservation programmes for over sixty years. Its General Conference adopted the very first global legal instrument on "landscape" as early as 1962, with the UNESCO Recommendation concerning the Safeguarding of Beauty and Character of Landscapes and Sites (UNESCO, 1962).

This was followed by the 1972 World Heritage Convention which, in its definition of cultural heritage in Article 1, included sites as "works of man or the combined works of nature and man" (UNESCO, 1972) and paved the way to truly recognizing cultural landscapes in 1992. This was paralleled by efforts at the European level which culminated in the Council of Europe's adoption of the European Landscape Convention (Florence, 2000).

In the twenty-first century, two significant evolutions should be noted: the attempts to establish a Global Landscape Convention and the adoption of the 2011 UNESCO Recommendation on the Historic Urban Landscape. They demonstrate growing interest in a holistic view, global collaboration and integrated approaches in addressing non-sustainable practices including degradation of ecosystems, growing uncontrolled urbanization, and over-use of limited land and natural resources.

This paper reviews these initiatives from a sustainable development perspective, including Resolutions by the United Nations General Assembly, and makes suggestions as to how landscape can be a unifying framework for future work.

1 The author is responsible for the choice and presentation of the facts contained in this article, and for the opinions expressed therein, which are not necessarily those of UNESCO.

Development of landscape approaches

Interestingly enough, the evolution of landscape approaches is intrinsically linked with global debates leading towards the sustainability concept in particular.

As early as the 1960s, worldwide debates emerged on nature preservation, protected areas and landscapes, including on the economic benefits of protected areas and landscape conservation for communities. Following a resolution adopted by the General Assembly in December 1962 on "Economic Development and Nature Conservation", the first World List of National Parks and Equivalent Reserves was published in 1961/62 with the help of the International Union for Conservation of Nature (IUCN), a global NGO established by UNESCO in 1949. Adrian Phillips reveals the history of this development:

"The emergence of a world-wide conservation movement after the Second World War encouraged the idea of a global framework for protected areas. This has been led by the IUCN network – or commission – of volunteer experts on protected areas. The International Commission on National Parks was established in 1960 under the leadership of Hal Coolidge. It soon became the Commission on National Parks and Protected Areas of IUCN (CNPPA); since 1996 it has been the World Commission on Protected Areas (WCPA). A 1959 resolution of the 27th session of the United Nations Economic and Social Council (ECOSOC) recognised that 'national parks and equivalent reserves are important factors in the wise use of natural resources'. In response, IUCN's new protected areas commission compiled a 300-page 'World List of National Parks and Equivalent Reserves'. This – the first version of the now familiar 'UN List' of protected areas – was published in 1961 and presented at the Seattle First World Conference on National Parks in 1962 ... At this meeting, the first proper debate about the 'nomenclature' of protected areas, which was based on a paper by C. F. Brockman, took place ..." (Phillips, 2004).

This growing awareness, in addition to related intergovernmental discussions, also led to the first ever global legal instrument in the field of landscape protection, the UNESCO Recommendation concerning the Safeguarding of Beauty and Character of Landscapes and Sites in 1962. Its preamble pre-empts later debates on sustainable development, as the concept did not exist yet as such:

"Considering furthermore that landscapes and sites are an important factor in the economic and social life of many countries, and are largely instrumental in ensuring the health of their inhabitants", ... and it also recognized "that due account should be taken of the needs of community life, its evolution and the rapid development of technical progress" (UNESCO, 1962).

While this Recommendation was "soft law" for Member States of UNESCO to consider, the following ten years leading to the First International Conference on the Human Environment (Stockholm, 1972) saw the development of further legal texts for the conservation of cultural heritage by UNESCO and ICOMOS and natural heritage by IUCN. But the emergence of the environmental movements (McCormick, 1991) and the evolution of holistic approaches for the human environment led to the merging of the texts leading to the World Heritage Convention (see for details Cameron and Rössler, 2013). The Convention Concerning the Protection of the World Cultural and Natural Heritage was finally adopted by UNESCO's General Conference on 16 November 1972. It was accompanied by the Recommendation Concerning the Protection, at National Level, of the Cultural and Natural Heritage adopted the same day. In its Preamble it specifically refers to the holistic approach and much needed global cooperation in this regard:

"Considering that the cultural and natural heritage forms an harmonious whole, the components of which are indissociable", and "Considering that a policy for the protection of the cultural and natural heritage, thought out and formulated in common, is likely to bring about a continuing interaction among Member States and to have a decisive effect on the activities of the United Nations Educational, Scientific and Cultural Organization in this field".

The World Heritage Convention already foresaw the concept of sustainable development before the word entered international debates, as Brown Weiss (1989) pointed out so eloquently: it took into account future generations in international law. It also brought forward the idea of shared heritage among humankind that is a "common patrimony" and thus the idea of "intergenerational equity". This idea is clearly reflected in Articles 4 and 5 of the Convention, recognizing that States Parties have the duty "of ensuring the identification, protection, conservation, presentation and transmission to future generations of the cultural and natural heritage", as well as "to adopt a general policy which aims to give the cultural and natural heritage a function in the life of the community and to integrate the protection of that heritage into comprehensive planning programmes". In this respect, the scope of the Convention goes beyond the specific properties included in its List of World Heritage sites, to encompass national heritage policies and wider development strategies.

However, one of the key features of this Convention, the protection of cultural and natural heritage together in one single instrument, did not lead to substantive considerations of landscape protection, enhancement of sustainable land-use practices and development of long-term management approaches in the early years – although some debates focused on the balance between natural and cultural sites and the protection of rural landscapes.

The inclusion of the cultural landscape concept and its development in the framework of the World Heritage Convention which culminated in 1992 has been extensively documented (see Cameron and Rössler, 2013). However there needs to be full understanding of the global context in which this Committee Decision was taken: due to the 1992 Rio Earth Summit (United Nations Conference on Environment and Development), awareness was growing about the environment and human action, similar to the global context of the 1972 Stockholm Conference (United Nations Conference on the Human Environment), when the World Heritage Convention was adopted.

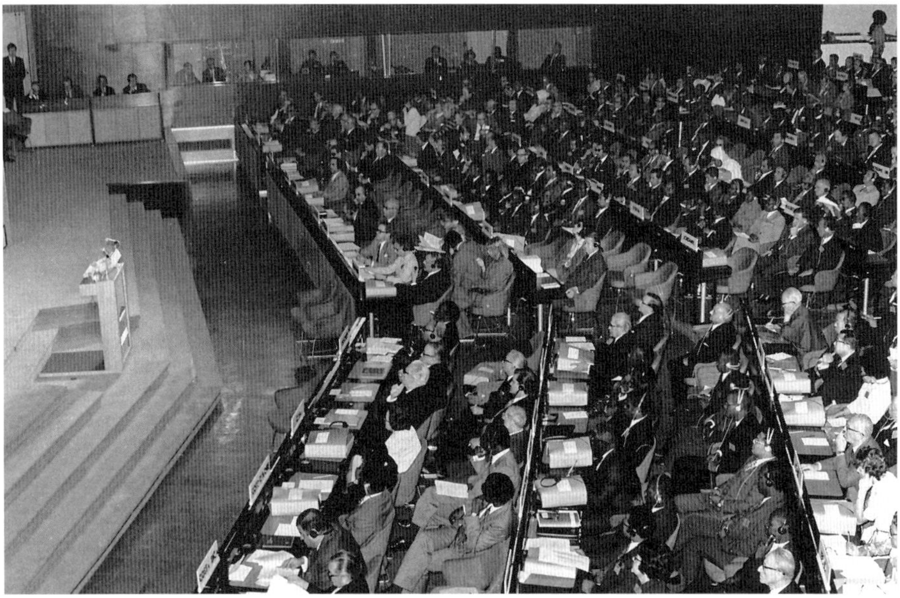

Fig. 1: The adoption of the World Heritage Convention at UNESCO's General Conference in 1972 – a document which already included the concept of intergenerational equity (© UNESCO)

This context can be clearly demonstrated by the wording introduced by Committee members at the 16th session of the World Heritage Committee in 1992 (Santa Fe, United States), including the key concept of "sustainable land-use". The Committee at that session finally acknowledged that a World Heritage cultural landscape is a site where the interaction between people and their environment is considered to be of Outstanding Universal Value. The Committee, when taking the decision to include cultural landscape categories into the *Operational Guidelines*, made the World Heritage Convention the first international instrument to recognize cultural landscapes and actively take action to protect them. Table 1 demonstrates the linkages between global debates and evolution of the international recognition of "landscape".

For the first time in this instrument, the notion of sustainability entered the *Operational Guidelines* in 1992, with reference to the "sustainable use" of cultural landscapes. Only in 2002, at the time of the implementation of the global commitments made ten years before in Rio, with the Johannesburg Declaration on Sustainable Development (2002), the World Heritage Committee adopted the Budapest Declaration, which stressed the need to "ensure an appropriate and equitable balance between conservation, sustainability and development, so that World Heritage properties can be protected through appropriate activities contributing to the social and economic development and the quality of life of our communities".

It took even more time, until 2005, for the overall notion of sustainable development to be introduced into the *Operational Guidelines:* "The protection and conserva-

Table: Linkages between global debates and UN Resolutions and international texts on landscapes or cultural landscapes

Date	International events	Discussions and development of approaches relating to landscape	International texts directly relating to landscape (legal instruments in **bold**)
1962-	UN General Assembly (1962) Seattle First World Conference on National Parks (1962)	Following a Resolution adopted by the General Assembly in December 1962 on Economic Development and Nature Conservation, which endorsed Resolution No. 713 of the 27th Session of the UN Economic and Social Council in 1959, recognizing national parks and equivalent reserves as an important factor in the wise use of natural resources, and leading to the compilation of the first World List of National Parks and Equivalent Reserves in 1962	**UNESCO Recommendation concerning the Safeguarding of Beauty and Character of Landscapes and Sites (1962)**
1972-	United Nations Conference on the Human Environment, Stockholm (1972) United Nations World Charter for Nature (1982)	Reflections on combined works of nature and man; natural and cultural heritage in one instrument discussed at Stockholm and presented by IUCN and by UNESCO and ICOMOS	**World Heritage Convention (1972)** **ICOMOS – Florence Charter (1981)**
1992-	Rio Earth Summit: United Nations Conference on Environment and Development: Rio Declaration Agenda 21	World Heritage cultural landscapes categories adopted in the framework of the World Heritage Convention (World Heritage Committee Decision, 1992): sustainable land-use introduced; Further discussions with the Habitat Agenda (including Chapter IV, Sustainable Human Settlements Development in an Urbanizing World including sustainable land use (http://www.un-documents.net/ha-4c.htm) and Agenda 21, including through Chapter 14, Promoting Sustainable Agriculture and Rural Development	Operational Guidelines for the implementation of the World Heritage Convention (1992)

Date	International events	Discussions and development of approaches relating to landscape	International texts directly relating to landscape (legal instruments in **bold**)
2002-	World Summit on Sustainable Development, (WSSD or Earth Summit), Johannesburg, South Africa: **Johannesburg Declaration on Sustainable Development (2002)**	Discussions on sustainable development by the United Nations The United Nations Environment Programme (UNEP) and UNESCO launched a Joint Programme on the Links between Biological and Cultural Diversity (JP-BiCuD) in 2010 to strengthen the linkages between biological and cultural diversity initiatives, and enhance the synergies between conventions and programmes	Ferrara Declaration celebrating ten years of cultural landscapes (2002) **European Landscape Convention (2000)**; Budapest Declaration (2002) by the World Heritage Committee Food and Agriculture Organization of the United Nations (FAO) Globally Important Agricultural Heritage Systems (GIAHS) (2002)
2011-	Rio+20: Outcome Document, *The Future We Want, inter alia,* set out a mandate to establish an Open Working Group to develop a set of sustainable development goals for consideration and appropriate action by the General Assembly	Preliminary study on the technical and legal aspects relating to the desirability of a new international standard-setting instrument on landscape http://unesdoc.unesco.org/images/0019/001917/ 191720e.pdf	**Recommendation on the Historic Urban Landscape (2011)** Florence Declaration on the Links between Biological and Cultural Diversity (2014) http://www.uniscape.eu/allegati/FLorence-UNESCO-CBDJP_Inst.pdf

tion of the natural and cultural heritage are a significant contribution to sustainable development" (para. 6). The *Operational Guidelines* further determined (para. 119) that World Heritage properties "may support a variety of ongoing and proposed uses that are ecologically and culturally sustainable". While in 1992 with the recognition of cultural landscapes, the role of communities in their protection and management was clearly identified, it took some more years to make the move broader for all types of sites and World Heritage conservation globally: At its 31st session (Christchurch, New Zealand, 2007), the World Heritage Committee decided to add "Communities" to the previous four Strategic Objectives, "to enhance the role of communities in the implementation of the World Heritage Convention" (Decision 31 COM 13B).

Regional levels: The European Landscape Convention

In the meantime, at the European level, the products of the close and intense interaction between people and their environment throughout European history, including through traditional farming and forestry practices, have been finally recognized. The European Landscape Convention (Florence, 2000) was the result of years of work identifying people's activities as crucial for creating resilient landscape patterns, varied biocultural resources also shaping the cultural identity in Europe's diverse regions.

With this process, "landscape" became one of the primary concerns of global and regional sustainability policies. It was seen as benefiting the local population's quality of life and economic potential, while creating a space for leisure activities, fulfilling emotional and spiritual needs, and contributing to a sense of identity. This led to more integrated planning and management strategies. Sustainable development has been the overarching goal of the international community since the 1992 Rio Earth Summit. This and the experiences with cultural landscapes under the World Heritage Convention were also taken into account in the implementation of the European Landscape Convention, which became an instrument for the enhancement of landscape policies in the European region, also reaching out to other parts of the world with a vibrant research network. Note that in other regions initiatives emerge for landscape approaches such as the Latin American Landscape Initiative (LALI).[2]

New and emerging initiatives

Another emerging approach is the concept of the Historic Urban Landscape (HUL) which derived from World Heritage Committee debates on integrating new architectural elements into historic urban settings. It was specifically discussed at a UNESCO conference in Vienna[3] in May 2005 as the *Vienna Memorandum on World Heritage and Contemporary Architecture – Managing the Historic Urban Landscape*. Following discussions with a broad range of stakeholders subsequent to this meeting, UNESCO's General Conference adopted a new Recommendation on the Historic Urban Landscape on 10 November 2011.[4] This Recommendation did not define a new category of cultural

---

2 http://www.csla-aapc.ca/sites/csla-aapc.ca/files/IFLA/120910%20LALI_EN-.pdf (accessed 4 July 2014).

3 UNESCO (2005) International Conference on World Heritage and Contemporary Architecture – Managing the Historic Urban Landscape, UNESCO World Heritage Centre in cooperation with ICOMOS and the City of Vienna at the request of the World Heritage Committee, adopted at its 27th session in 2003.

4 Recommendation on the Historic Urban Landscape, 10 November 2011: http://portal.unesco.org/en/ev.php-URL_ID=48857&URL_DO=DO_TOPIC&URL_SECTION=201.html.

landscape, but was intended as a tool to integrate policies and practices of the conservation of the built environment into the wider goals of urban sustainable development respecting cultural and landscape contexts. UNESCO's 2011 Recommendation on the Historic Urban Landscape applies to all urban heritage, not only to World Heritage properties: the urban context is now seen in a holistic way with its multifaceted historical, environmental and cultural layers.

As a follow-up to the International Conference on Biological and Cultural Diversity: Diversity for Development – Development for Diversity (Montreal, 2010) organized jointly by UNESCO and UNEP's Convention on Biological Diversity, a joint programme of work on biological and cultural diversity led by the secretariat of the Biodiversity Convention and UNESCO was established.[5] Enhancement of "biocultural diversity" is now firmly recognized in international conservation efforts. A close cooperation with FAO has been established on agricultural landscapes, in particular with the Globally Important Agricultural Heritage Systems (GIAHS) initiative since 2002, which develops an integrated approach combining sustainable agriculture and rural development.[6] Both advances are firmly rooted in the sustainable development concept and evolved with the global debates outlined above. Note that another aspect for integrated sustainable development was taken into account with the recognition of intangible cultural heritage, as defined in the 2003 UNESCO Convention for the Safeguarding of the Intangible Cultural Heritage. This evolution reinforced UNESCO messages for integrated heritage conservation by means of different conventions to enhance traditional knowledge and practices so fundamental to heritage conservation and the safeguard for long-term sustainable development benefiting future generations.

In 2010 UNESCO was approached by the International Federation of Landscape Architects (IFLA) for the development of a Global Landscape Convention, as the 47th World Congress of IFLA in 2010 had adopted a Resolution and a Proposal to further enhance the recognition and conservation of landscapes globally (Global Landscape Convention). UNESCO therefore held a small international expert workshop to discuss the matter and prepared a preliminary study on the technical and legal aspects (UNESCO, 2014).

Among the arguments presented were growing global change, including climate change and land degradation, unsustainable economic development, quality of life and governance, but most of all the piecemeal approach to landscapes globally. After

---

Further explanation and background on its development: http://whc.unesco.org/en/activities/638/.

5 Based on the working document adopted by the Conference: http://www.unesco.org/mab/doc/iyb/icbcd_working_doc.pdf (accessed 4 April 2014).

6 On this programme see FAO web page: http://www.fao.org/giahs/giahs-home/en/and on cooperation *World Heritage Review* No. 69 on agricultural landscapes: http://whc.unesco.org/en/review/69/ (accessed 4 April 2014).

considerable and substantive debates, the Executive Board of UNESCO took the following Decision:

"Takes note of the draft preliminary study on the technical and legal aspects of a new standard-setting instrument on landscape (186 EX/21)" and ... "Requests the Director-General to consider taking specific measures, under the existing standard-setting instruments, for the protection of landscapes."[7]

UNESCO and many other agencies, including UNEP and FAO, and the Council of Europe, are working jointly to overcome the crucial issues outlined above and to ensure inclusive sustainable development and integrated approaches for global landscape conservation.

Conclusions

Global landscape conservation is at the heart of encompassing sustainable development with clear benefits for local communities. While by definition, sustainable development is an overall goal for the international community, its implementation requires integrated territorial, regional and local strategies. This was taken into account for the Recommendation on the Historic Urban Landscape (2011), the last of a series of legal instruments dealing with landscape. This paper describes the evolution of landscape concepts and its relationship to the emergence of the sustainable development agenda globally.

Several conclusions can be drawn from this remarkable history: at each critical moment in time the links can be demonstrated between United Nations debates on people and their environment, land-use practices and sustainable development, and steps taken for specific legal instruments,. Moreover, UNESCO has over time become the house of dialogue on global landscape debates beginning with the first legal instrument in 1962, factors however that cannot be seen in isolation from growing awareness and international discussions in the field.

The fundamental principles of the 1972 World Heritage Convention of transmitting places of Outstanding Universal Value to future generations have been implemented in practice at World Heritage sites. Future generations have the right to the heritage of the past for their resources, identity and diversity, and to unique cultural landscapes linking cultural and biological diversity.

A broad recognition of cultural landscapes came at a time when links between cultural and biological diversity were increasingly being discussed, thus further raising awareness and influencing other legal instruments such as the 2000 European

7 Decision 186 EX/21. http://unesdoc.unesco.org/images/0019/001930/193025e.pdf (accessed 4 July 2014).

Landscape Convention or the 2011 UNESCO Recommendation on the Historic Urban Landscape.

The relationship between the evolution of the global debate on sustainable development and the increased awareness and concern about landscape over the past sixty years can be seen in three phases:

- very early attempts, prior to the notion of sustainable development, in the 1960s;
- a consolidation phase with a response in the form of a number of legal instruments of global importance, and the emergence of substantive protection measures at global, regional and national levels;
- a new debate on landscape in the twenty-first century addressing emerging needs with a more holistic approach and providing national and local authorities with new tools to face new challenges.

In terms of future evolution, especially for the Post-2015 Development Agenda, both the landscape and the cultural landscapes approach in particular, are well placed to link long-term sustainable development with conservation practices thanks to the active participation of local communities in these sites. Rapid globalization, including demographic changes, migration, climate change and growing poverty due to unlimited resource and land use, continuing land degradation and uncontrolled urbanization, will certainly lead to new challenges. Based on pioneering experiences and the intrinsic interconnectivity between people and their land, the landscape approach can provide new perspectives to innovate, and better respond to these emerging needs in the face of climate change and global social, economic and cultural change.

References

Brown Weiss, E. 1989. *In Fairness to Future Generations: International Law, Common Patrimony and Intergenerational Equity.* New York, Transnational Publishers.

Cameron, C. and Rössler, M. 2013. *Many Voices, One Vision: the Early History of the World Heritage Convention.* Dorchester, UK, Ashgate.

Fowler, P. J. 2002. *World Heritage Cultural Landscapes 1992–2002.* Paris, UNESCO World Heritage Centre. (World Heritage Papers No. 6.) http://whc.unesco.org/en/series/6/

Luengo Anon, A. and Rössler, M. (eds). 2012. *World Heritage Cultural Landscapes.* Elche, Spain, Ayuntamiento de Elche.

March 2014 Roundtable Proceedings http://www.patrimoinebati.umontreal.ca/documents/Proceedings_2014_FINAL.pdf

McCormick, J. 1991. *Reclaiming Paradise. The Global Environmental Movement.* Bloomington, Ind., Indiana University Press.

McCormick, J. 2004. The history of the international system of protected area management categories. *Parks,* Vol. 14, No. 3, p. 6. http://cmsdata.iucn.org/downloads/14_3lowres.pdf

Rössler, M. (ed.). 2003. *Cultural Landscapes: the Challenges of Conservation.* World Heritage 2002. Shared Legacy, Common Responsibility. Associated Workshops, 11–12 November 2002, Ferrara, Italy. Paris, UNESCO World Heritage Centre. (World Heritage Papers No. 7.) http://whc.unesco.org/en/series/7/

Rössler, M. and Folin Calabi, L. 2008. The cultural landscape and the historic urban landscape approach as a tool to protect important views in historic cities. Paper presented to the Round *Table Le Patrimoine Mondial/World Heritage: Définir et protéger les "perspectives visuelles importantes" Defining and protecting "important views"* Montreal 18–20 March. http://www.patrimoinebati.umontreal.ca/pdf/PV_Table_ronde_2008.pdf

Taylor, K. 2013. The challenges of the cultural landscape construct and associated intangible values in an Asian context. In: K. Da Silva and N. K. Chapagain, *Managing Asian Heritage: Contexts, Concerns and Prospects*. New York, Routledge, pp. 189–211.

UNESCO. 1962. Recommendation concerning the Safeguarding of Beauty and Character of Landscapes and Sites, adopted by the General Conference at its 12th session, Paris, 11 December 1962. http://portal.unesco.org/en/ev.php-URL_ID=13067&URL_DO=DO_TOPIC&URL_SECTION=201.html (Accessed 4 April 2014.)

UNESCO. 1972. Convention concerning the Protection of the World Cultural and Natural Heritage, adopted by the General Conference at its seventeenth session, Paris, 16 November 1972. http://whc.unesco.org/archive/convention-en.pdf (Accessed 4 April 2014.)

UNESCO. 2004. *Linking Universal and Local Values: Managing a Sustainable Future for World Heritage*. Paris, UNESCO World Heritage Centre. (World Heritage Papers No. 13.) http://whc.unesco.org/en/series/13/

UNESCO. 2010. *World Heritage Cultural Landscapes. A Handbook for Conservation and Management*. Edited by N. Mitchell, M. Rössler and P.-M. Tricaut. Paris, UNESCO World Heritage Centre. (World Heritage Papers No. 26.) http://whc.unesco.org/en/series/26/

UNESCO. 2011. Recommendation on the Historic Urban Landscape. Paris, 10 November.

UNESCO. 2013. Report on the International World Heritage Expert Meeting on the Mainstreaming of the methodological approach related to the Recommendation on the Historic Urban Landscape in the Operational Guidelines Rio de Janeiro, Brazil, 3–5 September 2013, http://whc.unesco.org/en/events/1071/.

UNESCO. 2014. Preliminary study on the technical and legal aspects relating to the desirability of a new international standard-setting instrument on landscape, presented to the Executive Board of UNESCO: http://unesdoc.unesco.org/images/0019/001917/191720e.pdf (Accessed 4 July 2014.)

von Droste, B., Plachter, H. and Rössler. M. (eds). 1995. *Cultural Landscapes of Universal Value. Components of a Global Strategy*. Jena, Germany, Fischer Verlag.

Sustainable Development and Intangible Cultural Heritage: Integrating Culture into Development

Shina Erlewein

Introduction

"Culture is what makes us who we are, it gives us strength, it is a wellspring of innovation and creativity, and it provides answers to many of the challenges we face today", said UNESCO Director-General Irina Bokova in her keynote address at the Blouin Creative Leadership Summit in 2012.[1] Culture is among the key emerging topics in international discussions today, and UNESCO is concentrating efforts to place culture at the heart of the global development agenda (UNESCO, 2012). Furthermore, sustainability is regarded as a fundamental, if not foundational aspect of development, together gaining increasing international importance. The concept of development has been expanded particularly since 1992, with thinkers such as Amartya Sen and Arjun Appadurai participating in the reconfiguration of meaning, and it currently faces a new conceptual shift, leading to the shaping of a new paradigm. For decades, the term sustainable development has been widely used in science and civil society as well as politics and, referring to a rather flexible concept, is frequently applied by a range of stakeholders and actors in the context of a variety of needs. However, no precise guidelines for operationalization and, even more so, no globally agreed criteria for assessment exist. Instead, a number of approaches are used at global, national and local levels. Due to this variety of applications and lack of clear-cut definitions, it has been argued that the term is losing its meaning today, and indeed the concept is open to precise definition and theoretical reconceptualization. Still, it goes without saying that a number of documents and international reports play a central role in enlivening this concept and making it useful and applicable on local, national and international grounds to the benefit of the global as well as the local population. In the context of this paper, the Brundtland Report (WCED, 1987) and the 1992 Rio de Janeiro Earth Summit, along with the Rio Declaration (UNCED, 1992*a*) and Agenda 21 (UNCED, 1992*b*) consolidating the paradigm of the three-pillar approach to sustainable development, reflecting environmental, economic and social goals, demand a brief mention, as this approach still lies at the heart of sustainable development strategies implemented today, with the economic pillar clearly taking central impor-

1 http://www.unesco.org/new/en/culture/themes/singleview/news/director_general_meets_the_secretary_general_of_the_united_nations_and_the_president_of_the_general_assembly_prior_the_67th_session_of_the_general_assembly/ (accessed 1 December 2014).

tance. However, in view of the increasing complexity of the world and particularly the variety of diverse societies and cultures all actively participating in the global community, underscoring their sociocultural significance and uniqueness, their particular perspectives, histories, needs and aspirations, and acknowledging the legitimate call for the recognition of cultural diversity in the world as a resource for humanity, today the cultural dimension of sustainable development is conceptualized as a fourth pillar.[2]

So far, culture has been largely ignored in implementation strategies, or has been looked at mainly as a means within the framework of the other dimensions. Indeed, culture impacts both on the activities and targets of the other three dimensions. For example, regarding the economic dimension, culture, referring particularly to cultural products and commodities, is produced and consumed in order to generate and enhance income, employment and economic growth, thereby ensuring prosperity and welfare, a perspective specifically recalling contributions by the creative sector. Culture also touches on the social dimension, as it enables the (re)creation of social cohesion and community, stability and peace, often even regulating the distribution of tangible and intangible resources, including health and education. And finally, culture is utilized in the environmental sense, for example in the promotion of specific community-based or indigenous perceptions and in the knowledge and usage of nature, of the environment and resources aiming, among others, at the protection and preservation of nature for future generations. However, I argue that even though culture permeates all the dimensions, as a signifying system influencing behaviour, values, attitudes and lifestyles and thus contributing immensely to the quality of life, it must be integrated as a fourth dimension in its own right rather than as a tool to enhance other dimensions.

As culture contributes immensely to sustainable development, linkages between intangible cultural heritage and sustainable development can indeed be defined. After first reflecting on the existing and the envisioned paradigms, outlining both the three- and four-pillar approach to sustainable development, this paper will then discuss the interrelation of sustainable development and intangible cultural heritage, particularly against the background of UNESCO's activities, debates and documents, giving special mention to the 2003 Convention for the Safeguarding of the Intangible Cultural Heritage and the Operational Directives given for its implementation. Finally, it will analyse the conceptualization of the recently drafted Operational Directives on sustainable development outlining its approach and thereby referring back to the above-mentioned paradigm of sustainable development.

---

2 Also, the international organization United Cities and Local Governments (UCLG) adopted, in Mexico City in 2010, the Declaration on Culture as Fourth Pillar of Sustainable Development, placing culture at the heart of sustainability.

UNESCO's Intangible Heritage Convention and sustainable development

In contrast to the World Heritage Convention (UNESCO, 1972), which does not refer to the notion of sustainability, the Intangible Heritage Convention, coming more than thirty years later, clearly reflects the idea of intangible cultural heritage as an enabler of sustainable development, with intangible cultural heritage going beyond the functional societal aspects of heritage and reaching out to be beneficial for the quality of life at large.[3] In its preamble, the Intangible Heritage Convention already acknowledges the importance of intangible cultural heritage "as a mainspring of cultural diversity and a guarantee of sustainable development", referring back to the 1989 Recommendation on the Safeguarding of Traditional Culture and Folklore, the 2001 Universal Declaration on Cultural Diversity and finally the 2002 Istanbul Declaration (UNESCO, 2003, preamble). The Convention defines intangible cultural heritage in Article 2 as the "practices, representations, expressions, knowledge, skills – as well as the instruments, objects, artefacts and cultural spaces associated therewith – that communities, groups and, in some cases, individuals recognize as part of their cultural heritage" (ibid., Article 2.1), already highlighting the central role given to communities and groups within this Convention.[4] The second part of the definition stresses that the intangible cultural heritage "transmitted from generation to generation, is constantly recreated by communities and groups in response to their environment, their interaction with nature and their history, and provides them with a sense of identity and continuity, thus promoting respect for cultural diversity and human creativity" (ibid.). Here the dynamic and processual character of intangible cultural heritage is clearly stated, hinting at the further development and thus change of practices, knowledge and skills in correspondence with the respective environment, touching upon natural as well as social and cultural aspects and aiming at mutual respect and the encouragement of cultural diversity worldwide. One essential feature of intangible cultural heritage is the transmission of practices from one generation to the next, hence introducing the component of intergenerational equity, itself being one of the

---

3 Note that UNESCO already underscored the role of culture as a driver for creativity and identity building, for value generation and social cohesion as well as international cooperation in the cultural sector during the 1980s – see for example the Mexico City Declaration (UNESCO, 1982) and the World Decade for Cultural Development (UNESCO, 1990)). Since the 1990s and particularly since the new millennium, UNESCO has clearly promoted culture as a dimension of development and their close alliance became explicit in the 2001 Declaration as well as the 2003 and 2005 Conventions (UNESCO, 2002, 2003, 2005).

4 Intangible Cultural Heritage manifests itself in the following five domains: "(a) oral traditions and expressions, including language as a vehicle; (b) performing arts; (c) social practices, rituals and festive events; (d) knowledge and practices concerning nature and the universe; and (e) traditional craftsmanship" (UNESCO, 2003, Article 2.2).

principles of sustainable development. The Convention even goes one step further, since in the last sentence, the scope of intangible cultural heritage in the context of this Convention is clearly described, specifying that intangible cultural heritage needs to be compatible with (1) human rights instruments, (2) mutual respect and (3) sustainable development. As such, cultural elements not satisfying these three conditions will not be inscribed on the lists of the Convention.[5] Consequently, sustainable development is not only encouraged or enhanced but rather can be conceived of as constitutive to intangible cultural heritage with regard to the processes and aims of this Convention.

Moreover, the Convention itself can be characterized as sustainable, as its underlying concept of safeguarding refers to the assurance of the viability of practices, highlighting cultural processes rather than products and specific manifestations of heritage (UNESCO, 2003, Article 2.3). The concept of viability, encompassing a number of safeguarding measures with transmission being among the most central ones, essentially mirrors the concept of sustainability as developed in the Brundtland Report. The Brundtland discussion in mind, sustainable safeguarding of intangible cultural heritage must enable contemporary practice, preservation and transmission, while taking into account also the needs and aspirations of future practitioners in exercising and enjoying the fruits of engagement with intangible cultural heritage practices and expressions in future.

But how can intangible cultural heritage contribute to sustainable development and how is sustainable development reflected within intangible cultural heritage?

Intangible cultural heritage and sustainable development

Commercialization, the economic sector and patronage

Initially, discussions at UNESCO on the linkages between intangible cultural heritage and sustainable development centred mainly on issues reflecting the economic dimension of development, its opportunities and challenges, while thereby also addressing social and cultural impacts. For example, at the 7th session of the Intergovernmental Committee in Paris (2012), the consultative body underlined the importance of intangible cultural heritage for sustainable development and the Committee debated on the relation of commercialization, safeguarding and sustainable development with a number of points being raised by States Parties. First of all, cultural and economic dimensions were considered complementary. It was also argued

5 Looking at the inscription criteria mentioned in the Operational Directives, criteria U1 and R1 clearly refer to Article 2 of the Convention and as such, nominated elements must respect sensitivities of communities and adhere to sustainable development, among others (UNESCO, 2014*a*).

that governments and economy can be involved in the safeguarding of intangible cultural heritage via the promotion of cultural tourism and craftsmanship. The importance of intangible cultural heritage in the creative industry and economy was emphasized, pointing to revenues gained through practice again contributing to the viability of intangible cultural heritage practices and expressions. Finally, it was stated that safeguarding and commercialization can be reconciled, keeping in mind the harmful effect of over-commercialization compromising the cultural character of intangible cultural heritage elements.[6]

Indeed, over-commercialization is a real risk to safeguarding, and here, States Parties, businesses and communities need to strive for a balance. Governments and agencies implementing the Convention need to equilibrate top-down and bottom-up approaches, encouraging communication within and among community members as well as utmost participation and collaboration on all safeguarding measures, involving in some cases mediators, cultural brokers or translators, in order to ensure that communities are the prime beneficiaries and that measures correspond with their wishes, needs and concerns, including those of women and young people, leaving them in power to broaden the scope of development and commercialization or to limit their respective activities and projects in case of negative effects. In this context it needs to be stressed that this Convention is essentially on the safeguarding of intangible cultural heritage and not on the promotion of tourism or development, even though discussed intensely these days, and the question as to whether economic aspects should be stressed or not is still an open one. Intangible cultural heritage should not be limited to economic assets and increase of market value, since cultural knowledge, skills, practices and expressions constitute fundamental elements of cultural and social integrity. It further needs to be recalled that inscription on the lists does not necessarily imply that safeguarding measures are sustainable by nature. Even well-intended measures aiming at sustainable development, focusing on cultural products rather than processes, can foster the de-valuation of culture and even encourage the deterioration of living heritage, in some cases jeopardizing the viability of the element and threatening the social cohesion of the respective community. Nevertheless, keeping in mind the potential harmful effects of (over-)commercialization, tourism and trade, and in view of the lack of patronage and livelihood of specific intangible cultural heritage practitioners, it can be argued that the economy can be developed for the benefit of the communities, enabling them to generate income from culture in a self-determined way. In fact, as my own fieldwork undertaken in 2012 on the safeguarding of Kutiyattam Sanskrit theatre in Kerala (India) shows, the lack of income is causing the younger and middle-aged generation of practitioners to disengage themselves, or temporarily leave active intangible cultural heritage practice

6 http://www.unesco.org/culture/ich/index.php?lg=en&pg=00473, audio recording on item 13a, 6 December 2013.

behind and seek other employment opportunities, often located in other professional areas, regions and even states. Lack of employment opportunities further discourages young people from non-hereditary families from working in the art form. Young males are expected to finance their families later on and many are not willing to undergo training, leading to a severe lack of male apprentices in government institutions and several Kutiyattam classes vanishing altogether.[7] Hence, employment and income generation can be regarded as crucial, enabling practitioners to be engaged full-time in the practice and transmission of their respective intangible cultural heritage, and encouraging young people to participate in practices. This is particularly important when few practitioners remain to uphold the tradition, when they themselves show strong dedication to their heritage but lack the financial means to engage in it on the long term. Indeed, long-term safeguarding can only be attained when financial security can be achieved among practitioners. Moreover, in these cases, financial support doesn't necessarily reflect the commercialization of intangible cultural heritage, as diverse forms of patronage of intangible cultural heritage practitioners have existed over centuries and can be considered complementary to intangible cultural heritage practice. However, some forms of patronage have broken away in the context of social change and transformation, or nation-building processes, leaving practitioners often unsupported. Thus, realizing the universalization of intangible cultural heritage and acknowledging the transformation of practices and spaces, changes in patronage also need to be envisaged, possibly involving new forms of such. In this context, intellectual and collective property rights also need to be addressed and States Parties could be encouraged, in close collaboration with the practicing communities, to create mechanisms for the protection of these rights also in their respective safeguarding policies.

Envisioning Operational Directives

As shown above, sustainable development reaches far beyond the theme of economics. Still, so far no guidance has been given in the Operational Directives with regards to how intangible cultural heritage can foster sustainable development, by what criteria it is considered compatible with sustainable development and vice versa. In addition, certain paragraphs in the Directives, such as paras. 116 and 117 on commercial activities related to intangible cultural heritage in Chapter 4 on awareness-raising (UNESCO, 2014*a*) seem too limited regarding the scope of this crucial and complex

7 In recent years at the government institution Kerala Kalamandalam, there was only one male student seeking advanced training in Kutiyattam.

issue, with paragraph topics also pointing far beyond the target of raising awareness of the intangible cultural heritage.[8]

In light of these concerns the Secretariat was asked to further develop the Operational Directives to the Convention providing guidance on the matter, also in view of the general implementation of the Convention (Decision 7.COM 7). During the 8th session of the Intergovernmental Committee in 2013, it was decided to develop a new chapter of the Directives which would go beyond commercialization matters and the contribution of intangible cultural heritage to the creative sector, and would take a broader perspective on the relationship between intangible cultural heritage and sustainable development. It would focus on implementation measures on the national level, and be meant to strengthen cooperation and exchange between UNESCO and WIPO on the matter (Decision 8.COM 13a). Last but not least, the outcome document of the Chengdu Conference on Intangible Cultural Heritage held on the occasion of the 10th anniversary of the Convention in July 2013, also asks the international community to enforce its commitment to intangible cultural heritage as a guarantee of sustainable development (UNESCO, 2013*a*),[9] with the evaluation report by UNESCO's Internal Oversight Service in October 2013 clearly pointing to a gap in guidance in the Operational Directives, regarding the compatibility and interrelation of the two, also regarding how intangible cultural heritage should facilitate sustainable development, whether specific manifestations of intangible cultural heritage are more suitable than others to the enhancement of sustainable development and finally regarding the connection between safeguarding measures and other development policies implemented on a national level (UNESCO, 2013*c*, para. 53).

Drafting Operational Directives

Subsequently, in order to fill this gap, a category VI expert meeting was conducted in Istanbul, Turkey, from 29 September to 1 October 2014, elaborating preliminary recommendations on draft Operational Directives on "Safeguarding intangible cultural heritage and sustainable development at the national level" and thus on the creation of a new single chapter in the Directives, to be discussed at the 9th and 10th sessions

8 The Directives also encourage the media "to contribute to raising awareness about the importance of the intangible cultural heritage as a means to foster social cohesion, sustainable development and prevention of conflict, in preference to focusing only on its aesthetic or entertainment aspects", without however giving further guidance how the connection shall be understood (UNESCO, 2014, para. 111). The Directives further specify that no contributions to the Intangible Cultural Heritage Fund can be accepted by entities engaging in activities not compatible with the principle of sustainable development (ibid., para. 73).

9 In the same month Morocco also organized an international expert meeting on "*Intangible Cultural Heritage and Economy*" held in Rabat.

of the Intergovernmental Committee in view of submitting the chapter for adoption by the General Assembly during its 6th session in 2016.[10]

The Concept Note to the expert meeting Document (UNESCO, 2014*c*) provides a number of examples recalling how intangible cultural heritage contributes to sustainable development. Among others, it mentions the contribution of intangible cultural heritage to social cohesion and inclusion, citing as an example the Brazilian Frevo, which links people with each other and with practices in the context of Carnival activities, thereby enhancing social ties and cultural identity. The Note further stresses the role intangible cultural heritage plays in the context of recreating, negotiating and also reshaping and developing further gender roles in societies. In the context of environmental sustainability, it cites the knowledge and practices of the Kikuyu women in Kenya involving the preservation of crops and seeds, thus fostering biodiversity, and Samoan mat-weaving practices and respected ecological knowledge and behaviours. Also, knowledge and strategies are addressed which enable community resilience in the face of natural disasters and the effects of climate change. In the context of the economic dimension, as an example, subsistence livelihoods of Estonian farmers are mentioned and finally under the section peace and security, the potential of the intangible cultural heritage to promote peace is exemplified by means of reference to the Manden Charter of Mali, one of the earliest human rights charters of the world and orally transmitted. Social practices such as the Murcia Council of Wise Men and the Valencia Water Tribunals are also cited as examples regulating resource usage and enabling local dispute settling and conflict resolution.

Building on this Concept Note, within the dimension of inclusive social development, the draft of the Operational Directives discusses the contribution of the intangible cultural heritage to food security, health care, access to clean water and forms of sustainable water usage, education, also recognizing traditional methods and models of education transmitting intangible cultural heritage, social cohesion and gender equality. Within the second dimension, environmental sustainability, particularly contributions in domain 4 of intangible cultural heritage manifestations, 'Knowledge and practices concerning nature and the universe' are mentioned, highlighting their contribution to biodiversity protection and preservation, to sustainable use and management of resources, as well as community-based resilience in face of natural disasters and climate change. In core dimension 3, inclusive economic development, the contribution of intangible cultural heritage to income generation, employment and decent work is stressed and the role of tourism considered. The final core dimension, peace and security, outlines the contribution of intangible cultural heritage to ensuring and restoring peace and security, dialogue, exchange and mutual

10 See UNESCO (2014*b*) for the draft chapter developed by the Secretariat and the Annex of Document ITH/14/9.COM/13b of the 9th Intergovernmental Committee session in Paris, (November 2014) for a revised version.

understanding, highlighting its potentials in dispute prevention and conflict resolution, leading to reconciliation of parties by means of peaceful measures or to the recovery of communities having experienced conflicts or disasters. The draft finally acknowledges the role of safeguarding intangible cultural heritage practices in the process of peace-building by fostering intercultural dialogue and respect for cultural diversity.

Besides the results of the expert meeting, the 2014 report by the subsidiary body also gives a few examples of how intangible cultural heritage can contribute to sustainable development, stressing the relation between intangible cultural heritage practices and the natural environment, as well as highlighting this year's nominations by Brazil, Niger and India, with Brazil underlining the contribution of intangible cultural heritage in the fight against oppression and racism, Niger highlighting the contribution of customary practices to dispute-settling among communities and the fight against social discrimination, and India pointing to the tradition of metalworking and its contribution to the economy (Document ITH/14/9.COM/10 Add., paras 71, 73).

Contextualizing Operational Directives

The proposed draft Operational Directives discussed here basically adheres to a framework established by the UN report, *Realizing the Future We Want For All*, organized around the four core dimensions established in that report. The report, written by the UN System Task Team on the UN Post-2015 Development Agenda, initiated by the United Nations Secretary General in 2011, builds on the results of the Rio Conference on Sustainable Development and acknowledges the importance of culture, stressing that "communities and individuals must be able to create and practice their own culture and enjoy that of others free from fear. This will require, inter alia, respect for cultural diversity, safeguarding cultural and natural heritage, fostering cultural institutions, strengthening cultural and creative industries, and promoting cultural tourism" (UN, 2012, para. 71). The report calls for transformative change and elaborates a vision and framework for the Post-2015 Development Agenda, placing three overarching principles at its core, namely the values of human rights, equality and sustainability, and defining four core dimensions of sustainable development in which transformative change must be pursued, namely inclusive social development, inclusive economic development, environmental sustainability, and peace and security, acknowledging further that no dimension constitutes a separate entity, but all dimensions are highly interdependent and mutually impacting (ibid., pp. 21–32). The report explicitly envisions a holistic approach, where synergies between the different dimensions can be effectively utilized, with the three above-mentioned principles informing and supporting activities in all dimensions. It is clearly stated in the report that the outlined approach "is consistent with the principles of the Millennium Declaration, which set out a vision of freedom from want and fear for present and future generations and which builds on the three pillars of sustainable development" (ibid., p. i, see also para. 53).[11] In the section on sustainability, the report declares: "Consistent with the Rio+20 Outcome, the focus on sustainable development should comprise these three dimensions – economic, social and environmental – and recognize their inter-linkages" (ibid., para. 63). Thus the verbatim report states that it asserts the three-pillar approach, thereby marginalizing the cultural dimension as an independent pillar. In fact, besides paragraph 71 mentioned above and referred to under the umbrella of inclusive social development, the report gives no clear mention of the role of culture in development. However, it does recognize various national policies implementing the agenda, reflecting the respective local situation and context, while keeping in sight the vision and principles expressed in the report (ibid., p. ii).[12]

In this context, the conference on Culture: Key to Sustainable Development, held in May 2013 in China, should also be mentioned. The background paper, *Culture in the Post-2015 Sustainable Development Agenda: Why Culture is Key to Development,* refers to the above-mentioned principles and core dimensions, but also proposes the option of conceiving of culture as a self-standing pillar and thus an independent development goal (UNESCO, 2013*b*). The subsequent *Hangzhou Declaration. Placing Culture at the Heart of Sustainable Development Policies,* which is considered the peak of UNESCO's efforts, brought together some 500 delegates from over eighty countries to discuss and finally explicitly promote the role of culture for development, encouraging that it be considered in the Post-2015 International Development Agenda as a "specific goal", being "based on heritage, diversity, creativity and the transmission of knowledge and including clear targets and indicators that relate culture to all dimensions of sustainable development" (UNESCO, 2013*d*, p. 6).

Concluding reflections

Today, development reaches far beyond the fragmentary concentration on economic growth and humanitarian tasks mainly involving human aids and resource-sharing, but rather takes a holistic approach, placing emphasis on equity, dignity and happiness as well as sustainability, embracing global peace, freedom of choice and the enhancement of welfare and well-being. Development is seen as a means to uplift the quality of life of populations and individuals, as reflected in economic, environmental, social but also intellectual, spiritual and emotional domains, thus integrating

11 The Millennium Declaration, which defines eight Millennium Development Goals, one of them being the insurance of environmental sustainability (UN, 2000), did not pay tribute to the cultural dimension of development or refer explicitly to cultural heritage.

12 At its 68th Session in 2013, the UN General Assembly acknowledged the link between culture and economic, social and environmental development as well as peace and security and recognized the role of culture as a driver and enabler of sustainable development, making the case for its inclusion in the Post-2015 Development Agenda (UN General Assembly Document A/C.2/68/L.69 N).

needs of the mind and the body. Development continues to address the eradication of poverty, but the latter is no longer only a matter of material ends and targets, of raising income and creating employment. Addressing poverty today also encompasses participation, access to culture, to cultural practices, expressions and related assets, enabling people to live the life they cherish and be the persons they aim to be, also and especially in an ever more complex global world.[13] This sort of well-being is essentially rooted in the local context and the aspirations of local communities, in its culture and capabilities, and both cultural diversity and cultural heritage can be considered crucial in this regard. As Appadurai (2002) believes, cultural diversity doesn't refer simply to differences in lifestyles and value systems, knowledge and practices, but rather to a "value through which differences are mutually related and reciprocally supportive" to a "value which expresses and implies other, even more fundamental values ... creativity, dignity and community .... And without these values, no vision of development can be sustainable, since it will not rest on the moral commitment of the actors and subjects of development, who belong to particular cultural communities" (p. 16). Looking now at the manifestations of intangible cultural heritage, it can be argued that intangible cultural heritage intrinsically and essentially relates to the above-mentioned values. It is a continuous source of cultural diversity, of creativity, dignity and community and it relies directly on the commitment and vision of its respective community, the practitioners.

As a final remark it can be stated that discussion and reflection on the subject of the interrelation of intangible cultural heritage and sustainability are still at the beginning stage, and further reflection, argument and exploration are truly needed. In fact, the three-pillar approach to sustainable development as applied in the *Realizing the Future We Want For All* report is reasserted in the current draft Operational Directives to the 2003 Convention, thereby missing the opportunity to further develop a four-pillar approach stressing the contribution of culture to development as a self-standing pillar. In the current Directives, culture, without being addressed on its own right, permeates and impacts on the other three pillars and thereby on sustainability goals. In so doing, culture, and intangible heritage as a component of culture, is reduced to a tool enabling the achievement of other goals. It becomes clear that culture and intangible cultural heritage can be considered economic drivers, sources of social cohesion and inclusion, sources for environmental protection and management, and sources for the promotion of peace and prevention of conflicts. Without meaning to question the importance and legitimacy of these goals and the contribution of culture to them, and hence that of the intangible cultural heritage as well, this paper wishes to encourage further reflection on the possibility of seeing culture as a

---

13 Access to and participation in cultural life and the freedom to engage in creative expressions and activities are fundamental human rights and mentioned as such in the International Covenant on Economic, Social and Cultural Rights (UN, 1966).

goal and a sector of activity in itself. In order to do so, the current draft Directives would need to undergo a fundamental revision.

But how can culture – as a self-standing pillar and at the same time interconnected with the other three pillars – be understood? The cultural dimension reflects and favours cultural diversity, creativity, human knowledge and skills, cultural practices, different peoples' lifestyles, attitudes and value systems as well as potentially a sense of place. It contributes to the shaping and assertion of identity, to community-building and its consolidation, enabling participation and access, dignity and equity; it contributes to the (re)generation of value, to patterns enabling orientation and meaning, making it possible for people to find their place in society and in the world and to enjoy meaningful lives. In another vein, it also promotes innovation, focusing on processes rather than products or quantifiable targets. It safeguards cultural and natural, tangible and intangible heritage, strengthens local resilience and adaptation to change. As a stimulant to the creative industry, to cultural tourism and cultural institutions and activities, it fosters learning, intercultural exchange, dialogue and communication, empathy and mutual respect, with a long-term vision of social and cultural integrity as well as social and cultural change, aided by science and technology.

Finally, the question remains whether or not it is possible to evaluate the contribution of intangible cultural heritage to development and to the enhancement of individual and societal well-being in quantitative terms, applying quantitative methods and specific indicators relating, for example, to economic growth or the broadening of life choices. Considering that the essential contribution of intangible cultural heritage to development and sustainability is largely qualitative in nature, the application of qualitative methods to intangible cultural heritage and sustainable development seems appropriate. This is particularly true as culture-sensitive and context-specific targets envisioned in development initiatives might differ from community to community. As such, ethnographic methods will be crucial, but methods developed in the disciplines of psychology, education and political sciences will also be beneficial. However, due to the scope of the task, it might also be worthwhile to take a look at indices already developed by Bhutan and Italy. Both the Gross National Happiness index and the Equitable and Sustainable Well-Being index integrate the social dimension of development and also try to evaluate quality of life and well-being in view of attaining sustainable development goals (UNESCO, 2013*b*).

References

Appadurai, A. 2002. Diversity and sustainable development. In *Cultural Diversity and Biodiversity for Sustainable Development.* Nairobi, UNESCO/UNEP, pp. 16–19.

UN. 1966. *International Covenant on Economic, Social and Cultural Rights*. New York, United Nations. http://www.ohchr.org/EN/ProfessionalInterest/Pages/CESCR.aspx (Accessed 2 February 2014.)

UN. 2000. *United Nations Millennium Development Goals*. Resolution adopted by the General Assembly. New York, United Nations. http://www.un.org/millenniumgoals/bkgd.shtml (Accessed 2 February 2014.)
UN. 2012. *Realizing the Future We Want For All*. Report to the Secretary-General realized by the UN System Task Team on the Post-2015 UN Development Agenda. New York, United Nations. http://www.un.org/millenniumgoals/pdf/Post_2015_UNTTreport.pdf (Accessed 2 February 2014.)
UNCED. 1992*a*. *Rio Declaration*. Final Declaration of the UN Conference on Environment and Development. Rio de Janeiro, UNCED.
UNCED. 1992*b*. *Agenda 21*. Document of the UN Conference on Environment and Development. Rio de Janeiro, UNCED. http://sustainabledevelopment.un.org/content/documents/Agenda21.pdf (Accessed 2 December 2014.)
UNESCO. 1972. *Convention on the Protection of the World Cultural and Natural Heritage*. Paris, UNESCO.
UNESCO. 1982. Mexico-City Declaration on Cultural Policies. In *World Conference on Cultural Policies: 26 July – 6 August 1982, Mexico-City: Final Report*. Paris, UNESCO, pp. 41–46.
UNESCO. 1990. *World Decade for Cultural Development, 1988–1997. Plan of Action*. Paris, UNESCO.
UNESCO. 2002. *Universal Declaration on Cultural Diversity*. Adopted in 2001. Paris, UNESCO.
UNESCO. 2003. *Convention for the Safeguarding of the Intangible Cultural Heritage*. Paris, UNESCO.
UNESCO. 2005. *Convention on the Protection and Promotion of the Diversity of Cultural Expressions*. Paris, UNESCO.
UNESCO. 2012. *UN Task Team on the Post-2015 Development Agenda. Culture. A Driver and an Enabler of Sustainable Development. Thematic Think Piece*. Paris, UNESCO. https://en.unesco.org/post2015/sites/post2015/files/Think%20Piece%20Culture.pdf (Accessed 2 December 2014.)
UNESCO. 2013*a*. *Chengdu Recommendations*. Chengdu. Document ITH/13/EXP/8. http://www.unesco.org/culture/ich/doc/src/20548-EN.pdf (Accessed 2 December 2014.)
UNESCO. 2013*b*. *Culture in the Post-2015 Sustainable Development Agenda: Why Culture is Key to Sustainable Development*. Background Note. http://www.unesco.org/new/fileadmin/MULTIMEDIA/HQ/CLT/images/Post2015SustainableDevelopmentAgendaENG.pdf (Accessed 2 December 2014.)
UNESCO. 2013*c*. *Evaluation of UNESCO's Standard-Setting Work of the Culture Sector: Part 1–2003 Convention for the Safeguarding of the Intangible Cultural Heritage*. Final Report by B. Torggler and E. Sediakina-Rivière. Paris, UNESCO.
UNESCO. 2013*d*. *The Hangzhou Declaration. Placing Culture at the Heart of Sustainable Development Policies*. Hangzhou. http://www.unesco.org/new/fileadmin/MULTIMEDIA/HQ/CLT/images/FinalHangzhouDeclaration20130517.pdf (Accessed 2 December 2014.)
UNESCO. 2014*a*. *Operational Directives for the Implementation of the Convention for the Safeguarding of the Intangible Cultural Heritage*. Paris, UNESCO. http://www.unesco.org/culture/ich/en/directives (Accessed 2 December 2014.)
UNESCO. 2014*b*. *Draft Operational Directives on Safeguarding Intangible Cultural Heritage and Sustainable Development at the National Level*. Paris, UNESCO.
UNESCO. 2014*c*. *Concept Note. Intangible Cultural Heritage and Sustainable Development*. Paris, UNESCO. Document ITH/14/EXP/2.
WCED. 1987. *Report of the World Commission on Environment and Development: Our Common Future* (Brundtland Report). New York, United Nations.

III Paradigms

From Mitigation to Adaptation: A New Heritage Paradigm for the Anthropocene

Giovanni Boccardi[1]

Introduction: The dawn of a new era

According to the Geological Society of London, among other bodies, the Earth might be currently transiting from the Holocene, a temperate and placid epoch which lasted around 10,000 years and saw the birth of agriculture and the industrial civilization as we know it, into the so-called Anthropocene epoch, defined by the irreversible impact of human activities on the environment (Irwin, 2011, p. 34). The Anthropocene, it has been suggested, is being caused by humans "disrupting the grand natural cycles of biology, chemistry and geology by which elements like carbon and nitrogen circulate between land, sea and atmosphere", which will lead to a "hotter, stormier and less diverse planet".[2] The effects of this new era will extend well beyond climate change, ranging from deforestation and soil erosion to the loss of biodiversity, the decline of food and energy sources and massive migrations. The range of challenges that the Anthropocene is posing to us are, to quote Jared Diamond, "time bombs with fuses of less than fifty years" (Diamond 2005, p. 498).

Experts are still debating whether the beginning of the Anthropocene is a contemporary event or if it should be placed at the time of the Industrial Revolution of the eighteenth century. At any rate, it is today that we seem to have become aware that the scale and range of our activities and their impact on the planet have passed a tipping point beyond which the nature of the relationship between humans and their environment has changed fundamentally. In this new world, the paradigms, ideas, attitudes and beliefs that emerged and developed in the past – across fields of knowledge as diverse as philosophy, religion, politics or economics – seem to be increasingly challenged.

One area that is likely to be particularly affected by the above trends is the field of tangible cultural heritage conservation, because it sits at the threshold between different and often conflicting societal interests associated with the use of land resources. The aim of this paper is to discuss the viability of heritage conservation in the Anthropocene by exploring the impact that this new epoch may have on its key principles and practice. In doing so, it focuses on some aspects that define its

---

1 The author is responsible for the choice and the presentation of the facts contained in this article, and for the opinions expressed therein, which are not necessarily those of UNESCO.
2 See http://www.anthropocene.info/en/anthropocene (accessed 25 July 2014).

fundamental relationship with the larger environment and the broader goals of society, with particular reference to the author's experience in implementing the World Heritage Convention.

Heritage vs. the rest and the strategy of mitigation

The birth of the conservation movement has been placed traditionally in the nineteenth century in Europe, as a reaction to disconcertion provoked by rapid changes and the loss of a familiar order following the emergence of modernity (Lowenthal, 1985). What raised concern in particular was the loss of those testimonies to our past whose meaning was thought to transcend the specific reasons that led to their original creation and which, because they had become in some ways symbolic of our identity, were thought to possess special value to society as its collective "cultural heritage". It has been noted, in this respect, how the notion of heritage as a testimony of the past worth preserving was directly associated with the contemporary rise of the historicist philosophy, which introduced the idea that the history of each epoch and nation, indeed of each individual, was unique (Riegl, 1982). According to Lowenthal and Binney (1981, p. 17), the urge to conserve heritage stemmed from "a threefold awareness of the past: that it was unlike the present, that it is crucial to our sense of identity, and that its tangible remnants are rapidly disappearing".

The realization that our world was undergoing dramatic and irreversible changes is also at the root of the birth, in the West, of the environmentalist movement. In his seminal book *Man and Nature*, published in 1865, George Pershing Marsh examines the negative consequences of human activities on the land and advocates the conservation of nature as well as of history. Lowenthal (1985, p. xvii) considers this book "the fountainhead of conservation consciousness".

It is thus apparent, how conservation is a field of activity that has defined its essence in opposition to trends and phenomena induced by humans that it wished to prevent – the destruction of the old and its replacement by the new – brought about by modernization and development. The confrontational and antagonistic nature of heritage conservation is also evident from the terminology that characterizes its policies and practice, as it developed over the course of the twentieth century. This is defined by words such as "protection" or "safeguarding" and concepts such as "boundaries", "buffer zone", "integrity" or "danger", which seem to be borrowed from a military or medical field handbook. From the beginning, conservation was *from* and *against* something. Underpinning this ideology, at least in Western societies, was the implicit belief that the timeline of human history is somehow cut into two separate parts. On one side, the past as a golden age, when people lived more in harmony with nature and knew instinctively how to build beautiful and lasting things, which somehow enriched, rather than spoiled, the existing cities and landscapes. On the other hand, the present, when – as a result of the rupture caused by modernity – we seem to have lost the ability to add our layer to the legacy of previous generations without compromising the whole thing and all we can hope to achieve, when intervening within a historic environment, is to address practical needs without causing too much harm.

This separation in the timeline is mirrored by a separation in space. An implicit tenet of conservation is that the world is divided into two: heritage and the rest. The idea that heritage is something that exists per se and is fundamentally different and separate from the rest is also reflected in the manner in which heritage is referred to in many languages. As Laurajane Smith has rightly pointed out, "there is no such thing as 'heritage'" (Smith, 2006, p. 13), in the sense that what we call heritage does not exist as such in its own right, but only as a social construct, the result of a continuous process "concerned with the creation and maintenance of certain social and cultural values" (ibid., p. 42) within a subject-object relationship. In the common conservation discourse, however, we often find that heritage is referred to through terms such as "property", "asset", "object", "element"[3] and so on, implying that certain things *are* heritage, in their essence, as opposed to others which are not.

Over the years, this duality has been reflected in the terminology of charters, recommendations, planning guidelines and legislation and informed the names, structure and language of global and national institutions and intergovernmental instruments devoted to heritage, such as the World Heritage Convention.[4] In this approach, places identified as heritage are treated as "islands" that are surrounded by a sea of non-heritage. Competent authorities and experts discover and then preside over these islands, by virtue of legal instruments and management plans whose aim is, citing as an example the provisions of the World Heritage Convention, to "ensure their safeguarding" as well as "protection against development and change that might negatively impact the(ir) Outstanding Universal Value" (UNESCO, 2012*a*, p. 25). In this process, what happens outside these islands is taken into consideration only insofar as it may pose a threat to the islands themselves. In the context of the World Heritage Convention, these threats are referred to as "factors affecting the property" (ibid., p. 109).

Coherently with this conflictual approach, over the past 150 years and in the face of increasing pressure from modernity in all its manifestations, the underlying strategy of heritage conservation has been that of *mitigation*, that is, "to make less severe, harmful, or painful"[5] the effects of perceived external factors on the subject of its interest.

---

3 For example, in the context of the UNESCO 2003 Convention for the Safeguarding of the Intangible Cultural Heritage.

4 The Convention concerning the Protection of the World Cultural and Natural Heritage was adopted by UNESCO in 1972. See more on its aims and activities at http://whc.unesco.org/

5 From Merriam-Webster online dictionary: http://www.merriam-webster.com/dictionary/mitigation (accessed 26 July 2014).

Mounting tensions

This approach worked more or less well at the initial stages of the conservation movement and for much of the twentieth century, when the focus of the heritage sector was on a select number of prominent monuments and sites, claims over which were more or less undisputed, while pressure from development was still relatively modest. The deal was clear then: heritage was a small portion of the land, possibly surrounded by fences and under the authority of some public institution. This was to be protected and conserved as it was, whereas changes could happen outside, where there was no concern for cultural values and sufficient space was available.

Progressively, however, radical changes in the context surrounding heritage conservation have put this paradigm under strain. A comprehensive review of these changes is beyond the scope of this paper. Suffice it to say that these include the extraordinary broadening of the scope of heritage, both in terms of typology and timeline, as a result of a new, larger understanding of what has cultural meaning; the democratization of decision-making processes relating to heritage and the corresponding growing role of civil society and local communities; the emergence of new regions of the world in the post-colonial era, which has brought new cultural perspectives in the international discourse on heritage; and the wider social, economic and environmental pressure associated with industrialization, growing populations, the depletion of natural resources and climate change.

As a result of all these trends, the boundaries between heritage and the rest became increasingly blurred and contentious, leading to growing tensions between heritage conservation and other societal or political goals, both in practical terms and conceptually. The World Heritage Convention offers an eloquent example of the issue. An analysis of the State of Conservation (SoC) reports prepared for the 2008 session of the World Heritage Committee (UNESCO, 2011, p. 3) has revealed, for example, how factors hindering effective management of World Heritage properties were related – in the vast majority of cases – to development threats and other forms of pressure associated with human activities, which came from outside the confines of the listed properties. In other words, the causes of most of the problems affecting World Heritage sites seemed to be rooted in a conflictual relationship with their wider physical and social environment and an unresolved dispute, within the concerned communities and national authorities, between what should be conserved and what should be allowed to change.

Controversies were bound to increase as the definition of heritage continued to expand its scope, both in typology and chronology. The World Heritage List has recently exceeded 1,000 properties and now includes more than 250 cities, numerous sites associated with so-called industrial archaeology and late testimonies to the architecture of the modern movement, such as the Sydney Opera House (inaugurated in 1973 and inscribed in 2007). The timespan between the past and the present, in fact, is getting smaller and smaller. In the 2010 exhibition *Cronocaos* at the Venice Biennale, the renowned Dutch architect Rem Koolhaas reflected on the growing scope of what our societies intend to preserve and underlined the ironic ambivalence of this desire to freeze the status quo at one moment in time and the underlying problem of how to ensure the survival of so much heritage. Elsewhere, Koolhaas had already noted, in this regard, how the current scope of conservation had reduced the chronological distance between us and "heritage": "in 1818, that was 2,000 years. In 1900, it was only 200 years. And now, near the 1960s, it became twenty years. We are living in an incredibly exciting and slightly absurd moment, namely that preservation is overtaking us" (Koolhaas, 2004, p. 2).

There is indeed a growing resentment for what many perceive as an obsession for preservation that undermines the ability of our generation to create and shape the environment according to our needs. An Italian architectural review, *Casabella*, published in 2012 a long article about World Heritage by the Spanish architect Beatriz Ramo (2012). It was not the usual series of postcards from the wonders of the world. This time, World Heritage was on the bench of the defendants for allegedly preventing societies from expressing themselves. "If UNESCO had been around in the thirteenth century", suggests the author, "today the vast majority of our heritage would simply not be there". For example, the famous Leaning Tower of Pisa would have never been allowed as "it affects the visual integrity of the pre-existing Cathedral, hampering its view from various key vantage points". The language made a deliberate and somewhat ironic reference to the arguments typically found in reports drafted by heritage experts when requested to assess the impact of a new development on a nearby heritage property. The article goes as far as to propose the establishment of a new type of international designation for areas reserved to development and creativity where all sorts of conservation regulations or other restrictions would be "strictly forbidden".

But regardless of the concern for freedom and creativity expressed by the architects, let us assume, for the purpose of our argument, that an ever-growing share of our built environment should indeed be recognized as "cultural heritage" and as such set aside for preservation. The real question is whether this would be feasible in the face of the increasing pressure associated with environmental, economic and social phenomena. Erica Avrami, from the World Monuments Fund, believes that "changing demographics and diminishing resources are making options more limited" (Avrami, 2011, p. 5). She notes that when considered against other pressing social, economic, and environmental priorities, such as clean air and water, reducing CO_2 emissions, job creation and the like, heritage conservation should "rationalize its cause and better align its goals and processes with those of sustainability planning for the built environment as a whole". That means, she adds, "questioning many long-held goals and practices about what to preserve and how" (ibid., p. 5). What this implicitly suggests is that, especially in developing regions of the world, it may become difficult if not impossible to maintain large numbers of cultural heritage assets, unless their use is aligned to the wider needs of their communities and sustainable in environmental terms. In certain areas most affected by climate change, such as coastal areas exposed to sea level rise or mountain regions with sensitive ecosystems, communities may not be able to support themselves and might be forced to migrate en masse, endangering the survival of entire cultures, let alone the conservation of their tangible heritage.[6]

Dissolving the boundaries

This raises a symmetrical and important issue that is often neglected: the seeming lack of concern by the discipline of heritage conservation for the areas currently not designated as heritage and for what is going to happen there. Almost all over the world, at the time of writing, new urban areas and industrial complexes are being constructed, especially in the suburbs of large metropolises of developing regions, which have no architectural quality whatsoever and are absolutely indistinguishable from one continent to the other. The product of this massive urban sprawl, with its often unhealthy and incoherent environment deprived of any harmony and character, will constitute the daily backdrop for the life of millions, if not billions of people. Regardless of the possible impact of these massive developments on identified heritage properties, should those concerned with the preservation of meaning and beauty (including, one would think, the heritage professionals) not also be concerned about this cultural disaster on a planetary scale? In a country such as Italy, which is reputed to have contributed significantly to the development of the theory and practice of heritage conservation, a stark contrast can be observed between beautifully preserved historic centres, which are subject to the strictest regulations and controls, and the chaotic ugliness of their anonymous surroundings where, on the contrary, a *laissez-faire* policy has often prevailed. Looking towards the future, the scale of the problem is mind-boggling. An issue brief published recently by the United Nations on sustainable cities and human settlements (UN, 2014, p. 1) states that "humanity is now half urban and expected to be nearly 70 per cent urban by 2050. ... During the next two decades the world will more than double the amount of land used for cities". The brief further emphasizes how "as cities lose density and sprawl, they lock themselves into unsustainable land use patterns where jobs and people are far from one another, transportation costs and congestion are high, infrastructure runs are longer and more costly, segregation of socioeconomic groups and land use types are more pronounced and environmental impacts are greater". How are these immense urban areas going to be built? Is this not a legitimate cause for concern for the heritage sector, a discipline whose original *raison d'être* was to protect an environment at the human scale from insensitive development? If our culture is 'one', should we not want to safeguard and promote it at 360 degrees, including both heritage and new creation? In the same

6 As an example, Bangladesh is expected to lose 17 per cent of its land by 2050 due to flooding caused by climate change, which may lead to as many as 20 million climate refugees.

vein, somewhat puzzling is the growing support, within our societies, for the preservation of heritage and, at the same time, the tolerance we seem to have developed for the poor quality and obsolescence of the things that we produce and use in our daily lives, such as the new buildings we construct, the cars, home appliances and clothes we buy, which we replace as soon as they get slightly worn or out of fashion. In other words, the same qualities we seem to appreciate in heritage, for example when we admire the timeless, exceptional design and the mastery of execution of the Parthenon Temple in Athens – which we may be able to visit once or twice in our life if we are lucky – appear to be much less of a concern than the things that are created now and surround us every day.

This sort of cultural schizophrenia was certainly not affecting those who built the places that today we consider outstanding cultural heritage properties. When Michelangelo Buonarroti was asked by Pope Paul III to rearrange the Capitol Hill in Rome (1536–46), the ancient seat of power and one of the most ancient and historically charged areas of the city, he conceived a grand oval piazza turned towards the new centre of power, the Vatican, thus reversing the classical orientation towards the Roman forum. This involved the demolition of some medieval buildings, the extensive rehabilitation of the old Senators' palace, including the moving of a bell tower on the axis of the new complex, and the construction of a new building to complete the symmetry of the design. In doing so, Michelangelo was not concerned with the preservation of the 'cultural heritage', in the sense that we attribute to this term today, and certainly did not respect the principles codified over 400 years later by international heritage charters and recommendations. Notwithstanding, he was able to realize something which was not only sensitive to the context, fitting to the needs of the time, durable and beautiful in itself, but also became a cherished symbol for future generations. Needless to say, if Michelangelo had lived today, he would never have been allowed to do what he did.

The current approach to heritage thus appears not only contradictory because of the artificial distinction between heritage and the rest, but also, to some extent, inherently unsustainable. On one hand, because the battle to preserve the existing remnants of the past is sooner or later going to be lost, as nothing lasts forever; on the other hand, because much of what our generation is producing is often of poor quality and will probably not survive the next 100 years, let alone become the heritage of the future. More significantly, at a time when the impacts of the Anthropocene seem to have the potential to undermine human civilization as we know it, and all efforts should be directed towards addressing this existential challenge, the heritage sector appears to be still locked within its intellectual precinct, preoccupied with finding an increasingly self-referential "cultural" value,[7] and with mitigating damage

7 And an even more abstract Outstanding Universal Value, in the case of the World Heritage Convention.

to a small portion of the planet from the adverse effects of "external factors". In doing so, conservation does not seem to have fully acknowledged that heritage is only a component of the larger ecosystem in which we live, and that "the network of relationships linking the human race to itself and to the rest of the biosphere is so complex that all aspects affect all others to an extraordinary degree" (Gell-Mann, 1994). Climate change and the progressive loss of environmental resources caused by the current development model are questioning the viability of our societies and the continuity of their cultures, whose safeguarding was the very reason why the conservation movement emerged. In the new circumstances, the heritage paradigm should thus be reassessed by dissolving the artificial boundaries that kept it for so long segregated from the non-heritage. At the same time, the mitigation strategy of heritage conservation would also need to be reconsidered. There seems to be no point in carefully preserving the portrait of an ancestor in the living room, if the entire house is at risk of being washed away.

From mitigation to adaptation

While the discussion on the relationship between heritage and 'development' has been going on for some decades now, it is only recently that the need to reconcile heritage conservation objectives with environmental, social and economic imperatives has really taken centre stage in technical symposia, the academia and international forums. New ideas and recommendations are being formulated, such as that by UNESCO in 2011 on Historic Urban Landscapes,[8] the International Council on Monuments and Sites (ICOMOS) Declaration on Heritage as a Driver of Development, also adopted in 2011,[9] or the new policy currently being elaborated to integrate a sustainable development perspective into the processes of the 1972 Convention (UNESCO, 2012*b*, p. 6). In shaping these new theoretical and practical frameworks, the idea that heritage is a "thing" and that the world is divided into heritage islands and a sea of non-heritage may have to give way to a new approach. One which appears more appropriate to describe reality is that of heritage as a *quality*, that is, the varying ability of things to convey cultural meaning and values, which in different degrees may be attributed to everything under the sun. To continue with our metaphor, thus, rather than islands in two dimensions, heritage might be better represented as the 'contour lines' of reliefs on a map, expressing the boundless peaks, valleys and plateaus of cultural value across the whole of our environment. The responsibilities of heritage agencies and experts, in this new approach, would not be limited to certain designated spots, but extend over the entire territory with the aim of representing one among

8 http://whc.unesco.org/en/activities/638
9 http://www.international.icomos.org/Paris2011/GA2011_Declaration_de_Paris_EN_20120109.pdf

other legitimate societal interests, all deeply connected within the bio-cultural continuum that the anthropologist Philippe Descola calls the "ecology of relations" (Descola, 2011). Naturally, the attention of heritage practitioners would be directed in particular towards the places where cultural meaning is deemed to be especially high, as these are the areas where risks and opportunities – from their perspective – are also greater.

The most significant change that may be required, however, is the redefinition of the purpose of what we call heritage and of its role in society. Initially, and for the past 150 years, we have been preserving heritage from the adverse effects of modernity, in a sort of reactive mode, to safeguard the symbols of our endangered cultural identity. In doing so, we were somewhat carried away by our enthusiasm, to the point where almost anything became potentially "heritage". In the Anthropocene, the question is likely to be reversed. In the face of what is possibly the greatest challenge that human civilization has ever faced, how can cultures, which developed over millennia of adaptation and interaction with the environment, come to our help? Could our historic cities and cultural landscapes, managed according to traditional knowledge, hold useful lessons that we can draw upon, in combination with modern science and technological innovations, to plan for the environment as a whole and finally change what appears to be a completely unsustainable pattern of production and consumption? From this perspective, what should we keep and repair and what should we let go? Which of the things we call heritage would contribute to our resilience against the disruptions of the Anthropocene and which, on the contrary, would add to our vulnerability? In answering these questions, of course, the ability of old things to provide us with a sense of identity and belonging – or just to make the world more beautiful – will play a significant role, but within a larger array of considerations. Places such as Stonehenge and the Taj Mahal will continue to be preserved as they are, but a more healthy proportion between the highly symbolic and the more worldly aspects of our environment should probably be established.

The future of heritage, in this new approach, might involve moving from the current strategy based on mitigation, that is, reducing harm, towards one based on *adaptation*, in which the systemic relationship between what we call heritage and the rest would be renegotiated to fit the new circumstances and serve newly perceived priorities. In the process, the artificial separation between the past and the present, the tangible and the intangible, as well as between heritage and creativity, should be overcome. Rather than an exclusive focus on the protection of the remnants of the past for their own sake, the goal should be the promotion of more sustainable ways of life that nurture cultural continuity by building on past experience (that is, heritage in the largest sense) while at the same time integrating the best of modern science within a single, holistic approach to the planning of the environment in its entirety.

In adapting to new circumstances, humans must be able to discern and select from these past experiences, retain what 'works' and integrate it in new and more effective strategies.[10] Adaptation is, by the way, the very process through which cultures have developed and prospered since the beginning of time, in all their diversity, when humans began responding to the pressure of their environment through behavioural changes and not simply by means of genetic evolution. Mitigation, on the other hand, has led many historic city centres to the all too familiar artificial, museum-like atmosphere that appears to be the contrary of a healthy, lively and creative culture which offers viable solutions to the challenges of our time. The question will be, then, if future generations will still find a use for the word 'heritage', a concept that developed out of a specific historical and cultural context and which, like many ideas in the past, may lose its relevance as a result of the dramatic, epochal changes that the world is expected to go through in the Anthropocene.

References

Avrami, E. 2011. Sustainability and the built environment, forging a role for heritage conservation. *Conservation Perspectives, The GCI Newsletter,* Spring Issue. Los Angeles.

Descola, P. 2011. *L'écologie des autres : l'anthropologie et la question de la nature.* Paris, Éditions Quae.

Diamond, J. 2005. *Collapse: How Societies Choose to Fail or Succeed.* London, Penguin Books.

Eco, U. 2011. Oral presentation delivered on the occasion of the launching of Encyclomedia (in Italian) http://www.laterza.it/index.php/index.php?option=com_content&view=article&id=415:umberto-eco-encyclomedia-per-la-scuola&Itemid=101

Gell-Mann, M. 1994. *The Quark and the Jaguar: Adventures in the Simple and the Complex.* New York, W. H. Freeman & Co.

Irwin, R. 2011. Welcome to the Anthropocene. Paris, *UNESCO Courier* 64th Year, No. 4, pp. 34–36.

Koolhaas, R. 2004. Preservation is overtaking us. *Future Anterior,* Vol. 1, No. 2, Fall 2004. Minneapolis, University of Minnesota Press.

Lowenthal, D. 1985, *The Past is a Foreign Country.* Cambridge, UK, Cambridge University Press.

Lowenthal, D. and Binney, M. (eds). 1981. *Our Past Before Us: Why Do We Save It?* London, Temple Smith.

Pershing Marsh, G. 1865. *Man and Nature.* New York, Charles Scribner.

Ramo, B. 2012. Merry Go Round; proposte per un manisfesto non troppo paradossale. *Casabella,* Italian review of architecture, No. 812, April. Milan, Mondadori.

Riegl, A. 1982, *The Modern Cult of Monuments: Its Character and its Origin.* Cambridge (Mass.) MIT Press.

Smith, L. 2006. *Uses of Heritage.* London/New York, Routledge.

UN. 2012. *Realizing the Future We Want for All.* Report of the UN Task Team on the Post-2015 Development Agenda to the Secretary-General. New York, United Nations. http://www.un.org/millenniumgoals/pdf/Post_2015_UNTTreport.pdf

10 The Italian semiologist Umberto Eco (2011) notes that one of the main functions of memory and culture is to enable us to forget what is no longer useful, lest we should all become like the idiotic character of Borges' novel, *Funes el memorioso,* who remembered everything and was therefore incapable of any generalization and of formulating any concept.

UN. 2014. *Issues Brief: Sustainable Cities and Human Settlements*. Prepared by the Technical Support Team co-chaired by the Department of Economic and Social Affairs and the United Nations Development Programme, New York. http://sustainabledevelopment.un.org/content/documents/2306TST%20Issues%20Brief%20Cities_FINAL.pdf
UNESCO. 2011. *Presentation and Adoption of the World Heritage Strategy for Capacity Building*. Paris, UNESCO World Heritage Centre. http://whc.unesco.org/archive/2011/whc11-35com-9Be.pdf (WHC-11/35.COM/9B.)
UNESCO. 2012*a*. *Operational Guidelines for the Implementation of the World Heritage Convention*. Paris, UNESCO World Heritage Centre. http://whc.unesco.org/en/guidelines/
UNESCO. 2012*b*. Decisions adopted by the World Heritage Committee at its 36th session (Saint-Petersburg, 2012). Paris, UNESCO World Heritage Centre. http://whc.unesco.org/en/sessions/36COM (WHC-12/36.COM/19.)

Social Sustainability of the Historic Urban Landscape

Michael Turner

Abstract

The transformation of urban communities has long been an issue around the world. However, with increased mobility, both real and virtual, the effects of the speed of change and the socio-economic dynamics of the city now necessitate a reappraisal of the ways these challenges and opportunities are sustainably met. Sustainability is interpreted as the needs and interests of present and future generations being fully safeguarded. Human generations of biblical times spanning thirty to sixty years have been reduced to between fifteen and twenty years, while generations of technology hardly make twelve months. With the urban complexities and speed of change, sustainability must now be seen not just in the context of history but also of geography. Karl Mannheim's essay on the problem of generations extends the definitions by including the socio-historical environment.

The conservation of the building as an object, as characterized in the Venice Charter and the World Heritage Convention, was extended to the city as a process and led to a global dispute culminating in the approval in 2011 of the UNESCO Recommendation on Historic Urban Landscapes. Originally debated within the World Heritage Committee, it presented a wider approach to include "social and cultural practices and values, economic processes and the intangible dimensions of heritage as related to diversity and identity".

Processes of gentrification are being scrutinized and the needs for social inclusion have brought together ideas and concepts defining the city's identity, thus providing the continuity of place rather than people. The Historic Urban Landscape approach strives to increase diversity through the "sustainable use of urban spaces", thereby pointing to the inclusion of previously marginalized communities. This has relevance to the favelas of Rio, the townships of Durban, the slums of Mumbai, the immigrant dock areas of London or New York and the banlieues of Paris. The opportunities provided by new communications, crowd-sourcing and technologies-for-all will be a factor for an integrative approach to urban design to manage the processes of transformation, creating new challenges for research.

The paper begins with the historical background, followed by an indication of social perspectives of the urban environment emphasizing coexistence and compromise and concepts of exclusion and inclusion, as an integral part of social sustainability, a critical aspect in social transformations. I conclude with an examination of the potential applications of the Historic Urban Landscape Recommendation to promote social sustainability.

Cities in transformation

The long and arduous process and dynamics of populating the world are an inherent part of the group effort that has resulted in the growth of our cities – essentially balanced between settlements and the agricultural hinterland. Historically, the symbiotic relationship between cities and hinterland was the epitome of sustainability; nature ensuring the environmental balance with wars, famine and plagues.

Decision-makers around the world during these centuries were not concerned with sustainability as we understand the term today, but the common thread was a tacit understanding of the limitations of technology and the hierarchies of the social organization of cities and their economic viability.

Archaeologists who have unearthed the tell at Jericho, with the remains of more than twenty successive strata, can attest to the earliest urban settlement some 9,000 years ago with a consistent layered footprint focused on the water source. Cities developed in surprisingly similar forms albeit in seemingly disconnected cultures. Between East and West, the city became a global phenomenon, being a manifestation of the human genes. The grids of Miletus and Xian, the gnomon for the Roman *cardo* and *decomanus*, and the Chinese *feng shui* with the Indian *vastu-purusa mandala*, all indicate the universality of the city. What made for the differentiation between one city and another was the social construct creating the economic and political structures of each society and its adaptation to different climates and biomes.

City states needed to find an indigenous sustainability for their footprint, which grew with the synoecism of the surrounding settlements, while empires embarked on global escapades initiating commercial interests that also brought greater cultural exchange and syncretistic customs and traditions. The extensive Greek and Roman Empires gave way to the Arab Caliphates of the eighth century amalgamating the countries from the Euphrates to the Maghreb with a single language, a single religion and a unified governing system. The caravan routes transmitted cultural ideas, knowledge and science to be applied to the economic structure and urban layouts and a strong socio-political pyramidal structure with large-scale cities such as Baghdad, Damascus or Cairo.

Further east, there were the inventions that made the large, bustling Chinese cities unique in their time and which included printing, paper money, porcelain, tea, restaurants, gunpowder, and the compass – the contributions of the Song dynasty (AD 960–1280). Subsequently, in the thirteenth century, the Mongol Empire extended from North-East Asia to Muslim South-West Asia and Christian Europe, butting up against religions of all three cultural areas for the most part in a bloodthirsty rampage. It took another century, a war and a plague before the European city broke away from the feudal system with the resulting development of trade within a new institutional framework and an urge for global exploration with the invention of the astrolabe and clock.

It was only in the eighteenth century, with the industrial revolutions around the world, that this trickle of movement from the countryside to urban areas became a massive influx. It was not just a change of place, but yet again, a change of social frameworks and hierarchies. The reactions to this revolution, generating the Garden City movement, were quick to follow while the pendulum swung with the Futurists, at the turn of the twentieth century, who turned their back on history and saw in the new machines of speed the future of civilization. Although a fringe group, it was this momentum and tempo that engaged the society of the period and heralded Modernism.

Since then, the speed of the transformation has grown exponentially, raising questions as to the new interpretations of sustainability. Moreover, with increased and faster mobility, both real and virtual, the socio-economic dynamics of the city have led to the need to reappraise the ways these challenges and opportunities are met sustainably, challenging the meanings of intergenerational responsibilities.

Cities, city-states and empires all followed similar patterns and left their indelible mark on the geomorphology and landscape of the city. In short, these meanings and interpretations are intractably tied to the socio-economic and political growth and their physical and architectural evidence. Urban conservation needs to include all these components. In the words of Ashbee, conservation of a city means "not only the things themselves, the streets, the houses, spires, towers, and domes, but the way of living, the idealism, the feeling for righteousness and fitness which these things connote, and with which every city with any claim to dignity and beauty is instinct" (Ashbee, 1924).

But the world does not stand still and many critics of the sustainability mantra recognize, as history has shown, that necessity is the mother of invention and innovation and renewal can change our lives and achieve our objectives. The Chinese inventions of the Song dynasty and the European scientific revolution from the sixteenth century of Copernicus to Newton contributed in their own way to renewing urban sustainability. How will the digital revolution meet the challenges of the next generations?

Time, place, people

The diverse definitions of sustainable development have been succinctly coined by de Vries and Petersen as "a quest for developing and sustaining qualities of life" thus encompassing the subjective and objective dimensions of human well-being, and inviting a truly trans-disciplinary approach (Petersen and de Vries, 2009). But a logical and reasonable universalism is being hotly debated. Marcuse, an avid urban protagonist wrote: "Sustainability as a goal for planning just doesn't work. In the first place, sustainability is not a goal; it is a constraint on the achievement of other goals. No one who is interested in change wants to sustain things as they are now" (Marcuse, 1998). Sustainability is essentially a means and not an end – it is an attitude and a state of mind through holistic thinking. Reid questions whether it is meaningful to talk of sustainable development when we have no certainty of the needs of future generations, their ecological, social and economic conditions as representing a "sustainable state" and how close we may be to such conditions. He implies that we need to consider whether this is an imprecise idealism unchecked by reality (Reid, 2013).

Sustainable development as most frequently quoted from *Our Common Future*, also known as the Brundtland Report (1987), suffices with: "Sustainable development is development that meets the needs of the present without compromising the ability of future generations to meet their own needs." (WCED, 1987, p. 247).

This preamble focuses sustainability on time and the intergenerational responsibilities. However the next sentences from the report are rarely quoted: "It contains within it two key concepts:

- the concept of needs, in particular the essential needs of the world's poor, to which overriding priority should be given; and
- the idea of limitations imposed by the state of technology and social organization on the environment's ability to meet present and future needs."

A decade later, in 1997, the UNESCO General Conference met in Paris and passed the Declaration on the Responsibilities of the Present Generations Towards Future Generations. It highlighted the responsibility of present generations to identify, protect and safeguard the tangible and intangible cultural heritage and to transmit it to future generations.

At face value this is a biblical term essentially identifying chronological periods of between thirty and sixty years. The average period was generally considered to be about thirty years, during which children were born, grew up, and began to have children of their own.

However, generations are now recognized as more than chronological periods. The 1923 essay of Karl Mannheim, *The Problem of Generations*, is considered seminal in this regard, although its application in the fields of cultural heritage has not been extensive. According to Mannheim's theory, the revolutionary events that have created generational identities include industrial, social, commercial, economic, environmental and technological revolutions, while other social incidents have, for example, coined generations as "post-war", "baby-boom" and "flower generations". Generations could have time-scales of fifteen and twenty years depending on local sociological conditions, whereas generations of technology can endure as briefly as twelve months.

Mannheim defined a generation not just chronologically, but as a group of individuals of similar ages whose members have experienced a noteworthy historical event within a set period of time, which raises an interesting interpretation of sustainability. He distinguished three categories "generation *location*", "generation *actuality*", and "generation *unit*" (Mannheim, 1952).

With the urban complexities and speed of change, sustainability must now be seen not just in the context of history but also of geography and sociology, evaluating the sustainability of place. Just as one generation cannot mortgage the assets of the future, one community cannot take over the assets of the other between physical territories. Balancing needs over time between generations must also include balancing needs between regions to provide for the world's poor through more equitable spread of resources and within current technological limitations and social organization. Each spatial level needs to be connected geographically to its surroundings through a hierarchy of neighbourhood, city, metropolis and region. Weber in discussing the nature of the city notes its historical relationship to agriculture and the presence of large acreages accessible to the self-sufficient, sustainable "urbanite" (Weber, 1958).

Mannheim identifies the cultural processes in five parts, focusing on the continuity and interactions between the generations that exist side by side with "my" generation boxed in by a "younger" and an "older" generation, essentially responding to a dynamic definition of sustainability.

All definitions of sustainable development require that we see the world as a system that connects space, as well as time and people.[1] The problems we face as a society are complex and serious – they cannot be addressed in the same way as when they were created. New mechanisms and technologies must be applied to generate innovative solutions.

Inspiration in this regard was provided in Athens with the culmination of the Congrès Internationaux d'Architecture Moderne (CIAM) Mediterranean voyage in 1933 and with the presentation of the Athens Charter, which in relation to heritage and continuity stated in para. 65 that: "Architectural assets must be protected, whether found in isolated buildings or in urban aggregations. The life of a city is a continuous event that is expressed through the centuries by material works – layouts and building structures – which ... form the city's personality, and from which its soul gradually emanates. They are precious witnesses of the past which will be respected, first for their historical or sentimental value, and second, because certain of them convey a plastic virtue in which the utmost intensity of human genius has been incorporated. They form a part of the human heritage, and whoever owns them or is entrusted with their protection has the responsibility and the obligation to do whatever he legitimately can to hand this noble heritage down intact to the centuries to come" (le Corbusier, 1973).

Agenda 21 for Culture, which was adopted by United Cities and Local Governments (UCLG, 2008), also provides a tool to enhance the role of culture in urban policies and as the fourth pillar of sustainable development (UCLG, 2010). While this approach has been recognized in other fora, I contend that the concept of culture as an enabler for sustainable development would better benefit from being a brace to the three existing pillars.

1 The Canadian-based International Institute for Sustainable Development.

Integrative system process: Recommendation on the Historic Urban Landscape

Cultural heritage in the urban age is no longer the recognition of the "monument", "groups of buildings" or "sites" as objects, characterized in the Venice Charter of 1964 and the World Heritage Convention of 1972. The UNESCO Nairobi Recommendation of 1976 and the ICOMOS Washington Charter of 1987 extended the city as a process but subsequently led to global dispute culminating in the approval in 2011 of the UNESCO Recommendation on Historic Urban Landscapes.[2] Originally debated within the World Heritage Committee, it presented a wider and more holistic and integrative approach to include "social and cultural practices and values, economic processes and the intangible dimensions of heritage as related to diversity and identity".

This approach accepts that socio-economic transformations are an integral part of the dynamics of the city, ensuring that community participation, academic research and public awareness are all part of capacity-building that is essential in culturally diverse settings. It should also provide support to communities in their pursuit for sustainable development and adaptation, while retaining the characteristics and values linked to their traditional knowledge, history and collective memory. It intertwines with traditions, the tangible and the intangible creating the spirit of place for livability and well-being giving an added dimension to the physical spatial configurations.

With the emphasis on the "object" and not the "subject", many forget that the first endeavour of the World Heritage Convention (UNESCO, 1972) is the adoption of "a general policy which aims to give the cultural and natural heritage a function in the life of the community and to integrate the protection of that heritage into comprehensive planning programmes" (Article 5(1)).

It should be emphasized that the new Recommendation on the Historic Urban Landscape does not come instead of the existing individual monument preservation codes but adds the urban dimension, embracing sustainability:

- Civic engagement tools should involve a diverse cross-section of stakeholders, and empower them to identify key values in their urban areas, develop visions that reflect their diversity, set goals, and agree on actions to safeguard their heritage and promote sustainable development (UN-Habitat, 2013).
- ... Heritage, social and environmental impact assessments should be used to support and facilitate decision-making processes within a framework of sustainable development.

---

2 General Conference36 C/23 Item 8.1 – Proposals concerning the desirability of a standard-setting instrument on Historic Urban Landscapes.

- Micro-credit and other flexible financing to support local enterprise, as well as a variety of models of partnerships, are also central to making the historic urban landscape approach financially sustainable.

The opportunities provided by new communications, crowd-sourcing and technologies-for-all will be factors for an integrative approach to urban design as a key discipline to accompany and manage the processes of transformation, creating new challenges for research. With their concentration of large and diverse populations, cities are the stage where the contest for social advancement is played. The two key concepts of Brundtland identify the challenges to be addressed, particularly among migrant populations, and introduce the social innovation that is the key to reducing poverty and increasing well-being. At the same time they are the focal points of social aspirations for increased quality of life, thus becoming the centres of influence on changing values in wider societies.

Innovative programmes in cultural heritage, arts and celebrations, conservation of historic buildings as cultural patrimony, and mobilization around cultural practices are generating economic opportunities and community cohesion. Culture as an enabler for sustainable development is a new indicator and Amartya Sen notes that "... cultural issues can be critically important for development. The connections take many different forms, related to the objectives as well as instruments of development. Cultural matters are integral parts of the lives we lead. If development can be seen as enhancement of our living standards, then efforts geared to development can hardly ignore the world of culture" (Sen, 2000).

Communications has always been the conduit for these exchanges, with printing and paper as a critical element in the dissemination of knowledge. The Song dynasty's expertise in moveable typeface probably reached Europe with the Mongol expansions, but it was only developed, perhaps autonomously, in the sixteenth century with Gutenberg in Germany. This, in turn brought about the printed flyer, enabling revolutions of the masses – an original version of Facebook. The invention of the radio did not go without comment, whereas the digital revolution has brought other dimensions to the city, changing yet again the urban rules.

Yet differing perspectives of the meaning and interpretation of any particular historic urban landscape can intensify an inherited rivalry of identities.

The human(e) city

The scheming tribune Sicinius calls:

Sic. Where is this viper
That would depopulate the city and
Be every man himself?
...

Sic.	What is the city but the people?
Citizens	True,
	The people are the city.[3]

Why is the city so volatile? According to the 2009 *Human Development Report*, there are about 1 billion persons, or one in seven, currently living outside their country or region of origin. It would be safe to say that, overall, one in three work or live in a city other than in the one they were born. Article 8 of the Nara Document outlines that "it is important to underline a fundamental principle of UNESCO, to the effect that the cultural heritage of each is the cultural heritage of all. Responsibility for cultural heritage and the management of it belongs, in the first place, to the cultural community that has generated it, and subsequently to that which cares for it" (Larsen, 1995). In the city, a major disparity – which is often a bone of contention in itself – exists between the community that "created" the heritage and the community that should be "caring" for it, resulting in two diverging groups.

Port cities as the entry points for migrants become the immediate haven for the new citizen. The upward-reaching younger generation moves quickly to new neighbourhoods, leaving the area for the next wave of change. These areas absorb the people and the urban fabric acts as a sponge, readapting itself to the needs of the communities. This is seen in cities from New York to London, Mumbai to Hong Kong and Naples to Melbourne. Some cities fare better than others and the sponge capacity is an indicator of urban resilience. The East End of London, for example, has successfully accepted the Huguenot weavers, the subsequent Methodists followed by continental Jewry and the Muslims of Bangladesh. Changes in these areas were generated by social reform or incidents of fire, transforming the sweatshops into street markets and small trader shops. Not so the Paris banlieue, which has fared much worse with social tensions, crime and violence.

These urban changes are accompanied by various interventions ranging from redevelopment to conservation and gentrification. Spaces change their function to reflect the new inhabitants, and houses in areas considered to be in uninhabitable slums in time undergo gentrification and are extolled for their qualities that are a product of generative processes that create layers of place, as exemplified in London and New York or alternatively, are condemned and then demolished.

---

3 *Coriolanus*, Act III. Scene I, Rome – a street; Sicinius.

Coexistence and compromise

How can the social and physical fabric be integrated with the dynamics of change to become an inherent value of the global city? Umberto Eco in debating migration, tolerance and the intolerable calls our current millennium "the great cross-breeding of cultures", with cultures co-existing and merging (Eco, 2010). He draws a distinction between immigration and migration, with immigration being individuals moving from one country to another while migration is the case where an entire people moves to a new territory, changing the existing culture. While immigration can be controlled politically, migration can be uncontrollable.

Social sustainability leaves room for the "other", openness for other narratives and space for future generations. Sen (2004) has indicated that "... historical objects, sites and records can help to offset some of the frictions of confrontational modern politics. For example, Arab history includes a long tradition of peaceful relation with Jewish populations. Similarly, Indonesian past carries powerful records of simultaneous flourishing of Hindu, Buddhist and Confucian cultures, side by side with the Islamic traditions. Butrint in Albania as a historical site shows flourishing presence of Greek, Roman and later Christian cultures, as well as Islamic history."

Toleration is "the practice of deliberately allowing or permitting a thing of which one disapproves. One can meaningfully speak of tolerating, i. e., of allowing or permitting, only if one is in a position to disallow" (Zagorin, 2003). This understanding requires mutual recognition that the evidence of the past can provide.

But to achieve tolerance and reject the intolerable, we need to focus on the interpretations of the city. There is more intra-group tension on the basis of diverse interpretations than inter-group tension based on the different values themselves. Cultural conflicts have been addressed in the 1994 Nara Document, the ICOMOS Burra Charter of 1998 (now updated to 2013) and the 2008 Ename Charter on Interpretation and Presentation, while the UNESCO 2005 Convention on the Protection and Promotion of the Diversity of Cultural Expressions underscores the need for freedom of expressions and social justice.

Social inclusion

Social inclusion is the reverse of the modern use of the term social exclusion which was coined in France during the 1970s, when no viable housing was then available for those who could not meet the required economic criteria. The roots of exclusion are deep, historical and indeed are continually reproduced in both old and new ways in contemporary society. There are multiple and varied sources of exclusion including marginalization, discrimination and lack of the right to the city in its broadest sense (Saloojee 2002). Exclusion was exacerbated with physical isolation, emphasized by roads and railways and other planning approaches of the period as single-use zoning with the accompanying socio-economic factors of gentrification. Communities were being marginalized through social, cultural and political hierarchies. However, sustainable urban conservation needs to extend its boundaries, to include areas that might not be considered viable, among them those considered socially disadvantaged.

The UNESCO Recommendation on Historic Urban Landscapes, in moving from the conservation of the building as an object to the city as a process, presents an approach to social sustainability providing a role for the NGOs, and thus expanding spheres of influence with the inclusion of previously marginalized communities. The favelas of Rio, the townships of Durban, the slums of Mumbai, the immigrant dock areas of London or New York and the banlieues of Paris are an essential component of this multicultural approach creating new challenges for research. The standard "conservation area" is no longer sustainable by itself and can only be considered in its wider context.

Gentrification

Processes of renewal in general and gentrification in particular are being re-evaluated and the needs for social inclusion have brought together ideas and concepts defining the city's identity and thus strengthening the continuity of place rather than people. The Historic Urban Landscape approach strives to increase diversity though the "sustainable use of urban spaces" thereby pointing to the inclusion of previously marginalized communities.

A look at East London in the 1880s would reveal a poverty-stricken slum, the rookeries, where records from the period describe it as a place of poor sanitary conditions, overcrowded and rife with criminal activity. What the planners could not do, the Second World War did, decimating those historic areas defined by Le Corbusier as slums. Subsequent to these dramatic changes, a study on working-class housing estates in the East End of London in the mid-twentieth century (Young and Willmott, 1957) revealed that kinship networks were deep and far more complex than previously understood. A strong correlation exists between impaired physical accessibility to places and areas of poverty (Vaughan, 2008). However, the values today in these traces of history have been overturned.

Examples of post-war renewal are seen in the work of architect Sir Denys Lasdun in Bethnal Green, where he strived to design a typical East End community in high-rise format, vertical streets with the flats arranged in two-storey maisonettes to recreate the feeling of urban life at street level. Here a reverse situation should be mentioned: the influx of middle-class people displacing lower-class workers in urban neighborhoods in London and its working-class districts, which was described in 1964 by the sociologist Ruth Glass, as "gentrification" (Glass, 1964, p. 342).

"One by one, many of the working class neighbourhoods of London have been invaded by the middle-classes – upper and lower. Shabby, modest mews and cottages – two rooms up and two down – have been taken over, when their leases have expired, and have become elegant, expensive residences ... Once this process of 'gentrification' starts in a district it goes on rapidly, until all or most of the original working-class occupiers are displaced and the whole social character of the district is changed" (ibid., p. xvii).

How did Sir Lasdun's two Bethnal Green buildings stand the test of time? While much thought and effort were put into these residential structures based on sociological research, they were ultimately unsuccessful and suffered from severe social problems.[4] Bradley House was demolished in 2005, while Keeling House has undergone gentrification and was recently transformed into luxury housing. The social changes of the family nucleus that are taking place around the world are exemplified in Bethnal Green. Cultural values are a moving target needing renegotiation not just for each chronological generation but the "generation *location*", the "generation *actuality*", and the "generation *unit*", as identified by Mannheim.

Conclusions

This paper began with an overview of the evolution of the city through synoecism to the empire-building of globalization. Sustainability must now extend the balance between location and actuality, redrawing the internal boundaries of the city to provide social inclusion. The social conditions of the urban environment must now emphasize coexistence and compromise. The intangible heritage forms an integral part of social sustainability that is now integrated in the contemporary context of innovation and the transfer of knowledge – a critical aspect in social transformations. The potential applications of the Historic Urban Landscape Recommendation to promote social sustainability allow us to coordinate the necessary efforts toward these goals.

The process of the evaluation of urban change should be part of an integrative system extending the Environmental Impact/Quality Assessment to include heritage. Partnership schemes to revitalize buildings and economic preservation incentives to owners of private structures are a few of the tools that need developing (Di Stefano et al., 2011). For example, Hong Kong has a unique formula with the Heritage Commission placed in the Development Bureau, and further studies should be shared to learn from this framework. In a similar vein, culture as a brace to the three pillars of sustainability would be a more compatible allegory.

The United Nations is undertaking the final touches to the Post-2015 Development Agenda to update the Millennium Development Goals. Among the key relevant topics raised were Culture: a driver and an enabler of sustainable development, migration

---

4 http://en.wikipedia.org/wiki/Keeling_House

and human mobility, sustainable urbanization and inclusive growth and employment. The city must become socially inclusive and meet the challenges of the digital age. The democratized values can only be comprehended through the identification of those urban components of change and the evaluation of the processes that generated the physical landscape. New urban attributes are needed to allow for opportunities provided by new communications, crowd-sourcing and technologies-for-all and to be a factor for urban design as a key discipline to accompany and manage the processes of transformation.

The complexities of these issues are a major challenge for the immediate future that might harness the new technologies for the benefit of the city and its citizens with social media, big data and smart, human(e) cities.

These transformations can translate into processes of evolution or revolution; the evolutionary course enabling urban resilience and better monitoring, as opposed to the potentially catastrophic results of revolutions in the urban fabric and its heritage, which can be particularly difficult to cushion. Cities are able to absorb shocks, and the higher the level of resilience the greater the shock that can be absorbed and vice versa. In the outline of their book on the resilient city, Vale and Campanella (2005) describe the city as a phoenix, able to regenerate from the ashes of destruction; it is the exception to the rule that cities are lost. Generating resilience is a complementary ingredient for managing the city, especially in light of large-scale changes.

The open secret for urban resilience is in the mixed uses of the city, its cultural diversity and sensitivities to the feedback from environmental assessment. While the latest UNESCO Recommendation on the Historic Urban Landscape underscores the need for an integrative approach to planning, these "mainstream" actions need to be expanded, as most urban development affected by climate change and other disasters is usually in areas that are environmentally unsustainable, areas that are "left-over urban spaces"[5] that are cheap and readily available. Too often it is the underprivileged that are affected by incidents in the city that involve urban disasters and the lack of social sustainability.

References

Ashbee, C. R. 1924. *Proceedings of the Pro-Jerusalem Society 1918–1922.* 2 vols. London, John Murray.

Di Stefano, L., Lee, H.-Y. and Cummer, K. 2011. *Hong Kong Style Urban Conservation.* ICOMOS General Conference, Paris, pp. 29–37.

Eco, U. 2010. *Five Moral Pieces – Migration, Tolerance and the Intolerable.* London, Vintage Books.

5 The term "space left over after planning" (SLOAP) was coined by Prof. Leslie Ginsburg of the Architectural Association in London during the 1960s.

Glass, R. 1964. *London: Aspects of Change*. University College London. London, MacGibbon & Kee. (Centre for Urban Studies Report, No. 3.)
Larsen, K. E. (ed.). 1995. *Nara Conference on Authenticity*. Trondheim/Tokyo, Tapir Publishers/ Agency for Cultural Affairs, Japan.
le Corbusier. 1973. *The Athens Charter*. Trans. A. Eardley. New York, Grossman Publishers.
Mannheim, K. 1952. *Essays: The Problem of Generations*. Ed. P. Kecskemeti. London, Routledge & Kegan Paul.
Marcuse, P. 1998. Sustainability is not enough. *Environment and Urbanization,* October, pp. 103–11.
Petersen, A. C. and de Vries, B. J. M. 2009. Conceptualizing sustainable development – an assessment methodology connecting values, knowledge, worldviews and scenarios. *Ecological Economics* (Elsevier), Vol. 68, No. 4, pp. 1006–19.
Rao, V. and Walton, M. 2004. *Culture and Public Action: A Cross-Disciplinary Dialogue on Development Policy*. Stanford, Calif., Stanford University Press. (Stanford Social Sciences.)
Reid, D. 2013. *Sustainable Development: An Introductory Guide, David Reid*. London, Routledge/ Taylor & Francis. (Business & Economics.)
Saloojee, A. 2002. Inclusion and exclusion. Bringing Worlds Together. Ottawa, Metropolis Project, pp. 34–54.
Sen, A. 2000. *Culture & Development*. World Bank meeting on development, Tokyo.
Sen, A. 2004. How does culture matter? In: Rao and Walton, op. cit., pp. 37–58.
UCLG. 2008. *Agenda 21 for Culture*. Barcelona, United Cities and Local Governments/Institut de Cultura.
UCLG. 2010. Culture: Fourth Pillar of Sustainable Development. Barcelona, United Cities and Local Governments/Institut de Cultura.
UNESCO. 1972. *Convention concerning the Protection of the World Cultural and Natural Heritage*. Paris, UNESCO World Heritage Centre.
UNESCO. 2011. *Proposals concerning the desirability of a standard-setting instrument on Historic Urban Landscapes*. Paris, General Conference, p. 36.
UN-Habitat. 2013. *Revised Compilation for Sustainable Cities & Human Settlements in the Sustainable Development Goals (SDGs) within the Post-2015 Development Agenda*. The Pando Team, December. New York, United Nations.
Vale, L. J., and Campanella, T. J. 2005. *The Resilient City: How Modern Cities Recover from Disaster*. New York, Oxford University Press.
Vaughan, L. 2008. Mapping the East End labyrinth. In: A. Werner, *Jack the Ripper and the East End Labyrinth*. London, Chatto & Windus, p. 288.
WCED. 1987. *Report of the World Commission on Environment and Development. Our Common Future*. (Brundtland Report). New York, United Nations. http://www.un-documents.net/wced-ocf.htm
Weber, M. 1958. In: G. Neuwirth and D. Martindale (eds), *The City*. Glencoe, Ill., Macmillan/Collier Macmillan (The Free Press).
Wilson Taylor, J. 1918. The Athenian Ephebic Oath. Classical Journal.
Young, M. and Willmott, P. 1957. *Family and Kinship in East London*. London, Routledge & Kegan Paul.
Zagorin, P. 2003. *How the Idea of Religious Toleration Came to the* West. Princeton, NJ, Princeton University Press.

Urban Heritage and Sustainable Development in South Asia: A Plea for a Heritage-Aware Approach

Jyoti Hosagrahar

Introduction

The built heritage of South Asia is rich and diverse: temples, mosques, tombs, forts, palaces, and dwellings of every kind abound. Archaeological ruins and sites dot the landscape, reminding us of the rich history of the region. In the cities, 1,000-year-old monuments sit cheek by jowl with steel-and-glass creations and small thatched huts. Preservation practice with its focus on material restoration very often remains fairly removed from culture, mythology, and society. Since the UNESCO World Heritage Convention was passed in 1972, twenty-five cultural heritage sites in India have been inscribed on the World Heritage List; six each in Sri Lanka and Pakistan; two each in Nepal, Bangladesh and Afghanistan; and none in Bhutan and the Maldives. The monuments inscribed so far represent a small fraction of South Asia's outstanding wealth of heritage. Despite this, the historic centres of only a few cities are inscribed on the World Heritage List: Lahore (Pakistan), and Galle and Kandy (Sri Lanka). In India, we are in the unique position of having an enormous treasure trove of urban heritage but no historic city or urban area has World Heritage status yet (although a few are on the Tentative List). Equally remarkable is that a vast majority of the sites are located in and around urban areas and in constant conflict with the pressures of urbanization.

In the context of rapid urbanization that is often uncontrolled and accompanied by excessive building and debilitating poverty, heritage properties in urban areas pose additional concerns for management. The pressures of development, inadequate infrastructure and employment opportunities, and the rapid growth in tourism both nationally and internationally, pose a variety of threats to the destruction of heritage properties and their values. At the same time, in a region faced with major issues of poverty, inadequate infrastructure, and a gross lack of employment opportunities, and a region with a young population (median age in India is 24), history and heritage cannot become a burden that must be cared for at the cost of basic needs (Government of India, 2011). Aspirations for improved living conditions, employment, and development benefits are real and cannot be stymied for preservation.

In the last two decades, we have experienced and observed unprecedented and incessant urbanization in South Asia. The rapid growth and globalized development have transformed cities and towns and posed a threat to the heritage assets, values, and identity of historic places. In response to persistent poverty and consistently exclusionary practices in the region that have resulted in an increasingly divisive society, several global and UN reports have identified poverty alleviation, inclusive social and economic development that give people the opportunities to improve their lives, and the provision of basic infrastructure as important goals of sustainable human development (UN, 2012). Increasing risks due to climate change and adaptation measures and strategies in and around heritage properties also need to be addressed.

This paper examines the challenges and opportunities of managing UNESCO World Heritage properties in urban areas in South Asia and their potential for contributing to the sustainable development of the communities and regions in which they are embedded. In the first section, I discuss the context of preservation practice in India and South Asia and its historical development, as well as the contemporary pressures of urbanization and development on historic cities. The next section proposes and considers a broader conceptualization of both cultural heritage and sustainable development, followed by a section on the challenges to sustainable development compatible with local heritage. I conclude with some normative policy recommendations for heritage-aware sustainable development in and around heritage areas.

Monuments and the city: Urban preservation in South Asia

The modern preservation movement found its first expression in eighteenth-century Europe with an emphasis on Greek and Roman antiquities. The earliest efforts included collections of historical works of art and artefacts that were placed in museums. Gradually, this led to government control of designated sites and the establishment of norms and legislation for the protection and administration of selected heritage properties. In Europe, the idea of protecting cultural heritage came to the forefront during the nineteenth century with the rise of the nation-state, the losses due to frequent wars, and rapid industrialization.

Modern notions of preservation came to South Asia through the British colonial state in the latter half of the nineteenth century. European fascination with and search for Indian antiquities, comparable to their pursuit of Greek and Roman antiquities, shaped the field of Indology. Ancient texts, scripts, inscriptions, cave paintings and other material remains were at the centre of the investigations. The interest in Indian antiquities, art and architecture became institutionalized as archaeological studies with the establishment in 1871 of the Archaeological Survey of India. Alexander Cunningham and other archaeologists discovered Buddhist stupas and unearthed ancient cities. They created lists and descriptions of the monuments they identified. The emphasis was on scientific study, documentation and conservation of ancient sites and archaeological remains, including monuments.

Monuments were recognized for their architectural style and artistic accomplishment. Heritage structures, celebrated as monuments, were objects to be visually admired, set apart as jewels. The Taj exemplified this approach for years. Neither the setting of the monuments, nor life within and around it, were considered in any way pertinent except for places of worship that remained active as such (Kavuri-Bauer, 2011). Cities and urban areas had no place in this classification. British preoccupation with constructing a narrative of glorious Indian antiquity and medieval decline (justifying British rule) could not justify valorizing or protecting contemporary, built environments, such as the medieval towns that continue to thrive even today (see Hosagrahar, 2005). Thus, urban preservation has remained a much-neglected area.

The legal and institutional frameworks inherited as a legacy of colonialism also endorse the protection of monuments and archaeological sites rather than cities with their living and thriving local communities. In India, the Ancient Monuments and Archaeological Sites and Remains Act (amended 2010); the Antiquities Act, 1968 (amended 1976) and the Immovable Antiquities Preservation Rules (1976) in Bangladesh; the Antiquities Act (1975) in Pakistan and a constitutional amendment and Act of 2010 that gave the full authority for the management of heritage in Punjab to the provincial government; the Ancient Monument Preservation Act, 1956 in Nepal; and the Antiquities Ordinance of 1940 (amended) in Sri Lanka, all of which were intended to provide protection to archaeological remains and monuments, have remained the key legal instruments for protecting and managing urban heritage.

Although the increase in tourism and visitation has brought a host of problems to heritage places, in recent years, urban preservation practice has also received some impetus from tourism particularly through the work of local NGOs and citizens' groups in various cities as well as some city development authorities. A large number of historic cities now have heritage walks in place to build awareness and educate. In India, for example, the Jawaharlal Nehru Urban Renewal Mission identified seventeen out of sixty-five cities as heritage cities in the first phase of the programme (Vaidya et al., 2010). This in itself created an enormous awareness of urban heritage. Many historic towns have undertaken efforts to list heritage structures and create inventories to help with monitoring and protection. In Sri Lanka a systematic approach to urban conservation has been applied in Kandy and the Galle Heritage Foundation has played a significant role in the management of Galle.

Heritage, sustainable development and the current pressures in historic urban areas

In recent years, urbanization in South Asia has been rapid, incessant and of gargantuan proportions. In the last two decades, cities and urban forms have experienced unprecedented transformation and development. A sense of speed, simultaneity and complexity accompany the urban transformation. In the current scenario of uneven economic development and depleting resources, built and natural heritage of urban areas are under severe threat from the speed and modes of development that have considered them irrelevant or inconvenient, and have at best cordoned them off for protection. For many in South Asia, cultural heritage in urban areas today is obsolete, burdensome and decorative at best. Occasionally there is an effort to milk them for their tourism value. There is an urgent need for heritage to have a more meaningful role in the development of a place and be relevant to the present context.

Discourses and practices in the last few decades have emphasized the conflicts between forces of economic development and preservation of cultural heritage. This has often pitted one against the other, demanding polarizing choices between progress and identity – comparable in many ways to the conflicts over development and preservation of the natural environment. Those involved in development, innovation and modernization of cities regard conservation of heritage as outdated, restrictive, irrelevant and backward-looking – or as exotic objects to be valued for their difference from contemporary urban life. Meanwhile, supporters and specialists of cultural expression and identity mourn the destruction of history and meaning when these unique and fragile built environments are sacrificed in the rush for rapid urbanization.

Broader definitions of sustainable development have asserted that social and environmental dimensions of development are as important as the economic. In the face of increasing risks of disasters and climate change, an integrative approach to planning for sustainable development has become all the more urgent. Although development efforts and strategies have in recent years noted the need to include the "cultural dimension" and international agencies and banks aiding development have recognized that preserving heritage structures and intangible heritage elements in development projects is an important responsibility.[1] Yet, in practice, a fundamental divergence between heritage conservation and development has persisted over recent decades, especially dominant modes of development focused on increasing GDP. The more recent Rio+20 and Post-2015 Development Agenda provide a small window onto a more integrative approach (UN, 2012). However, culture and cultural heritage have remained marginal in this debate. One consequence has been that contemporary urbanism everywhere is increasingly characterized by fragmentation, with local cultures having to find a place in the interstices of new urban development.

Expanded view of cultural heritage and sustainable development

Heritage is that which is handed down from the past. Particular to a time and place, heritage expresses the cumulative knowledge and experience of generations, affirming and enriching cultural identities. Cultural heritage is commonly perceived as historic monuments, museums, archaeological sites and masterpieces of art and

---

1 The World Bank and the Asian Development Bank, for example, both provide international assistance for infrastructure development related to cultural heritage tourism. See e. g. http://www.worldbank.org/en/country/china/research/all?teratopic_exact=Culture+and+Development&, and http://www.adb.org/search?keywords=heritage (accessed 17 November 2014).

architecture. More broadly conceived, it includes the cultural relationships and practices with respect to the natural environment, land management and water systems particular to a place and time, as well as a variety of material things and immaterial practices including inherited physical artefacts, monuments, buildings and places.

Cultural heritage includes not only the grand ensembles of structures and remarkable natural features, but also the cultural and natural processes that help to sustain them and provide them with contextual meaning. This would include their role in livelihood creation, practices of land and natural resource care and management, building, land use, institutional mechanisms (both formal and non-formal), markets and infrastructure systems that often call for a judicious and careful husbanding of resources. From such a perspective, heritage is a critical resource for sustainable development: the very connective tissue linking the natural and built worlds, spatially as well as temporally, connecting the past and present with aspirations for the future.

Geography, place and natural heritage can in themselves be valuable assets for the development of a city. Local knowledge and practices of ecosystem management can also be valuable resources for sustainable development of particular locales. Sometimes inherited knowledge and systems are rendered obsolete by the new pressures, conditions and aspirations. An integrative solutions approach evaluates and modifies these traditional systems with the objective of reducing obsolescence.

From identifying single monuments, protection for cultural heritage has expanded to include historic districts and territories. In addition, preservation efforts have moved from concentrating solely on the structures of the powerful and wealthy to an appreciation of their interconnectedness to the vernacular fabric in which they are situated. Gardens, open spaces, streets, festivals, folk music and dance, religious and artistic practices, are the connective tissue that binds the built world into an organic whole. Such a conceptualization of heritage includes both grand monuments and vernacular structures that constitute the unique identity of streets, townscapes and historic urban landscapes.

Rather than being static, the relationship of the community or group to their heritage is constantly evolving in response to changing pressures and circumstances. Local livelihoods, hereditary occupations and economies may be dependent on some of the inherited forms and practices that may be threatened with the loss of the particular heritage. As an expression of accumulated local knowledge, the heritage forms and practices may be essential for the very survival or sustainable development of the place, ecosystem or residents.

In South Asia today, the pressing needs for economic development and modernization have resulted in the unwitting destruction of heritage and along with it the identity and knowledge of those communities. The loss of heritage elements is a challenge to sustainable development in numerous ways. Preserving the richness and diversity of people's creative genius is as important for cities and towns as biodiversity is for natural environments. In a world with market-dominated globalization and a homogenized modernity, recognizing a variety of achievements and ways of thinking are crucial counter-balances. This diversity of knowledge systems, potentially invaluable for sustainability, would be lost to us by allowing heritage to be thoughtlessly erased.

Sustainable development today has become a catch-all phrase that means many things to many people. Sustainability as a concept came about in response to the environmental degradation and over-consumption in the highly industrialized economies. The Brundlandt Commission defined the objectives of sustainability as the improvement of human well-being in the short term without threatening the local and global environment in the long term (WCED, 1987).

In face of increasing risks of disasters and climate change, planning for sustainable development has become all the more urgent. Various dimensions of sustainability including heritage, forests and natural environment, water, waste, power, disaster risk preparedness, health, education and finance are all interrelated. Local institutions and knowledge systems play a key role as important resources essential for sustainable development. The management of resources needs to embrace a variety of levels and diverse practices, ranging from the formal private and state sectors to community-managed local systems. Enabling and facilitating the adoption of a diversity of solutions, appropriate to the context, and facilitating their integration so as to enhance the goals of sustainable development, is a critical challenge. A robust understanding of heritage includes the numerous and varied historical and traditional systems of building, providing necessary utilities and services as well as extracting and caring for natural resources.

Global imperatives of responding to climate change urge the adoption of low-carbon and zero-carbon technologies that are primarily aimed at making buildings and transport more energy efficient and less dependent on fossil fuels. Thus concepts of sustainability in urban areas have become universally operationalized in terms of energy efficiency. The more expanded view of sustainability that includes the social, cultural, economic and environmental dimensions are often overlooked in the rush to achieve labels of sustainability. History, heritage and traditions are critical resources for localized and contextualized approaches to achieving sustainability.

Challenges to heritage and sustainable development

South Asia faces unprecedented urbanization and increasing pressures of development. The greatest challenge in places with a rich heritage is balancing the conflicting pressures of preservation of the heritage elements with sustainability and local economic development. Pressures for development have made modernization a priority in much of South Asia. However, modernization projects such as road and drain building in urban areas, are often formulaic solutions based on universal models and global technological capabilities that are insensitive to local resources and cultural frameworks. Aspirations to join the global economy have also resulted in overexploiting some local resources at the cost of others. As a consequence they reject, neglect, and in the end are destructive to local context and heritage.

Faced with the pressures of rapid urban growth, inadequate infrastructure and debilitating social inequities, those in favour of large-scale modernization interventions, pit development against conservation in the allocation of scarce funding. With the promise of greater economic returns from grand modernization projects, businesses and many local communities, political representatives, and other stakeholders have been complicit in turning a blind eye to the neglect and destruction of cultural heritage. Furthermore, heritage threatened by the inadequacy of infrastructure in many places is compounded by a paucity of legal and financial instruments to safeguard heritage at national and local levels, as well as a lack of institutional capacity to manage a range of issues relating to the cultural impacts of development interventions.

Rapid and excessive urbanization and the pressures of commercial development also have a negative impact on urban heritage. With increasing real estate values and commercialization of all properties, even where a group of heritage structures has been protected, in metropolitan areas they are in danger of becoming isolated in a jungle of concrete and glass towers that overwhelm their context, character and identity. On the one hand, the real estate value of property has overwhelmed the identity and character of a heritage area with high-rise towers or destroyed heritage structures; on the other hand, history and heritage have themselves been commodified and marketed for the exotic and unique experiences they offer. Consequently a bias has been created for the aspects of inheritance that are easily made imageable and commodified.

Tourism that is inadequately planned and managed can add to the pressures of development in and around historic towns and cities. When excessive and insensitively designed, tourists and tourism facilities can destroy the character and identity of an area. The flow of capital, the demands of tourists for familiar modern amenities, and the environmental externalities of tourism have distorted the value of heritage and destroyed the fragile systems that nurture it.

Disasters, both natural and human-made, have destroyed heritage and infrastructure in many places. Earthquakes and floods have severely affected heritage in recent years as much as wars, ethnic conflicts, and the deliberate privileging of a dominant culture. Much heritage is destroyed during war and conflict – at times as accidental collateral of war as in Iraq in recent years, and at times as the targeted icon of a specific community. This has been painfully true in Afghanistan. Heritage places and structures representative of the dominant cultural group are generally cared for much better than those of subordinate or minority groups. The neglect or destruction of iconic and life-sustaining heritage elements has become another weapon in dominating an ethnic, religious or racial group.

Challenges of managing urban heritage in India

Beyond the threats of modernization and commercialization, there are several other challenges of managing urban heritage in India and South Asia that are of immediate relevance to our discussion of the deterioration and destruction of heritage.

India's vast geographical and cultural diversity has resulted in a wide variety of urban heritage from medieval forts (e. g. Jaisalmer) to colonial cities (e. g. Mumbai and Chennai), temple towns (e. g. Madurai and Srirangam), and modern planned cities (e. g. Chandigarh and Jamshedpur). Existing legal and administrative instruments, aimed at preserving monuments and archaeological sites in the colonial period, are inadequate to support the complex problems of managing living urban heritage. Even recognizing some of these as heritage is an enormous leap within existing administrative and legal structures in the Indian context.

Apart from those monuments and archaeological sites listed and protected by central and state agencies, elements such as streetscapes, elevations, skylines, riverfronts and public spaces remain largely unrecognized, unprotected. Furthermore, intangible heritage in urban areas are not comprehensively inventoried and integrated with the preservation of built heritage. Comprehensive inventorying and mapping of historic urban areas and their heritage assets beyond individual monuments is essential.

For a variety of reasons, in much of South Asia, the socio-economic condition of communities in many historic towns and historic parts of cities is much poorer than of those in contemporary cities (for a detailed analysis see UNESCO, 2010). The historic parts of cities and towns are often places of poverty, congested and overcrowded with inadequate infrastructure services, informal economy, decrepit housing stock and marginal access to global technology and markets. The structures often require not only material restoration and repairs but also updating of infrastructural services and adapting to contemporary uses. With changing political and economic circumstances, many traditional occupations find themselves increasingly obsolete in the contemporary city. Vanishing crafts and the loss of traditional livelihoods in historic towns compound the economic problems in these urban surroundings. In many places, the need for poverty alleviation programmes seems as urgent and important as the protection of heritage assets.

Maps and property records are often woefully inadequate. With a majority of properties in private ownership and many grey areas of community spaces, ownership is hard to establish. Ownership records are often complicated and messy in historic urban areas and the jurisdictions often need greater clarification. Moreover, as a majority of the ordinary buildings are under private ownership, conservation work is constrained by the limitation of public expenditure on private property. Financial incentives and benefits to private property owners are necessary reforms to promote the protection and improvement of private properties.

A major challenge in managing urban heritage in South Asia is coordination between agencies. When we consider new building construction, streets, drains, water supply and sewage, lakes, wells, plant material, master plans, building by-laws, tourist facilities and housing developments, including affordable social housing, then a large number of agencies and departments are involved. Agencies and departments not charged with managing culture and cultural heritage have little training on heritage issues and have typically given them no consideration. The absence of coordination between agencies and a multidisciplinary approach implies that, for example, incompatible tourism facilities, poorly managed traffic movement, poorly located parking facilities and inadequate solid-waste management can destroy the heritage value of a historic urban area both visually and in the use of urban spaces.

At the other extreme of destruction by routine and formulaic modernization efforts is the destruction of the authenticity of heritage when it is commodified and marketed for its exoticness. A bias exists for the aspects of inheritance that are easily commodified. When the physical, social, ecological and economic fabric of a historic urban area has been transformed or destroyed, the built fabric stands in danger of becoming a pastiche of hollow, consumable images with structures, settings and rituals that caricaturize a sanitized and aesthetic past. Some critics regard this selection of the delectable and delightful in a heritage place as entertainment and not as a repository of knowledge. The process of constructing exotic and picturesque heritage has, at times, falsified a place.

A heritage-aware approach for sustainable development

The need to find ways to integrate cultural heritage and sustainable development in urban areas is particularly pressing. Beyond monuments and museums, the cultural particularities of places including local knowledge and practices have often been discarded in the rush to modernize. Furthermore, the processes of globalization and the social transformations accompanying it have altered the terms of dialogue between different communities and groups and, into the bargain, local knowledge and identities have been eroded. By emphasizing locality, context, historical continuities and identity, a heritage-aware approach to development promises greater opportunities for achieving goals of equity and social justice. The success of endeavours for sustainability will hinge on the ability to identify and engender solutions that balance the needs of global sustainability with local, historically informed practices, and place-based cultural heritage with modern technocratic practice.

As a response to the fragmentation and polarization between development values and conservation values, I propose an integrated approach that aims to reconcile the sometimes-conflicting goals of heritage conservation, urban development, tourism development and sustainability (UNESCO, 2012). From the perspective that the cultural attributes of a town are its assets and should be valued as resources that need to be carefully utilized and nurtured for longevity, with an expanded view of cultural heritage, and a broader conception of sustainability, I argue for heritage-aware design and planning for sustainable development in South Asia. There is a growing awareness of the need to judiciously use and protect resources with a view to sustainability. Inherent in the idea of sustainability is development and change: the idea of making careful use of resources and of finding ways to replenish and enrich in protecting for the future. Similarly, conservation of heritage does not mean return to a pre-modern past or a pristine nature but finding ways of negotiating identities and forms of the past with the future through heritage-aware strategies for development. Rather than viewing the protection of cultural heritage as pitted against development and change, a heritage-aware approach to sustainable development would seek to reconcile and integrate heritage conservation goals with development goals in a manner that is sustainable and minimally intrusive. The concept of a heritage-aware approach to sustainable development consists of minimizing the negative impacts of proposed projects on heritage and maximizing the value of the heritage elements.

Integrative solutions are those that focus on preservation and restoration of monuments but also manage growth and change, implying that experts and consultants involved with the management of urban heritage also need multidisciplinary skills and approaches. While multidisciplinary teams are valuable, a fundamental training in integrative thinking and urban preservation planning is necessary so that development activities, tourism, growth and change can be as effectively managed as the material restoration of the heritage structures. Guidelines for urban regeneration can help guide new construction in historic urban areas to manage their identity and character, visually, in terms of their building process, and in their meaning to the fullest extent possible.

The UNESCO World Heritage Convention already places a great deal of emphasis on the involvement of local communities in the protection and management of heritage properties. The Historic Urban Landscape (HUL) approach, with its emphasis on guiding growth and change for continuity of identity and character, requires even greater engagement of stakeholders at every stage of intervention. Without systematic processes for stakeholder engagement, community engagement can be reduced to ineffective tokenism.

A framework for integrating heritage conservation with sustainable development:

First, an integrated approach to conservation and sustainable development is essential for living heritage such as in many historic cities in South Asia. In historic urban areas that have been continuously inhabited since they were established and where traditions and practices of living and working have built upon the beliefs and knowledge of generations, solutions that integrate heritage conservation and development more effectively use the wealth of cultural resources.

Second, by including local knowledge, practices and the natural environment as heritage assets, a heritage-aware approach to sustainable development recognizes the relationship of built heritage with its social, economic, geographical, historical and ecological context. Seeking continuities in the built fabric by preserving and regenerating as many of the relationships as possible promotes sustainability. In many instances, in places vulnerable to certain types of natural hazards, such an approach might help to build resilience to natural disasters.

Third, integrating sustainable development with heritage management demands looking upon heritage assets as resources for socially and economically inclusive development and poverty alleviation, where heritage resources could generate improved livelihoods in low-income areas.

Fourth, in evaluating and guiding proposed development through a variety of mechanisms such as master plans, development control guidelines and cultural and environmental impact assessments prior to their implementation, a heritage-aware approach to sustainable development can protect cultural resources by mitigating the negative impacts rather than addressing them post facto. Thus, a heritage-aware approach is valuable for management of all heritage properties in urban areas.

Fifth, reforms and modifications to existing and creation of new legal, administrative and financial instruments are necessary to support an integrated approach to conservation and sustainable development, since existing structures and instruments are inadequate. Institutional coordination between various responsible agencies also needs to be carefully managed and streamlined.

Finally, engaging, including and benefiting the communities that live in and around the heritage properties is important for sustainable development of the areas around them. Community engagement empowers a diverse cross-section of stakeholders. Efforts to strengthen local communities and involve local stakeholders are essential for decentralized governance of historic urban areas. Community participation and stakeholder involvement is also a matter of policy and needs to be treated as such.

From the above discussion, it is clear that the current practices of conservation in India and South Asia need to be critically examined and modified in response to relentless urbanization, commercialization and haphazard urban development. These pressures and local projects urge a broader conceptualization of cultural heritage beyond unique artistic and aesthetic value and of sustainable development as both local and cultural. Recent destruction wrought by floods in Kashmir and Uttarkhand and the ongoing conflicts in Afghanistan are reminders of the urgency and importance of mitigating disasters, both natural and those wrought by humans, and building resilience with culture and cultural heritage (BBC News Asia, 2014). The World Heritage Convention aims to encourage the establishment of robust national systems of heritage conservation, in addition to and with the listing of selected properties. Conservation strategies that are integrated with sustainable development and development strategies that are heritage-aware are essential for mediating dynamic continuity for historic urban areas and socially and economically inclusive sustainable development for local communities, reflecting the fundamental spirit of the World Heritage Convention.

References

BBC News Asia. 2014. *What the Floods did to Kashmir's Grand Heritage*. 20 October. http://www.bbc.com/news/world-asia-29685904 (Accessed 25 November 2014.)

Government of India. 2011. *Census of India*. http://censusindia.gov.in/2011-common/censusdata-online.html (Accessed 25 November 2014.)

Hosagrahar, J. 2005, *Indigenous Modernities: Negotiating Architecture, and Urbanism*. London/New York/New Delhi: Routledge.

National Portal of India. n. d. Rescue and Relief in Uttarakhand. http://india.gov.in/spotlight/rescue-and-relief-uttarakhand (Accessed 25 November 2014.)

Kavuri-Bauer, S. 2011. *Monumental Matters: The Power of Subjectivity and Space of India's Mughal Architecture*. Chapel Hill, NC, Duke University Press.

UN. 2012. *Realizing the Future We Want for All*. Report to the Secretary-General. New York, United Nations. http://www.un.org/millenniumgoals/pdf/Post_2015_UNTTreport.pdf (Accessed 25 November 2014.)

UNESCO. 2010. *Historic Districts for All-India: A Social and Human Approach to Sustainable Revitalization*. New Delhi, UNESCO House.

UNESCO. 2012. *Culture: A Driver and an Enabler of Sustainable Development – Thematic Think Piece*. UN System Task Team on the Post-2015 Development Agenda. https://en.unesco.org/post2015/sites/post2015/files/Think%20Piece%20Culture.pdf (Accessed 25 November 2014.)

Vaidya, C., Dhar, V. and Dasgupta Sur, N. 2010. Knowledge Sharing Programme under JJNURM (India). *Context: Built, Living, and Natural*, Vol. 7, Issue 2, October, pp. 75–82.

WCED. 1987. *Report of the World Commission on Environment and Development. Our Common Future*. (Brundtland Report). New York, United Nations. http://www.un-documents.net/wced-ocf.htm

Recognition of Indigenous Peoples' Sacred Natural Sites and the Cultural Dimension of Sustainable Development

Robert Rode

Introduction

Sacred natural sites (SNS) have been described in a broad way as "areas of land or water having special significance to peoples and communities", which are associated with emotional affections. The terms "sacred" and "natural" refer to an open concept of a set of cultural values that different social groups such as indigenous peoples attach to places. "Sacred" implies that these sites are connected with belief systems of those groups, but the term also implies different meanings to different groups of indigenous peoples representing their distinct belief systems that interact with nature. International organizations have taken different actions to introduce the concept of SNS into the debate on sustainability and heritage protection, for example the recognition of cultural landscapes under the UNESCO World Heritage Convention in 1992 or the elaboration of the IUCN-UNESCO Guidelines for the Conservation and Management of Sacred Natural Sites in 2008. Furthermore, this new international discourse depicts indigenous communities as "custodians" of SNS. This representation of indigenous communities as "custodians", however, may point to a reappearance of mythmaking in political narratives of environmental conservation that has been criticized as a manifestation of the "ecologically noble savage". Nevertheless, the discourse also introduces biocultural approaches into environmental conservation strategies by referring to different domains of human well-being – i. e. natural, cultural, spiritual and socio-economic. Since the adoption of the United Nations Declaration on the Rights of Indigenous Peoples (UNDRIP) in 2007, these approaches have accelerated the transformation of the policies and the political governance structures of environmental conservation at different geographical scales – i. e. individual/local, national and international.

The spread of the discourse on sacred natural sites (SNS) has transformed the relationship between conservation practitioners and indigenous communities, which is characterized by an internal social structure of world society. As a sociological approach to globalization phenomena, world society theory seeks to explain the contingency of local problematic circumstances under global conditionality (Wobbe, 2000, p. 16). By employing world society theory, which considers the reorganization of global order since 1945 as a point of departure regarding the scope of normative expectations and references, this paper investigates the idea that that SNS represent a distinctive field of social interaction facilitating cooperation at different geographical scales, coupled with interaction opportunities for conservation practitioners and indigenous peoples.[1] Sustainable development, which as a specific notion of development has been connected with the transformation of global order, represents a manifest field of the study of world society. This paper stresses that the United Nations (UN) as well as its specialized agencies such as the United Nations Educational, Scientific and Cultural Organization (UNESCO) have provided the information and data for the formulation of world societal problems in relation to sustainable development by transforming the relevance and expectations of nature conservation. After looking into the history of the term "sustainable development", this paper shows that despite the contingent emergence of the notion in global relations it has become a reference point particularly for nature conservation practitioners and indigenous peoples.

Sustainability: An accidental ideal or guiding principle of development?

International politics often seem to be driven by buzzwords, and the debate on sustainability as the guiding principle of development in the last forty years or so possibly reaffirms this contention. The German social scientist and journalist Iris Pufé and the German historian Ulrich Grober both stress that although the term itself has gained considerable attention in different scientific disciplines, at present there is no unam-

1 In the field of sociology authors have also criticized the notion of "world society", because they question whether the entire world may constitute a "society" in terms of identity, shared norms and values, a coherent political governance framework comparable to a nation-state, and congruence of general living conditions. However, in her recent study of world society as a scientific discourse the Austrian sociologist Veronika Wittmann (2014) stresses that sociology possibly holds to a notion of "society" that can no longer be maintained. Most "national" societies bear much resemblance to what many sociologists might understand as a more or less congruent or homogeneous society. Against this backdrop Wittmann considers world society as an approach to reflect on global transformations, which transcend societal boundaries confined by the nation-state. In this regard, she suggests six characteristics of world society: (i) socio-economic inhomogeneity; (ii) global processes of sociability (in German "Vergesellschaftung"); (iii) dynamic cultural particularities that are simply part of world society; (iv) global norms and processes of regulation beyond national legislation; (v) transnational identities; and (vi) integration into global structures through a plethora of organizational forms (ibid., pp. 51–5). The world society discourse, therefore, seeks to trace global consequences in local events and the complexity of social interactions as a globalized context. Although this paper does not discuss the entire debate on world society it is important to understand at this point that as a scientific discourse it stresses integrative moments in an era of globalization despite continuous incongruence, inhomogeneity, instability or uncertainty in social relations and interactions.

biguous definition of the principle (Grober, 2010, pp. 16–18; Pufé, 2014*b*, pp. 15–16). Since the definition of the term used in international politics is equivalent to intergenerational justice it was integrated into a broad framework of political goals and actions through the definition of sustainable development. But what does "sustainable development" mean in contrast to "sustainability"? Pufé emphasizes that this new understanding of sustainability implies a development strategy at the intersections of environmental protection, poverty reduction and economic growth (2014*a*, p. 42). The relative success and popularity of the term sustainable development, however, sometimes disguises its conceptual history and contingent re-emergence in the 1980s.

Frank Uekötter, reader in environmental humanities at the University of Birmingham (UK), highlights that environmental issues have caused concern among earlier generations – despite the commonly accepted thesis that in the past people lacked "ecological awareness" – and the origins of environmental policies today can be traced back to the nineteenth century. In the post-war era other terms such as "environment", "ecology" and "participation" dominated the debate. Although the environmental protection movement originated to a considerable degree in civil society in industrialized countries, which faced the ecological consequences of unprecedented economic growth during the "golden age of capitalism" (Maddison, 1982) during the post-war era from 1950 until 1972, governments also supported this movement (Uekötter, 2014, p. 13). Civil society organizations called for immediate solutions to problems of environmental degradation and pollution. Although there was no agreement on how to solve these problems, how to protect the environment or how to preserve nature, governments and international organizations began to conceive of "environmental problems" as international concerns.

Uekötter stresses that the relative success of sustainable development as a new strategy was also a matter of "chronology" (2014, p. 14) because in 1986 the catastrophic nuclear disaster in Chernobyl preceded the publication of the report. In 1992, the Rio Conference sought to bring environmental concerns and the question of development together, as well as to adopt internationally binding instruments. Although today the discrepancy between knowledge and action is obvious – in particular in view of the failed "remake" of the Rio+20 Conference in 2012, which did not produce any substantial results, unlike the 1992 Summit. Pufé argues that through this 1992 Summit the ideal of sustainability found its way into international politics (2014*a*, p. 51). Nonetheless, progress towards legally binding instruments including enforceable rights has not yet been achieved.

In addition, the definition of sustainable development remains unsettled due to the fact that often, governments, international organizations and civil society organizations could not agree on establishing a framework of actions to implement sustainable development. Sustainable development is still dominated by an environmental protection perspective, because industrialized countries apprehend its underlying assumptions in terms of environmentally sound economic development (Pufé, 2014*a*, p. 103). In order to avoid further confusion with regard to the term sustainable devel-

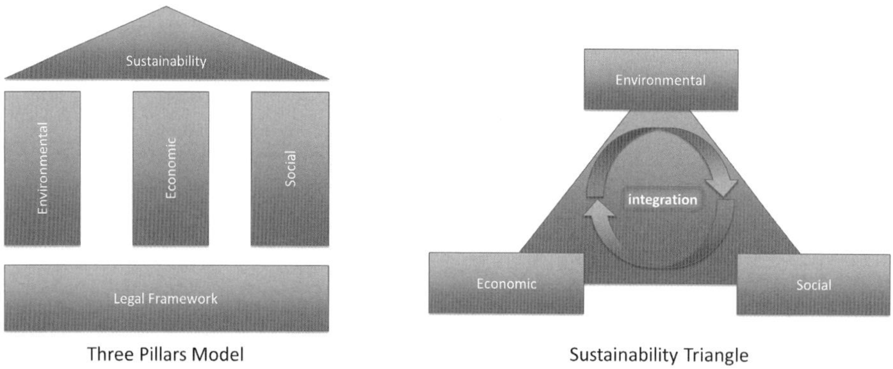

Fig. 1: Three Pillars Model and Sustainability Triangle showing the interrelationship of the environmental, economic and social dimensions (Pufé, 2014*a*, p. 125 [English translation by R. Rode])

opment, applications such as the "Three Pillars" or the "Sustainability Triangle" have been used, for example, in implementation strategies of Agenda 21 (Figure 1). Here, policy-makers attempt to demonstrate the interrelationship between the environmental, economic and social dimensions of sustainability. Nevertheless, these applications may not measure the impact or importance of each dimension holistically. For example, as the first model in Figure 1 shows, sustainability may be achieved with only two pillars or dimensions. Regardless of these shortcomings, policy-makers and scientists as well as indigenous activists have used these models to approach the cultural dimension of sustainable development, as the next section demonstrates.

SNS and biocultural approaches to heritage conservation

In the process of expanding the designation of protected natural areas worldwide, the question of sustainable development has come to the fore, particularly with more reliable data available concerning environmental degradation and the resulting loss of biodiversity. Because of their high levels of biodiversity, SNS have drawn attention from the environmental protection movement. In its specific SNS conservation guidelines the International Union for Conservation of Nature (IUCN) argues that "in many societies, traditional sacred natural sites fulfil similar functions as legal protected areas" (IUCN, 2008, p. 5). Commonly, the use of these sites has been restricted in history as a result of their specific cultural or spiritual significance to certain communities. According to IUCN, even if human influence is greater at some SNS, often, they continue to retain high levels of a variety of animal and plant species. It is however impossible to reach agreement on the significance of the sacredness of spaces, and the meaning of the term "sacred" has been challenged, because people have rejected the literal truth of specific belief systems. In cultural anthropology, for example, differences in nomadic and sedentary understandings of sacred spaces have been discussed in various cultural contexts, and show, for example, the central importance of the interaction between physical and spiritual life for nomadic people (Vitebisky, 2005). This paper cannot, however, venture into the broad debate on the significance of sacredness but acknowledges that SNS reflect a spiritual and cultural relationship between certain communities' faith with natural sites. The understandings of these complex and intangible relationships are often shared by local communities – but also by entire communities of faith – and it is therefore difficult to define them unambiguously.

In a report by the World Wide Fund for Nature (WWF) and the Alliance of Religions and Conservation (ARC), international protected natural areas experts Nigel Dudley et al. have attempted to define three categories of SNS, which reflect furthermore a broad array of challenges to their recognition, conservation and management (Dudley et al., 2005, pp. 18–20). In their report, the experts distinguish between sacred natural sites (e. g. forests, woodlands, coasts, mountains), sacred semi-natural sites (e. g. modified landscapes), and built sites with remaining natural vegetation (e. g. constructed sacred sites that maintain natural parts free of interference). In addition to these approximate categories of SNS, other experts have also identified two further classifications in the world: "[SNS] established by indigenous and traditional peoples in the context of their spiritual beliefs and customary institutions, or created by institutionalized religions or faiths" (Oviedo and Jeanrenaud, 2006, pp. 84–5). Differences arise from the age of the sites and property relationships. SNS established by institutionalized world religions such as Christianity or Buddhism may have been created in the last centuries, whereas indigenous peoples' SNS may often have their origins in Palaeolithic times or at least before colonization. And in the case of indigenous peoples' SNS, "ownership" differs substantially from legal property institutions as for example the Roman Catholic Church. Indigenous communities rather value and safeguard sacred places through their beliefs and practices (ibid., p. 86). Although disputes over definitions and significance of SNS persist, indigenous communities as well as other faith communities attach values to specific natural sites all over the world. Thus, an understanding of how different indigenous communities seek to maintain and manage them has to be based on the local communities' cultures and belief systems.

As mentioned above, SNS – and in particular indigenous peoples' SNS – are considered important reservoirs of biodiversity by various international bodies and organizations. Various international organizations concerned with nature conservation and sustainable development have come to the conclusion that the ecological diversity in these reservoirs may be a direct or indirect result of customary management practices. In 1999, a comprehensive study by the United Nations Environment Programme (UNEP) established a framework for understanding the importance of biodiversity for indigenous communities. In their contribution to the report, Andrew Gray and other experts on the subject highlighted that the fundamental relationship between biodiversity and indigenous communities lies in local knowledge or a "traditional ecological knowledge of indigenous and tribal peoples" (1999, p. 73). For conserving biodiversity, as the UNEP report adds, the uniqueness of traditional indigenous knowledge is critical, because here the term "traditional" does not refer to the relics of an individual community's past but rather seeks to draw attention to the ways these practices are acquired and used by those communities in their environment and territories (ibid., p. 75). An important feature of the conservation practices at indigenous peoples' SNS is a specific group of people, who have watched them over a very long period of time. This group is often described as "custodians" of the spiritual and biological values of SNS, and international bodies such as IUCN have adopted this notion in their guidelines for identifying the relevant stakeholders for the conservation of such sites.

From SNS to the fourth pillar of sustainable development: Recognition of indigenous peoples' rights and the question of misconceptions in nature conservation

In accordance with the UNEP report, the IUCN guidelines draw attention to the complexity of the situation of conservation at individual SNS, which is unique in every case. Thus, a comprehensive stakeholder analysis or mapping has to be approached with care, and although custodians often constitute central stakeholders in this activity, "identifying and interacting with custodians of sacred natural sites ...", as the IUCN guidelines point out, "requires great sensitivity, respect and trust building, sometimes in historically difficult, politically charged and very tense situations" (IUCN, 2008, p. 7). Custodians may range from individuals to whole communities, and can represent an authority with clear leadership structures. However, sometimes the leadership or authority of custodians may appear diffuse to other stakeholders such as protected areas agencies. In these specific protected areas contexts, conflicts may arise among indigenous communities, between indigenous communities and non-indigenous communities, between indigenous communities and other institutions or the state, and there may sometimes exist different long-standing historical conflicts. Thus, indigenous peoples and SNS experts have called for recognizing indigenous communities' systems of decision-making. According to indigenous peoples and SNS experts, important standards for engaging indigenous communities as well as SNS custodians have been set by the UN Declaration on the Rights of Indigenous Peoples (UNDRIP), in particular the concept of free, prior and informed consent (FPIC), laid down by Article 32 of the declaration (Colchester and Ferrari, 2007, p. 20; IUCN, 2008, p. 8; IWGIA, 2013, pp. 56–9; Verschuuren et al., 2010*a*, p. 11).

Research on human rights has pointed out that the UNDRIP as an instrument in the context of the UN is unparalleled, because "it is ... the only specifically collective human rights instrument recognized by the UN, this being the essence and distinctive character of the text and 'indispensable' for the 'existence, well-being and integral development' of indigenous peoples" (Morgan, 2011, p. 17). Being the result of the first UN Decade of the World's Indigenous Peoples (1995–2004), which the UN so designated to draw attention to the need for a specific human rights instrument for the protection of indigenous peoples (Pufé, 2006, p. 129), the key provisions of the declaration also reflect the fact that the completion of the document took almost twenty-five years, and thus they contain relatively widespread sources of relevant principles in international law, such as UNESCO's 1972 Convention concerning the Protection of the World Cultural and Natural Heritage and UNESCO's 2003 Convention for the Safeguarding of the Intangible Cultural Heritage. For example, Article 12 affirms the right of indigenous peoples to "maintain, protect, and have access in privacy to their religious and cultural sites", and Article 13 calls specific attention to indigenous peoples' cultural "practices, expressions, knowledge and skills" that are essential for their revitalization, use, development and transmission to future generations. Moreover, FPIC as a key principle of the UNDRIP that recognizes indigenous peoples' right to self-determination also reflects the concern for conservation and the role of indigenous communities' sovereignty over their land, territories and natural resources, which had already been stressed by IUCN's Inter-Commission Task Force on Indigenous Peoples in 1997:

"Experience shows that when Indigenous Peoples enjoy territorial security and are given freedom to make their own decision … they tend to exercise their right to development in ways which provide long-term environmental benefits. Conservationists and developers must be prepared to cede decision-making powers to Indigenous Peoples, while understanding local priorities and criteria for sustainability. If not, conservationists will continue to clash with Indigenous Peoples" (IUCN, 1997, p. 86, in Pufé, 2006, p. 131).

The UN and its specialized agencies, such as the International Labour Organization (ILO) and UNESCO, as well as Advisory Bodies such as IUCN, have lobbied and advocated for binding legal human rights instruments that protect indigenous peoples and their lands, territories and resources. Against this backdrop, Pufé argues in her study of international climate change alliances in the Amazonian region, that it is fundamental to assist indigenous communities in determining and qualifying their own experts, who will be capable of participating actively in the conservation and management of their lands and resources (2006, p. 137). IUCN's guidelines also contain this idea when they refer to the role and importance of SNS custodians, both of which are linked to the interest in including cultural and spiritual values of indigenous peoples into conservation approaches (Verschuuren, 2010, p. 65).

According to Bas Verschuuren, scientific inquiry has increasingly developed analytical frameworks that consider the reciprocity of biological (e. g. number of species) and cultural diversity (e. g. number of languages, cultural practices) in terms of measuring biocultural diversity, which in turn might be applied in nature management and conservation strategies (Verschuuren, 2010, p. 67). Following this idea of bridging the nature-culture divide in conservation, biocultural conservation approaches appear particularly suitable for the conservation of SNS. However, biocultural approaches entail the need to reconceptualize conservation strategies across different geographical and policy-making scales, i. e. individual/local, national, international. According to Dudley et al., conservationists still lack an understanding of biocultural approaches to SNS, which is partly due to the difficulty of establishing effective management frameworks in cooperation with indigenous custodians of SNS (Dudley et al., 2010, p. 26). Despite the necessity of effective measures that seek to foster indigenous self-determination from the point of view of the nature conservationist movement and international organizations, the discourse on biocultural approaches to nature conservation, or more specifically to SNS, falls short of acknowledging that this framing may suggest a re-emergence of problematic misrepresentations of indigenous peoples across these different geographical and policy-relevant scales. The cultural anthropologist Ter Ellingson has shown in his work on *The Myth of the Noble Savage* (2001, p. 356) that despite the awareness in anthropology today of its formation as an academic discipline in the nineteenth century, which is closely connected to the problematic construction of savage nobility in European colonies that fuelled racist agendas, this rhetoric was apparently introduced into the ecological debate in the 1990s.

Ellingson criticizes this misconception as rhetoric of the "ecologically noble savage" that has caused controversies on the eve of the twenty-first century among conservationists, ecologists and anthropologists concerned with nature conservation and indigenous peoples' livelihoods. Scientists as well as conservation practitioners have attempted to collect empirical data to prove that "indigenous peoples possess an intimate knowledge of their environment" (Alvard, 1993, p. 363, in Ellingson, 2001, p. 350) that enables them to manage their lands and resources in a sustainable way. Thus, the shortcomings of the strategies envisaged for example by IUCN result from a subtly biased representation of indigenous communities as the "other" in absolute distinction from "us". Following the critique of the ecologically noble savage rhetoric, the "other" here refers to a particular notion of conservation that contends that indigenous peoples are unable to damage their environments. Ellingson stresses that the moralization and globalization of the ecologically noble savage rhetoric obfuscates the distinction between very different social groups across the world, who cannot be perceived exclusively in a dichotomy of indigenous peoples versus the state – or versus the international community. For example, Katsuhiko Masaki has shown in his study of river control projects in Nepal that advocates of rights-based and participatory approaches to development have used the idea of FPIC rather as a "straightjacket" in the implementation of these projects, and consequently failed to acknowledge intra-community conflicts among indigenous communities caused by new forms of social differentiation as a result of party politics and gender struggles (Masaki, 2009). Thus, the cooperation of indigenous communities, conservation practitioners and researchers would require revising assumptions with regard to the ecologically noble savage rhetoric in order to avoid unrealistic responses to the conservation needs at particular SNS. More precisely, participatory strategies envisaged by biocultural approaches to conservation of SNS might become blurred by ignoring the issue of misrepresenting identity struggles of indigenous peoples.

The recognition of indigenous peoples by international organizations, however, has fostered their active participation in global forums on the future of sustainable development as the guiding development principle. Inspired by advocates of Agenda 21, indigenous peoples have called on the international community in the preparation of the 2012 Rio+20 Conference to include culture as the fourth pillar of sustainable development (IWGIA, n. d.). In fact, creating the post of the UN Special Rapporteur on the Human Rights and Fundamental Freedoms of Indigenous Peoples in 2001, the establishment of the UN Permanent Forum on Indigenous Issues (PFII) in 2000 as a subsidiary body of ECOSOC with membership of indigenous peoples' representatives, as well as the adoption of the UNDRIP in 2007, has facilitated the harmonization of activities concerning indigenous issues across the UN (Morgan, 2011, pp. 29–32). Although Rio+20 and other UN forums concerned with sustainable development may not have produced satisfactory results, indigenous peoples as well as others such as UNESCO through its Hangzhou Declaration (2013) have attempted to put the cultural dimension of development on the Post-2015 Development Agenda. In September 2015, the UN and its Member States will attempt to adopt new Sustainable Development Goals (SDGs) building upon the Millennium Development Goals. From the point of view of world society theory, which seeks to understand globalization with regard to the spread of norms, institutions and values, the debate on the biocultural conservation strategies for indigenous SNS – as well as the claims by indigenous peoples to include culture as a dimension of sustainable development – supports the idea of normative globalization. In recognizing indigenous rights across different geographical scales and sectors (i. e. the UN, research, nature conservation), indigenous peoples build connections with similar organizations. Furthermore, the questioning of the levels of agreement or the values and norms that do not appear to be shared across these sectors as shown by Ellingson, rather points, from the perspective of world society theory, to the authority of specific groups (Barthel-Bouchier, 2013, p. 39).

Although world society theory places emphasis on how norms, institutions and values spread globally, as an analytical perspective it understands global cooperation and consensus in terms of conflict and opposition. Thus, the results of this study on biocultural approaches in the conservation of SNS allude to the issue of how conservation practitioners, indigenous peoples, decision-makers and researchers struggle to elaborate a set of norms using sustainable development as a reference point. The inclusion of culture, or more specifically biocultural conservation strategies, into the SDGs may appear to provide indigenous peoples with opportunities to argue their cause. Nevertheless, world society theory would contend restrictively that, as the history of the term sustainable development has shown, the relative success of including culture into nature conservation strategies may or may not contribute to the incorporation of culture into the SDGs when the nation-states have competing interests or priorities.

Conclusion

These considerations show how indigenous peoples, nature conservation practitioners, policy-makers and researchers seek to merge the concern with SNS with the discourse on sustainable development. It is precisely the contingent history of the term itself that has allowed these different sectors to formulate normative ambitions and expectations globally, which seek to transform the understanding of nature conservation. In the context of the UN, sustainable development as a new ideal of development may appear to be imposed from above on other geographical and political scales. However, it is the ambiguous use of the term that also creates openness and inclusiveness, and its meaning no longer exclusively refers to the environmental, social and economic dimensions of development. The global concern with SNS and the attempts to establish a framework for biocultural approaches to conservation indicate a broader scope of global cooperation in nature conservation, and conflicts, opposition and competing interests reflect the increased authority of the cultural dimension in this field.

By referring to the idea of SNS custodians, international organizations attempt to involve indigenous peoples in nature conservation and management strategies to further the conceptualization of sustainable development. As Grober puts it, the "elasticity" (2010, p. 280) of the term allows these different sectors to adapt its substance to specific conditions. Overall, determining sustainable development will have to answer the questions as to how the different conservation strategies reduce environmental degradation and enhance human well-being. In this regard, the debate on the rhetoric of the ecologically noble savage suggests that including culture as another equivalent dimension of sustainable development also needs to create awareness of unrealistic expectations due to misrepresentations of indigenous communities.

References

Alvard, M. S. 1993. Testing the "ecologically noble savage" hypothesis: interspecific prey choice by Piro hunters of Amazonian Peru. *Human Ecology*, Vol. 21, No. 4, pp. 355–87.

Barthel-Bouchier, D. 2013. *Cultural Heritage and the Challenge of Sustainability*. Walnut Creek, Calif., Left Coast Press.

Colchester, M. and Ferrari, M. F. 2007. *Making FPIC – Free, Prior, Informed Consent – Work: Challenges and Prospects for Indigenous Peoples*. Moreton-in-Marsh, UK, Forest People Programme http://www.forestpeoples.org/sites/fpp/files/publication/2010/08/fpicsynthesisjun07eng.pdf (Accessed 1 September 2014.)

Dudley, N., Bhagwat, S., Higgins-Zogib, L., Lassen, B., Verschuuren, B. and Wild, R. 2010. Conservation of Biodiversity in Sacred Natural Sites in Asia and Africa: A Review of the Scientific Literature. In: Verschuuren et al. (eds), op. cit., pp. 19–32.

Dudley, N., Higgins-Zogib, L. and Mansourian, S. 2005. *Beyond Belief, Linking Faiths and Protected Areas to Support Biodiversity Conservation*. A research report by WWF, Equilibrium and the Alliance of Religions and Conservation (ARC). http://assets.panda.org/downloads/beyondbelief.pdf (Accessed 1 September 2014.)

Ellingson, T. 2001. *The Myth of the Noble Savage*. Berkeley/Los Angeles, Calif., University of California Press.

Gray, A. et al. 1999. Indigenous Peoples, their Environments and Territories. In: *Cultural and Spiritual Values of Biodiversity. A complementary contribution to the Global Biodiversity Assessment*. Nairobi, United Nations Environment Programme, pp. 59–118.

Grober, U. 2010. *Die Entdeckung der Nachhaltigkeit. Kulturgeschichte eines Begriffs*. Munich, Verlag Antje Kunstmann.

IWGIA. n. d. *Sustainable Development and Indigenous Peoples*. Copenhagen, International Work Group for Indigenous Affairs. http://www.iwgia.org/environment-and-development/sustainable-development (Accessed 1 September 2014.)

IUCN Inter-Commission Task Force on Indigenous Peoples. 1998. *Indigenous Peoples and Sustainability. Cases and Actions*. Utrecht, Netherlands, International Books.

IUCN, 2008. *Sacred Natural Sites. Guidelines for Protected Area Managers*. http://cmsdata.iucn.org/downloads/pa_guidelines_016_sacred_natural_sites.pdf (Accessed 1 September 2014.)

Maddison, A. 1982. *Phases of Capitalist Development*. Oxford, UK, Oxford University Press.

Mallarach, J. and Papayannis, T. (eds). 2007. *Protected Areas and Spirituality*. Proceedings of the First Workshop of the Delos Initiative, Montserrat, 23–26 November 2006. Gland, Switzerland/Montserrat, Spain, IUCN/Publicaciones de l'Abadia de Montserrat.

Masaki, K. 2009. Recognition or misrecognition? Pitfalls of indigenous peoples free, prior, informed consent (FPIC). In: S. Hickey and D. Mitlin (eds), *Rights-Based Approaches to Development. Exploring the Potential and Pitfalls*. Sterling, Va., Kumarian Press, pp. 69–84.

Morgan, R. 2011. *Transforming Law and Institution. Indigenous Peoples, the United Nations and Human Rights*. Burlington, Vt., Ashgate.

Pufé, I. 2006. *Klima – Wälder – Indigene Völker. Umwelt- und Entwicklungspolitik im Rahmen des "Klima-Bündnisses" zur Erhaltung von Natur und Kultur in Amazonien*. Munich, oekom.

Pufé, I. 2014*a*. Nachhaltigkeit. Stuttgart, Germany, UTB.

Pufé, I. 2014*b*. Was ist Nachhaltigkeit? Dimensionen und Chancen. *Aus Politik und Zeitgeschichte*, Vol. 64, No. 31–32, pp. 15–21.

Oviedo, G. and Jeanrenaud, S. 2006. Protecting Sacred Natural Sites of Indigenous and Traditional Peoples. In: Mallarach and Papayannis (eds), 2007, op. cit., pp. 77–99.

UN. 2007. Declaration on the Rights of Indigenous Peoples. New York, United Nations. http://www.un.org/esa/socdev/unpfii/documents/DRIPS_en.pdf (Accessed 1 September 2014.)

Uekötter, F. 2014. Haus auf schwankendem Boden: Begriffsgeschichte. *Aus Politik und Zeitgeschichte*, Vol. 64, No. 31–32, pp. 9–15.

UNESCO. 2013. The Hangzhou Declaration. Placing Culture at the Heart of Sustainable Development Policies. http://www.unesco.org/new/fileadmin/MULTIMEDIA/HQ/CLT/images/FinalHangzhouDeclaration20130517.pdf (Accessed 1 September 2014.)

Vásquez, M. A. and Friedmann Marquardt, M. 2003. *Globalizing the Sacred. Religion across the Americas*. New Brunswick, NJ/London, Rutgers University Press.

Verschuuren, B. 2010. Arguments for developing biocultural conservation approaches for sacred natural sites. In: Verschuuren et al. (eds), op. cit., pp. 62–71.

Verschuuren, B., Wild, R., McNeely, J. A. and Oviedo, G. 2010*a*. Introduction: sacred natural sites the foundations of conservation. In: Verschuuren et al. (eds), op. cit., pp. 1–13.

Verschuuren, B. (eds). 2010*b*. *Sacred Natural Sites. Conserving Nature and Culture*. London, Earthscan.

Vitebisky, P. 2005. *Reindeer People: Living with Animals and Spirits in Siberia*. London, Harper Perennial.
Wittmann, V. 2014. *Weltgesellschaft. Rekonstruktion eines wissenschaftlichen Diskurses*. Baden Baden, Germany, Nomos.
Wobbe, T. 2000. *Weltgesellschaft*. Bielefeld, Germany, Transcript.

Culture, Heritage and Solidarity in the Context of Sustainable Development

Manuel Peters

Introduction

Since its adoption in 1987 by the World Commission on Environment and Development (WCED) the term sustainable development has gained worldwide acceptance as a "visionary development paradigm" (Drexhage and Murphy, 2010, p. 2). Sustainable development was thus adopted almost universally as a guiding principle among governments, businesses and civil societies. As is true for every concept that is broadly accepted, there are many existing definitions of sustainable development. It is agreed upon, however, that sustainable development, if properly understood, goes beyond one-dimensional understandings of development that focus, for example, only on processes of economic growth. Notwithstanding, Drexhage and Murphy (2010, p. 7) describe sustainable development as a very flexible concept allowing a great variety of stakeholders to adapt it to their own purposes. Accordingly, there is still the tendency to see the environmental dimension and/or economic development as the focal point(s) for sustainable development – often to the disadvantage of recognizing the complex (and) convergent nature of the economic, social and environmental dimensions of sustainable development. This certainly has to do with the predominant role that (neoliberal) economic relations and institutions play in the international arena (Stiglitz, 2002).

Culture as basis for an informational perspective on sustainable development

Against the backdrop of the definitional and practical ambiguity of the concept of sustainable development, it is of great importance to always clarify the applied understanding. To this end, Amartya Sen, an important contributor to the debate, sees the need to refer to an overarching informational approach that allows for measuring, judging and informing practices and definitions of sustainable development in non-economic terms. Too often, he argues, informational approaches that are applied in measuring the application and outcome of practices around sustainable development are based on economic criteria, e. g. on the gross national product (GNP) or the gross domestic product (GDP). Sen criticizes this focus sharply by accusing it of confusing "ends with means" (Sen, 2010, p. 226). A proper assessment of the state of development, he argues, has to take into account that people have values in their lives and usually value the freedom to choose between different opportunities. The mere focus on outcomes or, as he calls it, "achieved functionings" (ibid., p. 236) is too narrow. Instead, "a person's capability to do things he or she has reasons to value" (ibid., p. 231) should stand at the centre of evaluation. Capabilities that individuals value, however, are not context-free. In other words, capabilities and values are always context-bound.

Against this background it makes little sense to define a "fixed list of relevant capabilities" (ibid., p. 242) that can be applied in each and every context. Instead, values of importance are dependent on cultures while cultures are changing, and values, ideally, are reasoned publicly. The informational perspective that Sen proposes therefore emphasizes the changing nature of social contexts and social relations – always unequal to differing degrees – by highlighting the importance of the sustainable development of the capabilities of individuals. Without reference to culture in concepts of sustainable development, the great importance that values play in peoples lives, i. e. that people "cherish their [context related] ability to reason, appraise, choose, participate, and act" (ibid., p. 250; my insertion) is easily forgotten. What is more, these abilities, in Sen's view (ibid., p. 251), should not just be sustained but – "(when possible)" – also expanded "without compromising the capability of future generations to have similar – or more – freedom".

As the importance of certain capabilities always unfolds only in certain contexts, Sen's informational perspective on sustainable development is of great importance for discussing the role that culture (can) play(s) in the context of sustainable development. The integration of culture into debates, for example, as the Fourth Pillar of Sustainable Development (UCLG, 2010), may therefore cast another light on the convergence of the three other pillars by linking them to the context-dependent opportunity of making choices. However, as I argue in the following, while the integration of culture into concepts of sustainable development is of great importance and should be seen as groundbreaking, history also shows that caution is required with reference to culture in the context of development.

What should also become visible by the inclusion of culture into concepts of sustainable development is the positionality of the knowledge that we apply. Consequently, we are asked to clarify the often implicit intentions behind development ambitions, due to the fact that these are often rather ambiguous.

Culture as a reminder of the positionality of knowledge about sustainable development

Reflecting on the positionality of knowledge present in approaches to development can be seen as of particular importance in the context of development "cooperation". Seen this way, development cooperation is not necessarily good and sustainable. On the contrary, when exercised without proper reference to the basic cultural ideas and interests behind the concept of development, the cooperation may be rather unsustainable (Brühl, 2011, p. 15). This is because development may thus represent a certain dominant development culture that does not fit very well in the context where it is applied. What is more, when development cooperation is put into historical perspective, it becomes clear that the concept of development has to be seen as a cultural product of the West that was introduced as a new strategic means in times of transition from colonialism to globalization. The reference to development, Brühl argues (ibid., p. 26 f.), filled the power vacuum that was the result of processes of decolonization and served as a counter-project to state socialist power blocs. The consequence was the stigmatization of the majority of the world's population as members of underdeveloped nations and cultures. A latent sociocultural racism was the consequence. This is not without irony, because those nations that, by then, had just recently been emancipated from colonialism and consequently had every reason to see themselves as developed, were now, again, referred to as underdeveloped and in need of assistance (see also Escobar, 1995, p. 23 ff.). Seen this way, the classical concept of development is suspect of anything but paying proper reference to the cultures and cultural values of the people living in the respective contexts that are in "need" of development. Behind uncritical concepts of development there often remains the idea of fostering a better, freer culture. Without reference to an informational perspective as described above and a context-bound process of self-definition of what a freer culture actually means, these conceptualizations of development more often than not result in rather paternalistic practices rather than empowering conceptions of sustainable development. This can go as far as seeing culture as a hindrance to development and the reasons for unsuccessful sustainable development in a missing culture for sustainable development.

The role of culture in sustainable development is thus very important. Without considering these cultural aspects of ambitions to develop, predominant concepts of development are prone to stay centred on the established difference between "developed" and "developing" countries. The inclusion of the concepts of culture and cultural heritage, though, can tell us that there is no single end-point to development, but that the definition of what development means is context-dependent. As a consequence, marking countries as "developing" and "developed" can be considered a hindrance to successful sustainable development. This is even truer when "developed" countries are considered as role models of successful development that, apart from concerns as regards their sustainable use of natural resources, are seen as more or less socially and economically sustainable. Drexhage and Murphy (2010, p. 7) argue that "developed" countries can be considered anything but role models because governments as well as civil society in "developed" countries lack the necessary engagement to address important issues such as their locally and globally unsustainable consumer culture and/or the fostering of more equal social, economic and environmental relations on a global scale.

There are thus several reasons why culture and cultural heritage should be considered an important part of concepts and practices around sustainable development, where they have at least a twofold role. First, the concept of culture highlights the positionality of the ways we act, perceive and think, and culture therefore "ultimately shapes what we mean by development" (UCLG, 2010). There is necessarily a wide diversity of conceptions of development. This may help to highlight the ambiguity behind all conceptions of development. Culture, in this sense, is about taking local knowledge, local practices, local values, etc. seriously and making them part of development processes. This contribution of culture to sustainable development is already a concern in heritage studies (Boccardi, 2012, p. 10 ff.). Second, the integration of diverse cultural heritages can bring different histories and conceptions of economics, of the social and the environmental to the fore. This may be seen as of great importance for finding alternatives to economic-centred approaches to sustainable development. Here, the integration of culture and, specifically, cultural heritage also has concrete political implications. How we understand cultural identity and cultural heritage therefore matters.

Cultural diversity and identity politics

In 1995, the report *"Our Creative Diversity"* (UNESCO) was published by the World Commission on Culture and Development. The report serves as an important anchor for UNESCO's concept of culture. It also stands as a milestone for its concerns with protecting the diversity of the world's cultures and their respective heritages. The understanding of culture presented in the report can therefore serve as a good starting point for understanding the complex role that culture and cultural heritage play in sustainable development.

Against the background of diverse forms of oppression that a diversity of cultural minorities experienced in the recent decades previous to its publication, the report spends a great amount of energy arguing the importance of the protection of cultural diversity on a world scale. This is done by reference to a "right to culture" according to Thomas Hylland Eriksen (2001, p. 127). The aspiration to thereby strengthen the protection of local conditions and local human resources cannot be valued highly enough. In the course of the 1990s, however, cultural identity was also instrumentalized in the form of brutal identity politics in many parts of the world. This leads Eriksen to blame the report for its concept of culture, which he says tends towards an "exoticistic bias" (ibid., p. 131). He explains that "throughout the report, cultures are implicitly and explicitly seen as rooted and old, shared within a group, to be treated 'with respect' as one handles aging china or old aunts with due attention due to their fragility" (ibid., p. 132). Culture, he criticizes, is mainly seen as tradition although it has to be seen as both tradition and "communication ... impulses, choice, the future, change, variation" (ibid.), that is, ordinary. Hybrid cultural forms appear in the report as artificial, "while tradition ... is profound" (ibid., p. 134). Hybridity is accordingly associated with modernity and tradition with ethnicity. This resulted in the assumption that cultural diversity is a "value in itself". But what, he asks, happens to the "right to *not* have a specific (usually ethnic) identity" (ibid., p. 135; Eriksen's emphasis). This is an important question, because group rights and human rights may sometimes stand in contradiction to each other. The focus, then, cannot be on the preservation of cultural diversity but rather has to be on individuals who may want to choose to be – or not to be – members of particular groups. It follows for Eriksen that local initiatives should be supported with reference to rights but without reference to culture:

"Since the word culture divides but an unqualified rejection of the relevance of local circumstances oppresses, this kind of ambivalent position is the only starting-point for a humanistic politics that tries to achieve the impossible: equality that respects difference, 'a sense of belonging to a community larger than each of the particular groups in question'" (Eriksen, 2001, p. 144).

Eriksen here binds the respect for difference to a sense of belonging that transcends the groups in question. This kind of understanding of the fostering of respect for difference was termed "solidarity" by Richard Rorty. I return to this below. Eriksen however does not dismiss the importance of culture in general but the relevance of the focus on a right to culture for UNESCO. It would follow for development practices that respecting and including local knowledge, local art, etc. are very important, but that, in order to do so, culture is the wrong reference. This is an important account, also because local knowledge, social status etc. are not evenly distributed within local contexts (see also Antweiler, 1998). The fostering of cultural group identity may therefore not result in the intended social inclusion and empowerment.

From a cultural studies perspective, narrowly defined group identities, bound by and rooted in tradition, have to be seen as an obstacle to "wider, more inclusive solidarities" (ibid.) as well. However, James Clifford argues that we have to be careful not to dismiss identity politics in general, because this may also have disenabling results. He goes on to explain:

"Throughout the world, people are caught up in, and excluded by, the powerful currents of capitalist markets, religious movements, and national projects. Embracing and resisting these forces they struggle to position themselves, to establish home bases, sites of collective support and action. Communities need to make 'room' for themselves (Turner, 1992, p. 14) in a crowded world. If in the late twentieth century they do this through cultural processes of ethnic, regional, tribal, class, racial, gender, and sexual identification (in tactical combination) this is not something we have the luxury, or the privilege, to lament" (Clifford, 2000, p. 96 f.).

In the citation above, Clifford positions cultural identity strategically and gives it an important role in struggles for participation in the world. Cultural identifications and corresponding struggles are thus seen as adequate when they are a necessary part of democratic mobilization processes. These, he argues, have to "work through the cultural discourses that situate groups, that provide them with roots (always spliced), with narrative connections between past and present (traditions), with distinctive social habits and bodies" (ibid.). Oppositions to such special claims to cultural rights, he argues, may mask another "unmarked, 'identity politics', an actively sustained historical positioning and possessive investment in whiteness" (ibid., p. 97).

Cultural identities in a cultural studies understanding are thus an object of politics. This, we cannot ignore. In politics, cultural identities are "made and unmade, connected and disconnected, in the interactive arenas of democratic, national and transnational life" (ibid., p. 95). Just as communities are not stable, as whom they integrate is constantly changing, national and transnational orders have to be seen as arenas of "continual struggle and negotiation, formation and breakup" (ibid., p. 96). Thus, according to Clifford (2007, p. 24), cultures and spaces have to be understood as historically contingent and, while probably persistent, without a natural shape to them.

Cultural formations, then, have to be seen as combining different, not necessarily associated, elements and spaces. The way those elements are associated, to take an example, whether pizza is seen as an all-Italian food or rather as belonging to the culture of north Italy or to that of south Italy or – because of its near universal adoption – to the world, has thus to be seen as a matter of (un-)successful politics, dependent on the position taken. In this sense, the role of culture in sustainable development lies, on the one hand, in the acknowledgement of local cultural knowledge in conceptions of sustainable development. On the other hand, it lies in the acknowledgement that cultural identity is always also politics and that recognition of cultures also falls into a realm of politics and political representation that structure communities and spaces. The way we work with cultures and cultural heritages is, therefore, also a matter of democratic engagement, and consequently, of solidarity. The concern for social inclusion and equity necessarily encompasses culture.

Solidarity as an alternative approach to sustainable development

"It is in the emergent sites, the things that don't quite fit, the remembered or revived alternatives, that we look for utopian, transformative visions and practices" (Clifford, 2000, p. 11).

David Featherstone (2012, p. 56), among others, writes that in the current conjuncture, international relations are "dominated by powerful forces, such as capital". The validity of this argument also shows in the tendency of practices and conceptions of sustainable development to focus on economic development, and to take possession of cultural heritage mostly in economic terms (Albert, 2013). Cultural heritage, on the contrary, may also serve as a reminder of other possible presents and "other trajectories into other futures" (Grossberg, 2010, p. 57). To this end, a focus on solidarity and on "hidden histories and geographies of internationalism" becomes a meaningful enterprise (Featherstone, 2012).

Solidarity, classically, is seen as a given. In a Durkheimian conception, for example, solidarity is something that is an "automatic outcome of social position and is determined by prior allegiance to clan or heritage" (ibid., p. 20) in "traditional" societies. In modern societies, Durkheim sees solidarity as deriving automatically from modern forms of interdependence, i. e. the division of labour. Solidarity is also often seen as evolving from belonging to a particular class or gender, with "innate capacities of solidarity" (ibid.) to the class or gender one belongs to. Another very powerful, but similar argument is that solidarity evolves from a "shared sense of 'humanness'" (ibid., p. 19). Calling Durkheim's understanding on solidarity into question seems quite easy. If it were true that solidarity is a direct outcome of the division of labour, why is there no global solidarity in a present of global production and consumption? A claim for global sisterhood or class-interest has been called into question, not only by postcolonial feminists, because of the fact that these claims were uttered mostly by white women in "developed" countries. The reference to shared sense of humanness is enticing but also problematic.

Some of these (different) assumptions of (different degrees of) universal relatedness to those who, in the end, are like me/us seem appealing at first sight. However, they miss a notion of identity politics that was discussed before, of the "tensions and conflicts over how solidarities are constructed" (ibid., p. 21). Likeness, instead of being already there, has to be understood as actively produced, since likeness, from a cultural studies perspective, is made and unmade in political processes and therefore contingent. Following Featherstone, practices of solidarity thus have to be understood as the active creation of "shared values" and "community solidarity, or political integration". There is thus no necessity for likeness to predate solidarity, which is always an activity. It is therefore important again not to understand values and communities as a given. Only then, does the creation of "a more expansive sense of solidarity than we presently have" (Rorty, 1989, p. 192, in Featherstone 2012, p. 22) become a meaningful project. In this understanding, solidarity emerges as a transformative potential and a productive force that shapes universalizing processes (ibid., p. 38). Universalisms, like the assumption of our shared humanity that we tend to refer to, we thus have to understand as actively produced, struggled over, and at stake in politics. They do not precede political participation. However, solidarities are not only a means of those movements and communities that we frame as good, and they do not have predictable outcomes. The highlighting of the active production of local, regional and international relations and correspondent (cross-over) communities that is in play in our choices, makes the concept of solidarity important for alternative conceptions of sustainable development.

From a cultural heritage perspective, then, alternative "texts, artefacts, and instances of political activity" (ibid., p. 64) that create different senses of international relations and of being modern and developed therefore have great importance for alternative approaches to sustainable development today. Those histories, however, are more often hidden than told as long as economy-centred conceptions prevail.

From such a perspective, we are also asked to reflect on our own involvement in sustainable development, in addition to working and struggling for alternative, more sustainable economic, social, environmental and spatial relations. This may also mean renouncing certain forms of consumption; it may mean working for different cultures of sustainability in "developed" countries. It always means looking for alliances with those who intend to do the same. This, as the concept of solidarity tells us, is also an act of world-making. Alternatives are always part of the present.

References

Albert, M.-T. 2013. Heritage studies. Paradigmatic reflections. In: M.-T. Albert, R. Bernecker and B. Rudolff (eds), *Understanding Heritage: Perspectives in Heritage Studies*. Berlin, De Gruyter, pp. 9–17. (Heritage Studies Vol. 1.)

Antweiler, C. 1998. Local knowledge and local knowing. An anthropological analysis of contested "cultural products" in the context of development. *Anthropos*, Vol. 93, pp. 469–94. http://www.jstor.org/stable/40464844

Boccardi, G. 2012. Working document for the expert meeting on "Heritage and Sustainability – from principles to practice", Toyama, Japan, 3–4 November. http://whc.unesco.org/document/128768

Brühl, D. 2011. Einführung in die Themenstellung Kultur und Entwicklung. In: D. Brühl (ed.), *Kultur und Entwicklung: Theoretische und praktische Beiträge zur soziokulturellen Ausrichtung der Entwicklungszusammenarbeit*. Oldenburg, Germany, BIS Verlag, pp. 15–44.

Clifford, J. 2000. Taking identity politicsseriously: "the contradictory, stony ground ...". In: S. Hall, P. Gilroy, L. Grossberg and A. McRobbie (eds), *Without Guarantees: In Honour of Stuart Hall*. London/New York, Verso, pp. 94–112.

Clifford, J. 2007. Indigenous articulations. In: R. Wilson and C. L. Connery (eds), *The Worlding Project: Doing Cultural Studies in the Era of Globalization*. Berkeley, Calif., North Atlantic Books, pp. 13–38.

Drexhage, J. and Murphy, D. 2010. Sustainable development: from Brundtland to Rio 2012. Background paper prepared for consideration by the High Level Panel on Global Sustainability at its first meeting, 19 September 2010.

Eriksen, T. H. 2001. Between universalism and relativism. A critique of the UNESCO concept of culture. In: J. K. Cowan, M.-B. Dembour and R. A. Wilson, (eds), *Culture and Rights: Anthropological Perspectives*. Cambridge, UK, Cambridge Escobar, A. University Press, pp. 127–48.

1995. *Encountering Development: the Making of the Third World*. Princeton, NJ, Princeton University Press.

Featherstone, D. 2012. *Solidarity: Hidden Histories and Geographies of Internationalism*. London, Zed Books.

Grossberg, L. 2010. *Cultural Studies in the Future Tense*. Durham, NC, Duke University Press.

Rorty, R. 1989. *Contingency, Irony, and Solidarity*. Cambridge, UK/New York, Cambridge University Press.

Sen, A. 2010. *The Idea of Justice*. Penguin Books, London.

Stiglitz, J. E. 2002. *Globalization and its Discontents*, 1st edn. New York, W. W. Norton.

Turner, T. 1992. Defiant Images: The Kayapo Appropriation of Video. *Anthropology Today*, Vol 8, No. 6, pp. 5–16.

UCLG. 2010. Culture: Fourth Pillar of Sustainable Development. Barcelona, United Cities and Local Governments/Institut de Cultura.

World Commission on Culture and Development, UNESCO 1995. *Our Creative Diversity: Report of the World Commission on Culture and Development*. 1. Aufl. Johannesburg, Pretoria: EGOPRIM.

IV Theory, Methods and Practices

Disciplinary and Epistemological Perceptions

Cultural Landscapes: Heritage Preservation as a Foundation for Sustainable Regional Development

Joaquim Sabaté, Mark Warren

Introduction

Many governments and institutions recognize and promote "cultural landscapes"; it is a complex term that essentially connotes the product of the natural landscape and human society's transformation thereof, including assigned meaning. The cultural landscape is more than a tract of land or series of monuments to preserve, however: it can provide the basis for a sustainable territorial planning framework. As our definition of heritage has expanded from the individual icon to broader landscapes, urbanism has grown in scope from single cities to comprehensive regions. Cultural landscapes are regional concerns that urbanism must necessarily address. Through regional projects, cultural landscapes can be given detailed plans designating patterns of use and growth, paving the way for official recognition and establishing channels for participation by residents. These regional plans based on appreciation of heritage as a social and economic resource provide a sustainable model: in addition to protecting the valued heritage, the measures are intended to attract economic activity (tourism, investment, commerce) and provide a programme for long-term growth. If plans allow for continuous adaptation and account for potential future development, they can turn heritage landscapes into economic drivers and foundations of regional reactivation. Ideally, by turning the landscape itself into a resource, the local community will be enriched in a permanent and sustainable manner.

Cultural landscapes can serve as a major component of sustainable urban planning at a regional level. By studying the experiences of a variety of cultural landscapes and heritage parks around the world, the authors propose some criteria to guide such planning and preservation projects. They do not intend to provide a systematic model but rather a framework for understanding the complex relationship between heritage and development, preservation and renewal, protection and planning.

The discussion of heritage has traditionally – and logically – looked backwards in time: we value heritage for its connection to the past, and interpret it chiefly in that context. Many heritage preservation projects therefore focus somewhat narrowly on the physical or cultural preservation of a site according to a static historical image. Historic preservation in the West, Robert Melnick notes with a nod to David Lowenthal, acts to halt change rather than accommodate progress (Melnick, in Alanen and Melnick, 2000, p. 22). A sustainable approach, however, demands that heritage be looked at primarily in the context of present use and future development. The cultural landscape is a heritage construct capable of providing such a sustainable framework, allowing for organic processes of change to continue while preserving sites' natural and cultural integrity for the present and the future. Moreover, the cultural landscape is an inclusive concept that can apply to any site or territory – although its application is not always easy.

The concept of sustainability has been defined and applied in very different ways, but at its core is the ability to meet present needs without compromising future generations' ability to meet theirs, as stated in the 1987 Brundtland Report (WCED, 1987). Ideally, sustainable development should even enhance those future generations' ability to meet their needs. In order for the preservation (itself a form of development) of heritage to be sustainable, then, it is not enough to address needs of the present day and obligations to the past: it must furthermore not harm future generations, and, if possible, should benefit them.

This is a thoroughly realizable goal. Heritage is a valuable asset whose worth is far more likely to increase than decrease over time. In an age marked by a loss of authenticity and a tendency toward environmental homogenization, heritage is a precious and vanishing resource. Although returns are not necessarily immediate or easy to measure, investment in preserving heritage is a sound long-term strategy for public and private actors (National Trust for Historic Preservation, 1976; Strauss and Lord, 2001). Particularly given the growth of the tourism and travel industries, and the increasing mobility of capital worldwide, the economic benefits of heritage preservation are difficult to deny.

In order to ensure a sustainable project with the greatest possible benefit in both the near and distant future, traditional preservation is insufficient. This is especially true of large, complex, and context-dependent sites such as cultural landscapes. We must adopt a far broader definition of preservation, one that includes the preservation of use patterns and cultural significance in addition to (or, in some instances, instead of) physical remnants, or that can allow for the full interpretation of a site's history rather than that of certain favoured eras or illustrious individuals. We must also recognize the act of preservation itself as a stage in the dynamic process of a site's development, with consequences of its own. And, of unsurpassed importance regarding project sustainability, we must also understand that heritage resources are intimately related with the local communities and individuals who are integral to their significance and integrity. They must receive the direct benefits of any preservation project, and their involvement and connection to the site is critical for its success.

Certainly, we must prioritize preservation efforts, especially given the broad potential applications of the cultural landscape definition. Just as any physical or philosophical artefact of the present is "heritage" to future generations, any site of any scale can be seen as a unique cultural landscape, whether a picturesque river valley or a mundane expressway interchange. It would be nonsensical to freeze all development to preserve the global landscape in a petrified form for the interpretive benefit of future generations, just as it would be unsustainable to constantly obliterate and replace the landscape, as is the tendency of modern development. We must instead find a sensible middle ground, sustainably preserving those elements, sites or areas that are of greatest present and potential value. This is a difficult, perhaps unavoidably subjective task, but one that is facilitated by the cultural landscape framework.

The US National Park Service and the development of cultural landscape preservation

The practice of historic preservation is a relatively recent one, whose development has hardly been without controversy. The narrative typically begins in Renaissance Rome, with official papal protection of ancient ruins; it resumes with the French Revolution's institutionalization of historic preservation and the continuing efforts of French cultural leaders during the first half of the nineteenth century. At this time the primary focus was on the preservation (often including the beautification, or "restoration") of specific monuments and their immediate environment, frequently at the expense of other historical and contemporary layers. Architect Eugène-Emmanuel Viollet-le-Duc's restorations epitomize this approach, arguably sacrificing the integrity of the extant structure in favour of conjectural reconstructions.

Restoration and reconstruction remained a common approach to heritage preservation well into the twentieth century, although it was no longer in vogue among most European academics and intellectuals. The prevailing trend was the tradition of more restrained preservation, as advocated by William Morris and John Ruskin, as noted in a 1935 report on historic preservation by J. Thomas Schneider, then Special Assistant to Interior Secretary Harold Ickes (Schneider, 1938, p. 122f.). Schneider's report was prepared to provide legislative and policy recommendations concerning the greatly expanded National Park Service (NPS), which had recently been given responsibility for all federally controlled historic sites and buildings (Schneider, pp. 8f, 19).

Restoration was not an uncommon approach to preservation in the United States: at Williamsburg, Virginia, the Rockefeller-funded preservation project's first phases involved the restoration of fifty-seven buildings, the reconstruction of sixty-five buildings and two business blocks, and the destruction of over 350 modern buildings. With surprising sensitivity, Schneider declares, "Every phase in the historical development of a monument should be preserved. The principle is that it is not for this generation to judge between epochs and styles, for we are but the temporary custodians of these monumental archives and we must pass them on to future generations in a condition the least offensive to posterity" (ibid, p. 124). Indeed, the last clause displays a remarkable prescience apropos of the above-mentioned Brundtland Report's definition of sustainable development, published fifty years later. However, Schneider's report does not highlight heritage as a tool for sustainability, but rather views "development of a greater national appreciation of the cultural values inherent in historic sites and buildings" as the main goal beyond physical preservation (ibid., p. 1) Later on, the report strongly advises against reconstruction except in special circumstances, and asserts that often "the original setting is as important as the original boards and bricks with which the structure was built" (ibid, pp. 171, 173). Based on the recommendations in this report, Congress gave the NPS the legislative authorization and policy guidelines to manage the nation's historic cultural resources.

The NPS had, prior to 1933, been responsible for the federal areas designated national parks, monuments and reservations, while other federal historic properties were administered by the Department of Agriculture and of War; executive orders by Franklin Roosevelt expanded the NPS and charged it with the administration of all federal historic sites (ibid, pp. 17, 19). State, local and private authorities had been and would continue to be responsible for other historic sites. The NPS would become a pioneer in the planning and management of heritage, drawing on other nations' experiences but also earning a reputation of its own. The growth of the NPS beginning in the 1930s was largely due to Depression-era federal spending programmes meant to create jobs and salvage the economy, but it is also indicative of a growing public interest in preserving the nation's cultural and natural heritage.

Only a few years earlier, Berkeley geographer and professor Carl Sauer had published his seminal *The Morphology of Landscape* (Sauer, 1925) an early exploration of the cultural landscape construct. Sauer defines the "cultural landscape" as the product of human activity impressed upon the natural landscape over time. "The natural landscape is being subjected to transformation at the hands of man," he writes. "By his cultures he makes use of the natural forms, in many cases alters them, and in some destroys them." Natural and cultural heritage are interdependent and interactive, creating unique and significant interpretive areas.

Over the following decades the academic discourse continued to develop, led by John Brinckerhoff Jackson and others, but it was not until the 1960s that the NPS began to regard cultural landscapes as a discrete type of heritage resource (Page, 1998, p. 10). The NPS had begun with the administration of national parks and battlefields, in addition to some individual historic buildings; this was its main charge from its creation in 1916 until its reorganization in 1933 (Schneider, 1938, p. 169). The inclusion of a greater number of large, culturally significant and actively inhabited and utilized sites required new methodologies, though the NPS initially maintained a far greater interest in preserving the physical natural and cultural record than it did in the communities that comprised the areas' living culture. During the creation of Great Smokies National Park in the 1920s and 30s, for example, the NPS effectively evicted much of the local population of Cades Cove, Tennessee, to create a static, historic park image that highlighted the vernacular cultural production whose development was halted by the very intervention that sought to preserve it (Alanen and Melnick, 2000, pp. 127 f.).

During the 1970s and 80s the NPS continued to study and experiment with the preservation and management of cultural landscapes, beginning with rural historic landscapes (National Park Service, 1985) but also, significantly, preserving the industrial heritage that represented much of the United States' past productivity as well as its contemporary urban decline. Lowell, Massachusetts, designated a National Historic Park in 1978, is perhaps the best-known example, and one that has served as an inspiration elsewhere in the United States and internationally (Dublin, 1992; Sabaté and Schuster, 2001). Not only have projects like that of Lowell preserved natural and cultural heritage and provided a venue for education and recreation; they have given new life to cities and regions reeling from the loss of industry and a lack of new development opportunities.

The NPS first recognized cultural landscapes as a specific heritage resource type in 1981 (Alanen and Melnick, 2000, p. 7). In 1988, the NPS formally listed "cultural landscapes" as a type of cultural resource in its park system, and established policies "to mandate the recognition and protection of significant historic, design, archaeological, and ethnographic values." This "recognized the importance of considering both built and natural features, the dynamics inherent in natural processes, and continued use" (Page, 1998, p. 7). The idea of preserving a cultural landscape is, in a sense, paradoxical: external intervention interferes with the prior cultural or natural processes of the system, threatening to upset them. The cultural landscape is at once process and product; preservation interrupts the process and alters the product (Alanen and Melnick, 2000, pp. 3, 16). Yet this must be weighed with the consequences of inaction and failure to protect the landscapes in question, and of allowing these cultural landscapes' futures to be determined instead by market pressures or occasional government or private intervention.

By the end of the twentieth century, the NPS's policies for the planning, management and interpretation of cultural landscapes adhered to criteria for sustainable development. The NPS defined the cultural landscape as "a geographic area ... associated with a historic event, activity, or person or exhibiting other cultural or aesthetic values," and divided cultural landscapes into four non-exclusive types: historic site, historic designed landscape, historic vernacular landscape, and ethnographic landscape (Alanen and Melnick, 2000, p. 8). As noted in the NPS *Guide to Cultural Landscape Reports* of 1998, "Cultural landscapes are not separate systems or characteristics, but integrated, living, dynamic constructs" (Page, 1998, p. 101). This comprehensive and cautious understanding is fundamental not only for successful preservation efforts, but also for recognizing cultural landscapes' potential for sustainable development. Physical change (according to traditional patterns of natural and cultural development and use) is not feared or avoided, but rather understood as an often-necessary aspect of the dynamic process of the landscape (ibid, p. 111). Changes that diminish the site's overall integrity, however, are seen as detrimental and are therefore unwelcome additions to or detractions from the landscape. "When land use is a primary reason for significance of a landscape," the *Guide to Cultural Landscape Reports* continues, "the objective of treatment is to balance perpetuation of use with retention of the tangible evidence that represents its history" (ibid, p. 106).

UNESCO, too, has established criteria for designating and preserving cultural landscapes, although the United Nations agency lacks the executive authority of the NPS and other national and local administrations. Its recognition, however, is a powerful tool that facilitates funding and stimulates development, thereby encouraging the protection of designated heritage sites and activities, while the World Heritage Convention provides a legal framework for listed sites. In 1992 UNESCO first recognized cultural landscapes as a specific category of heritage, with language somewhat different from that of the NPS. UNESCO divides cultural landscapes into three main categories: clearly defined landscapes designed and created intentionally by man, organically evolved landscapes, and associative cultural landscapes, which may lack material cultural evidence. Organically evolved landscapes are further distinguished between those whose process of evolution has already ended and those that are active "continuing landscapes" (UNESCO, 2013).

The semantic distinctions in definition are telling: the NPS focuses on cultural landscapes as historic record, while UNESCO understands them as active elements that form both our heritage and our legacy. Both are important. The emphasis on the past does not inherently make the NPS strategy unsustainable, but it creates a bias that needs to be accounted for in its preservation projects and their management.

In compiling his report on historic preservation for the Secretary of the Interior and for Congress, Schneider travelled to a number of European countries to produce a comparative analysis of preservation trends and techniques; Canada, Mexico and Japan are also included. "A cursory examination reveals that practically every nation, excepting the United States, with any substantial background of history was long before this interested itself in preserving the best and most significant products of man's handiwork" (Schneider, 1938, p. 35). Schneider shows his appreciation for the United Kingdom's National Trust and the open-air museum of Skansen at the Nordic Museum in Stockholm, Sweden (which had already inspired the American re-creations of Ford's Greenfield Village in Michigan and Storrowton in Springfield, Massachusetts). Over all, Schneider encountered a great variety of methods and practices, organizations and instruments, policies and goals from country to country. But he observed that preservation was typically carried out by those "within the fields of education and fine arts" and that "the technical problems of conservation and preservation serve only as a means to its basic and ultimate end in promoting and stimulating the cultural arts" (ibid, p. 108). Where the NPS was concerned, it was the "educational, inspirational and recreational worth of such sites and monuments [that] furnish the fundamental and constitutional bases of justification" for federal involvement (ibid, pp. 175 f.) – these can still be considered active and sustainable goals. But since historic preservation in the United States fell not to a separate specialized bureau but to the NPS, the integration of landscape and culture in preservation projects was perhaps inevitable.

A basis for sustainable development

Historically, preservation policies and practices have not always met current criteria for sustainability. Those projects that have involved the displacement of communities or the destruction of their livelihood are the most obvious offenders, but even those that have had positive local effects are not necessarily sustainable – that is, they may harm future generations. Tourism booms that lead to growth and employment can be followed by busts that leave decaying hotels and empty restaurants. Renovated historic districts in urban areas can drive housing costs up and traditional residents out. Commercialization of heritage can destroy its integrity and replace authenticity with kitsch.

However, we live in an age of accelerating development, in which transformations of our environment that once took generations are realized in a matter of years or months. Preservation is essential to the survival of our physical and cultural heritage; but we cannot believe that preservation is an authorless act devoid of value judgements, cultural and historical biases, or economic and political interests, nor can we pretend that preservation does not interrupt its object's history and redefine its future. Our interest is not merely in establishing the value of heritage and demanding its protection, but in utilizing these resources to benefit given territories' local development, education and quality of life.

A methodology for sustainable development entails understanding that the future is not certain and maintaining the flexibility to adapt to changing conditions. If we recognize that the future is ambiguous and that we are limited to our own perspective in the present, we can create the conditions for the sustainable preservation of our past.

The cultural landscape paradigm can certainly be a sustainable system for heritage preservation: the NPS and UNESCO guidelines reflect that commitment to sustainability. Because the cultural landscape can – and should, some might argue – define all territory, it can furthermore be incorporated as a key facet of urban and regional planning, assuring its real power in the political and legal fields, and contributing to local and regional development in a positive and sustainable way. A sustainable cultural landscape preservation plan can serve as the foundation for a broad regional plan based on the same sustainable ideals.

The relationship between heritage and local development is complex, but by nearly any standard heritage constitutes a valuable asset in the global market: heritage is rare, fragile, in limited and diminishing supply, and cannot be reproduced. It is an important instrument for attracting people and capital as the easy movement of each accelerates. By preserving heritage, we hope not only to save its present value but also to cause that value to increase in the future, reinvesting the gains in the community. The sustainable use of heritage for this purpose can aid local development, while maintaining the mission of its preservation.

Some methodological criteria

The importance of involving the individuals that comprise a heritage site's local community cannot be stressed enough. Their interdependence with their heritage is essential to any intervention, for if they become alienated the heritage that remains loses its authenticity except as a historical record. If they continue to feel a sense of entitlement to their heritage, however, the community‘s esteem will grow in its own eyes, serving as a foundation for perpetuating the preservation of their heritage going forward. Moreover, strong local involvement has proven crucial to heritage projects' success, providing insight in the planning, management and interpretation phases.

Sustainable cultural landscape preservation programmes are well suited to serve as foundations for regional plans because they require the involvement and cooperation of groups from grass roots to government, including economic and social interests. Diverse agents and interests focus on common goals for mutual benefit, with a long view toward the future.

If managed properly, cultural landscapes can help regions to generate economic activity and create jobs, attract tourism, and continue to reinforce communities' self-esteem. This has proven important for the revival of Lowell and other industrial cities and regions whose economies had been in seemingly inescapable decline. The preservation, rehabilitation and sustainable reuse of obsolete historic structures have given old buildings new value and new life.

The standard procedure for preserving cultural landscapes is to inventory resources and assets, research and document the site, choose a narrative or narratives that allows the site to communicate its story, build a support structure of routes for circulation and other necessary infrastructure and services, provide guidance for the site's interpretation, and stipulate its sustainable management in the future. To this, we might today add the rehabilitation and reuse of obsolete or dilapidated structures, if appropriate, to promote local development through the community's own heritage resources. Beyond that, we could include integration with regional plans to coordinate efforts and assets, for the benefit of the community and the broader region.

Today interventions in cultural landscapes are growing, with new heritage parks dedicated to industry, mining, farming, rivers, historic routes, battlefields, archaeology, ecology, etc. (Sabaté, 2004).

By analysing the most significant of these projects we can draw an initial conclusion: the intelligent management of heritage resources is a key factor for economic development, because heritage attracts tourism and investment, generates jobs and economic activity, and reinforces the community‘s self-esteem, a fundamental aspect concerning projects' sustainability, to wit, its future viability. The post-industrial decay in these communities hides the very keys to their future transformation. We can see the signs of decadence, vestiges of past splendour, as blight, or we can learn to utilize them to build a new future by treating them as resources and assets.

Cultural landscapes and heritage parks are becoming an increasingly important part of regional development. They are communicative spaces that retain and transmit information about our past. Just as cities play a leading role in the information age as centres of interaction and exchange, cultural landscapes assume an ever more relevant function as places where histories, narratives and messages are tied to spaces and forms. To better understand cultural landscapes and their roles, beginning in the 1990s researchers at the Catalonia Polytechnic University and the Massachusetts Institute of Technology examined a variety of examples, learning from earlier experiences to better plan future ones (Sabaté and Schuster, 2001).

Our interest is not only in establishing the value of heritage and demanding its protection. Our duty as professionals entrusted with the well being of individuals and the territories they inhabit is to utilize the resources comprised by cultural landscapes to benefit a given territory's local development, education and quality of life. Our commitment, and our goal, is ultimately to improve the lives of the local community (Sabaté, 2009).

Cultural heritage is a social construct, a complex of sacrosanct symbols and relics legitimized not by its authenticity, but rather by our appreciation of it. Heritage exists only as an abstract concept until specific assets are appraised and the discourse begins to take shape. Once appreciated only for its aesthetic value or as architectural monuments, heritage has come to be interpreted much more broadly, as places of memory. It ceases to enclose itself in privileged museums and cities and demands recognition in its actual context. It begins to realize its value as the inheritance of a given community and its territory.

This opens new perspectives on what the revaluation of cultural resources means for regional development. The traditional outlook implies recognizing and inventorying assets, establishing their organization and management, and developing the conditions of their reuse, essentially for tourism and leisure. But this method distances the resources from the community. Today we maintain a wider and more integrated view of heritage and its worth. We have changed our emphasis from its simple protection to increasing its value and potential. By closely integrating the function of natural and cultural resources with their territory, we transcend preservation and arrive at a feasible and sustainable increase in value.

This brings us to the relationship between heritage and local development. Since the 1992 Rio de Janeiro Conference on Environment and Development (Earth Summit) we have understood environmental protection to be tightly linked to communities' development. Likewise, the improvement of cultural resources should be related to achieving higher levels of well being among the population of their territories. But we must go beyond this trope and learn to articulate the issue in both dimensions: heritage and local development working together, not in an abstract sense but rather applied to concrete examples of heritage and their territory.

In the space of a few years heritage has gone from being seen as a source of large public spending with little in the way of social returns, to constituting a central factor in the most relevant socio-economic initiatives and, significantly, their image. There has truly been a conceptual reappraisal of heritage, not only in its theoretical bases but also in its regional implications, and in the politics tied to its management. Today heritage, once essentially monumental but now a variegated collection of resources, is the basis of much touristic, cultural and educational activity, with many positive consequences. Particularly important are the reinforcement of communities' self-esteem and the creation of social capital.

But at the same time we must ask whether all the effects are beneficial, and whether they truly contribute to positive processes of local development. We know that the exploitation of heritage has not always favoured its authenticity; we also understand that not all the heritage resources are implicated in the economic processes that seek development by attracting visitors.

Our goal in studying the keys to successful heritage parks is to determine how to use them to spur development and enhance the heritage resources themselves. The following are lessons and hypotheses we have drawn from the study of various examples (Sabaté, 2009, 2010):

- Assets of the territory must be made useful to the community that occupies it; bearing in mind that heritage is the basis of identity and popular solidarity.
- The preservation of heritage and related development must be sustainable, without exceeding its carrying capacity or affecting the authenticity or integrity of the resources.
- Development is a process, not a final goal. We must therefore continually reexamine and reformulate models and policies regarding heritage.
- Complex legal and executive instruments are needed for effective management, to coordinate the many different agents and groups involved.
- The local population must be involved in the process of recognizing and valuing heritage.
- To maximize the gains on investment in heritage, projects must take advantage of synergy of the individual and the collective, at local and regional levels.
- It is necessary to develop strategies that incorporate heritage and its benefits in a context that reaffirms the shared values and resources of a community.

In a recent text that reviewed the evolution of the treatment of cultural landscapes over the past thirty years, we demonstrated the development of ever more complex and broad-reaching instruments of intervention (Sabaté, 2010). These involve the first inventories, catalogues and documentary work; isolated projects to rehabilitate and reuse individual structures; plans and projects that integrate heritage in ambitious and coordinated proposals; and, finally, territorial plans in which the heritage constitutes a focus of the programme and can become a motor of local development. Ultimately the heritage of industry and labour seeks the same treatment under territorial plans and projects as natural heritage, while culture and nature can become axes of reflection, recording the extent of our interventions on the landscape.

Cultural landscapes and heritage parks are becoming more important in regional economic development strategies. But we should not consider this the end of the road. The majority of territorial plans in the twentieth century emphasized population dynamics and industrial development, and used massive infrastructural projects and zoning as fundamental instruments. Today, however, some notable regional plans have begun to recognize a new dichotomy: nature and culture. Nature and culture as parts of a single concept: heritage. And cultural landscapes can constitute a vehicle to achieve this framework, protecting diverse environments with distinct identities.

Thus should we direct our efforts, understanding landscape, in its broadest sense, including the natural and the cultural, the physical and the intangible, as the foundation for planning instruments and design? Landscape is not the finished product of a culture or cultures, but rather a continuously evolving reality. We must go beyond simply preserving our society's cultural inheritance. We have seen how it can generate opportunities for development that allow historic appreciation and neoliberal economic policy to coexist. We must overcome a purely conservationist approach to heritage and work with the available resources to protect heritage while continuing necessary processes of transformation. Today's construction, too, can reinforce identity, and it may become heritage tomorrow.

Conclusion

The concept of the cultural landscape is a relatively recent phenomenon, and our idea of sustainability more recent still. Neither is easy to define or measure. These are complex, interdisciplinary themes that will benefit greatly from further study and careful application.

One of the greatest challenges is posed by the fields' subjectivity. It is impossible to preserve and interpret all of natural and cultural history's infinite layers together: preservation efforts necessarily privilege certain elements over others. Issues also arise where preservation and development cannot be reconciled, and one must be given preference. Value judgements must be made where these conflicts arise, with no easy solution. In addition to relying on experts and professionals from various disciplines, the local community must be involved in such decisions. If nothing else, it means the inhabitants of the landscape will continue to determine their own future, preserving their authentic connection to and control of their environment.

References

Alanen, A. R. and Melnick, R. Z. (eds). 2000. *Preserving Cultural Landscapes in America*. Baltimore, Md., Johns Hopkins University Press.

Dublin, T. 1992. *Lowell: the Story of an Industrial City*. Washington DC, US Department of the Interior.

National Park Service. 1985. *Land Use Plan, Cultural Landscape Report, Boxley Valley, Buffalo National River, Arkansas.* Washington DC, US Department of the Interior.

National Trust for Historic Preservation. 1976. *Economic Benefits of Preserving Old Buildings.* Washington DC, Preservation Press.

Page, R. R. et al. (eds). 1998. *A Guide to Cultural Landscape Reports.* Washington DC, US Department of the Interior.

Sabaté, J. 2004. Paisajes culturales. El patrimonio como recurso básico para un nuevo tipo de desarrollo. *Urban,* No. 9, pp. 8–29.

Sabaté, J. 2009. Algunas pautas metodológicas en los proyectos en paisajes culturales. In: *La práctica del urbanismo.* Madrid, Editorial Síntesis.

Sabaté, J. 2010. Paisajes culturales y proyecto territorial: un balance de treinta años de experiencia. *Identidades: Territorio, Cultura, Patrimonio,* No. 2, Barcelona, December, pp. 7–26.

Sabaté, J. and Schuster, M. (eds). 2001. *Designing the Llobregat Corridor: Cultural Landscape and Regional Development.* Barcelona, Universitat Politècnica de Catalunya/Massachusetts Institute of Technology.

Sauer, C. 1925. The morphology of landscape. *University of California Publications in Geography,* Vol. 2, No. 2, pp. 19–54.

Schneider, J. T. 1938. *Report to the Secretary of the Interior on the Preservation of Historic Sites and Buildings,* 1935. Washington DC, US Department of the Interior.

Strauss, C. H. and Lord, B. E. 2001. Economic impacts of a heritage tourism system. *Journal of Retailing and Consumer Services,* Vol. 8, No. 4, pp. 199–204.

UNESCO. 1994, rev. edn. 2013. *Operational Guidelines for the Implementation of the World Heritage Convention.* Paris, UNESCO World Heritage Centre.

WCED. 1987. *Report of the World Commission on Environment and Development. Our Common Future.* (Brundtland Report). New York, United Nations. http://www.un-documents.net/wced-ocf.htm

A Reflection on Methodological Approaches in Assessing and Implementing Social Sustainability in Historic Public Spaces

Solmaz Yadollahi

Introduction

The human self is shaped and developed thanks to social interactions with other persons. Although modern technological developments have caused a growing number of social interactions to take place in the virtual public sphere, the unique value of face-to-face interaction is undeniable: it is in physical public space that the members of a society share the control and use of space. Public space is, and historically, has always been a space for practicing social co-existence and a basis for social sustainability.

Furthermore, having been shared by contemporary and past societies, historical public spaces have the exceptional power of connecting generations to one another, and these public spaces, if protected, can extend connections to future generations. In other words, by telling the story of the construction of societies, historical public spaces can be sources of identity for present and future societies.

In this paper, I will clarify, through a literature review, the meaning of public space and reflect on theoretical approaches to and methods of assessing the ability of urban public spaces to enhance social sustainability. I will explain how the definition of public space and approaches to urban planning share concepts with social sustainability. Finally, reflecting on examples of empirical research that attempt to link physical and social components of public spaces, I will point out the methodological strengths and weaknesses in the field.

Given that approaches to and methods of studying public space in urban planning and urban heritage conservation overlap in many areas, I will not separate the two fields here. However, the empirical works presented are examples of research on historical public spaces. The position of this paper towards historical public spaces, urban heritage, and their relationship with social sustainability is based on a dynamic understanding of heritage.

One of the most recent publications on heritage, *Understanding Heritage,* edited by Marie-Theres Albert and others, gives a comprehensive perspective on the subject of heritage. Through her paradigmatic reflections on the notion of heritage and heritage studies, Albert (2013), views heritage as a dynamically created phenomenon and a cultural process. She links cultural heritage to the concept of "human development",[1] arguing that "the protection and use of heritage is conceived of as a potential that shapes identities and builds peace" (Albert, 2013, p. 14). She suggests that the notion of heritage protection should be seen in the framework of sustainable development. The following discussion approaches urban heritage in the framework of that understanding of heritage. In other words, urban heritage encompasses the tangible and intangible components of the dynamic city.

The relation between urban heritage and sustainability is discussed in the UNESCO Recommendation on the Historic Urban Landscape (HUL). The HUL approach calls for the sustainable use of urban spaces by changing the focus from the traditional monumental approach to one that takes into account the social and economic development process. In fact, HUL advocates "a new use and enjoyment of the urban space that defines the city as a living heritage" (Bandarin, 2012, p. 224). HUL is an effort to sustainably protect urban heritage for the coming generations, and to balance the forces of conservation and urban development (Turner, 2013).

As defined by the UNESCO Recommendation on the Historic Urban Landscape, urban heritage can be categorized in three main typologies: first, monumental heritage of exceptional value; second, public, open spaces and streets; and third, urban infrastructures (UNESCO, 2011). Accordingly, in this paper, historical public spaces are considered in the context of the second category of urban heritage in the HUL Recommendation.

Viewing historical public spaces as the most dynamic category of urban heritage, in direct relationship with the members of society, this paper attempts to understand how these spaces contribute to social sustainability and asks how effective the currently used methods are in assessing this contribution.

Social sustainability and its relation to public space at a conceptual level

Social sustainability

Initiated with the 1972 Stockholm Conference, the concept of "sustainability" became popular through the Brundtland Report on the 1987 United Nations' World Commission on Environment and Development, then evolved in the course of different international meetings. These debates placed the *needs* of communities and their *limits* in an ethical framework (WCED, 1987).

---

1 In the United Nations Development Programme, "human development" is generally understood to mean enlarging people's choices as regards their standard of living, in areas such as health, education and political freedom (UNDP, 2014).

The environmental aspect dominated the discourses on sustainability from the late 1980s to the mid-1990s, after which the economic aspect attracted the focus of debates. The feature of *social sustainability* began to be considered more seriously from the mid-2000s onwards (Colantonio and Dixon, 2011).

The focus of this paper is on social sustainability and how it is implemented in urban planning. From a semantic perspective, social sustainability can be defined as the ability of a society to sustain itself. It is about people. Naturally, the environmental and economic aspects of sustainability can be achieved thanks to people's ability to sustain their society within their limited resources. In *Urban Regeneration and Social Sustainability*, Colantonio and Dixon (2011) define social sustainability as how individuals and groups gather together and decide what they want for themselves, taking into account physical boundaries and environmental limits. Manzi et al. (2010) provide a conceptual framework that presents a multidimensional understanding of social sustainability involving the relationship between concepts of *participation, justice, democracy*[2] and *social cohesion* with economic competitiveness and environmental efficiency.

In short, we can suggest that social sustainability reflects the ability of a society to share, maintain and develop its environmental and economic resources in a way that allows *social justice, equality* and *participation* within and outside the community, with consideration for the needs of future generations. This paper develops its argument based on the fact that social sustainability depends on human relations. By linking the key concepts embedded in social sustainability with the meaning of public space, I will first discuss how physical public space can contribute to social sustainability, then give examples and discuss the research challenges in this regard.

The meaning of public space

Patrick Geddes (1854–1932), the Scottish thinker and town planner, talks about giving people places in which they can flourish (Colantonio and Dixon, 2011). These simple words show the nature of the contribution of physical urban spaces to the enhancement of social sustainability. Since the focus of this paper is on public space, I will continue with a short review of various understandings and definitions of public space. Since research on public space has always been interdisciplinary, we will examine the viewpoints of the different disciplines.

---

2 When Manzi and others use the term *democracy* they do not refer to a specific understanding of it. In general, they state that terms such as participation and democracy refer to the system of responsibility-sharing in a community. In this paper, democracy is understood as "government by the people exercised either directly or through elected representatives" (*American Heritage Dictionary of the English Language*, 2000, democracy).

Many scholars, such as the urban planner Madanipour (2003) and the political scientist Parkinson (2012), call public space the sphere of "interpersonal communication".[3] The urban historian and architect Hayden (1995) explains how social and physical spaces are linked through public spaces that are influential in "social reproduction".[4] Interpersonal communication which leads to social flourishing and, as Hayden puts it, social reproduction, of course, needs a physical space in which it can take place. This is the most important function and value of public spaces.

Historical public spaces have another important characteristic because of their ability to tell the stories of a society. The idea of "storytelling" is reflected in the literature on historical monuments and urban spaces. For example, according to Hayden (1995), social memory relies on storytelling, and "place memory" can trigger social memory through the urban landscape.[5] In fact, she believes that memory is "naturally place-oriented" or at least "place-supported", because places engage all human senses (sight, sound, smell, touch and taste), thus making them powerful sources of memory. She argues that the relationship between places and social memory is the key and most powerful reminder to citizens of historical urban places of their public pasts, one that helps them to be connected with those who share a common past. Hayden calls urban landscape a "resource for public history". Similarly, Madanipour (2003) argues that historical public spaces create the opportunity for us to share the experience of being together in the same physical spaces. In his view, being in a historical public space is experienced by past and present generations. If it is conserved, it can be perceived by future generations. In other words, the experience of being in historical public spaces can bond generations.

The above-mentioned factors associated with public space show that physical public spaces are necessary for face-to-face communication among members of a community, as well as for making the latter aware of their common history. This creates solidarity and a sense of belonging to the community, a basis for social sustainability.

Another way to understand the role of physical public spaces in helping societies to flourish is to explore the key concepts used to define public space. As we shall see, scholars in different disciplines define public space in a similar manner, which shows

3 Interpersonal communication is an area of study. In this paper however, it refers simply to the act of exchanging information between two or more human beings through verbal or non-verbal messages. The term "communication" here does not refer to the communication theory, which is also a specific scientific field.

4 Here, Hayden does not give an exact definition for "social reproduction". However, considering the context of her book, one can conclude that by the term "social reproduction" she means the process in which social structures are recreated so that the whole social system can continue.

5 Hayden chooses to use the term "place" instead of space, because for her, place carries the meaning of the special *personality of a location* in the city, which is why people become attached to that place.

that the key concepts that construct the meaning of physical public space are commonly agreed upon. A clarification of these definitions also shows how the physical and social components of public space are intertwined and how social sustainability relates to public space at a conceptual level.

Viewing physical public space through a political lens, Parkinson (2012) argues that democracy[6] depends heavily on the accessibility of "physical public space". Although a political scientist, Parkinson is mainly concerned with physical space, and his definition can help open a discussion on the relation between the social and physical components of public space. Parkinson gives a fourfold definition of physical public space, which takes into consideration its *legal, social, political* and *architectural* aspects. In his definition, public space is "openly accessible, and/or uses common resources, and/or has common effects, and/or is used for the performance of public roles" (Parkinson, 2012, p. 16). In this definition, *openness, accessibility,* and being *common* are the key attributes of public space.

These attributes are to be found in other definitions. Under the title *Common Ground,* Orum and Neal (2009) have collected some of the most important literature on public space from disciplines such as sociology, political science, art and urban studies. They define public spaces as "all areas that are open and accessible to all members of the public in a society, in principle though not necessarily in practice" (ibid., p. 2). According to Orum and Neal, a space is *open* when people are free to use the space regardless of their political opinions, religion, age or gender. A space is *accessible* when its use is not limited by barriers of language, physical or mental ability or geographic mobility. According to this definition, public spaces are theoretically supposed to be open and accessible to all members of the public, though for reasons such as a lack of facilities or the indirect discouragement of users, they might not meet these criteria. In general, the attributes of *openness* and *accessibility* play the key role in their definitions of public space. Of course, as this suggests, openness and accessibility to public space represent a common right for all members of the public.

Madanipour (2003) provides a similar definition of public space, using the criteria of *access, agency* and *interest.* In his view, public space is shared by all members of a community, controlled by the public (governmental) authorities, and is open and available to everyone. For Madanipour, the factors that define public space are *openness, accessibility* or availability, *control,* and being *shared* by the community members. However, he argues that a generalized definition of public space becomes "an ideal type", because real-world public spaces may or may not be managed by legitimate agencies, and may or may not be accessible to all members of a community. Therefore, he suggests that a more precise definition of public space would be based on the observation of real-world cases of public spaces. In that sense, the broad discussion

6 Parkinson has a liberal conception of democracy.

in this paper of the ways in which physical public space contributes to social sustainability would demand a certain amount of nuancing when applied to a specific local context.

In short, public space represents the physical and durable basis for face-to-face interaction of members of society and a basis for social sustainability. In principle, it is where members of a society equally share physical space and the memories associated with it. Public space can tell the shared stories of a society and become a catalyst for solidarity. From the literature reviewed here, it can be concluded that an ideal public space is a space of human *communication* that allows *diversity* of people and ideas. Furthermore, historical public spaces can be sources of public history and the *collective identity* of a society. On an abstract level, the key concepts that construct the meaning of public space are *commonness, openness* and *accessibility.* Some authors also point out the notion of *equality.* Hence it is not surprising that the key concepts of social sustainability (*social justice, participation* and *communication*) are hidden in the very meaning of physical public space.

These shared concepts can be seen in urban planning research that attempts to measure or enhance the public-ness of public spaces, or in other words, to study the capacity of public spaces to implement social sustainability. Further on I will give examples showing how the theoretical understanding of social sustainability and the abstract meaning of public space are used in research.

Urban planning approaches that link the social and physical components of public space

The reviewed scholars of urban planning agree that the forces that shape cities are the market, government, and civil society. Newman and Kenworthy (1999) add urban experts to these forces, as advisors to these three groups. Like many others, they argue that the market and government are of a short-term nature, whereas civil society is the guardian of the values of the community, shaping the society's long-term direction. As a non-governmental and non-profit actor, civil society can represent and safeguard the values of a society without being influenced by political or economic interests. Since a city's public spaces are the main arenas bringing members of the civil society together, we can suggest that the role of urban planning is to facilitate the face-to-face communication of the guardians and long-term directors of the social development process. Of course, this assumption is an optimistic one – in actual fact, the success of a public space strongly depends on the level of equality and the state of democracy of the society using it, a notion reflected in the commonness of control and use of public space, which is a purely political matter. However, urban planning can influence other social aspects of publicness.

Over the twentieth century, schools of thought in architecture and urban planning progressed from functionalism and formalism to more socially sustainable approaches.

The last century saw the dominance of the modernist approach in urban planning, the creation of rationally structured, automobile-dominated urban spaces divided into areas such as business and residential zones. The outcome of this modernist urbanism was the so-called "auto-city", formed through a top-down planning approach that resulted in environmental and social damage (Newman and Kenworthy, 1999). The shift in urban planning approaches in reaction to the auto-city phenomenon took place in the late twentieth and early twenty-first centuries.

For example, the Sustainable City movement was launched as a reaction to the modernist approach and was concerned with all aspects of sustainability, the environmental in particular. Similarly, urban planning and regeneration movements such as New Urbanism, the Right to the City movement, the launching of "Selfmade City"[7] projects, and the Placemaking movement arose later as a reaction to modern urbanism. These movements commonly advocated the bottom-up approach in urban planning and provided cities with lively and welcoming public spaces for all.

Among these urban planning movements, the Placemaking approach deals more specifically with public space. A short review of its background and methods reveals how urban planning attempts to make a contribution to social sustainable development.

The Placemaking discourse was almost simultaneous with debates on the sustainable city. According to Newman and Kenworthy (1999) and the Massachusetts Institute of Technology (MIT, 2013), academics and professionals who believed in the necessity of changing the modernist approach in urban planning began to advocate improving street life in cities, urban heritage conservation and enhancement of the quality of urban public spaces by creating walkable and pedestrian-friendly rather than car-dominated cities. In short, the aim was to give urban public spaces back to the public.

MIT's 2013 publication on Placemaking gives a useful overview of this approach and its background. According to MIT, the movement began in the 1960s in the United States through the efforts of a group of urban thinkers, among whom were Jane Jacobs, Kevin Lynch, Christopher Alexander and William Whyte. The core of the Placemaking approach is the creation of places *by people* and *for people*, the urban planner considered only as an adviser body. It advocates the fundamental right of citizens to the city and concerns issues such as healthy living thanks to safe and fun public spaces. It also encourages the use of existing resources through urban heritage conservation (ibid., 2013).

---

7 The idea of "Selfmade City" is also one of the urban planning approaches that considers social and economic issues of urban governance and focuses on small-scale projects. This approach advocates the right of local people to shape the urban space they live in. For example, *Selfmade City, Self-Initiated Urban Living and Architectural Interventions*, edited by Kristien Ring (2013), introduces the "Selfmade City" approach and shows sample projects in Berlin.

The methods used in the Placemaking approach are mainly based on behavioural observations. In *The Social Life of Small Urban Spaces*, Whyte (1980) provides a detailed analysis of public life in plazas by observing what people do and interviewing them. His main data-collecting method is behavioural observation through time-lapse cameras.

Inspired by Whyte's work based on observations and interviews, a group of professionals and researchers following the Placemaking approach have developed a set of indicators for assessing the capability of public spaces to host public life. The tools they use for this purpose are introduced in their official web page, *Project for Public Spaces*.[8] They categorize their indicators under the four attributes of *sociability, uses and activity, access and linkage*, and *comfort and image*. In this framework, the number of women, children and elderly, identifiable social networks, volunteerism, evening use and street life in urban spaces indicate their *sociability*. To assess *uses and activity* they study factors such as land-use patterns, property values and rent levels. For *access and linkage*, they use indicators such as traffic data, pedestrian activities and parking usage patterns. Finally, for assessing *comfort and image*, they study crime statistics, the sanitation rating of spaces, built and natural environmental data.

In the following section I will provide examples illustrating how social life is studied in public spaces, and how the ability of public spaces to host sustainable social life is evaluated.

Methods used in empirical research on social sustainability in public space

Today, sustainability indicator checklists are tools used by governments to assess urban planning projects in many countries. Before discussing a few research-based examples of the use of these indicators, I would like to say a few words about a work on the broader understanding of social sustainability in the urban context. In *Social Sustainability in Urban Areas*, Manzi et al. (2010) present a collection of published articles. The case studies they present are mainly of a qualitative nature and interest me for two reasons. First, they present the Egan Wheel as a tool for evaluating the social sustainability of communities. The Egan Wheel shows the capacities of a community to develop social sustainability, thus helping to understand which aspects of social sustainability can (theoretically) be enhanced by a well-designed and high-quality built environment, as well as an active and inclusive social and cultural life. The Egan Wheel provides a schematic view of how social sustainability is seen through the lens of urban planning (Figure 1). Second, although in the Egan Wheel the influ-

8 http://www.pps.org/

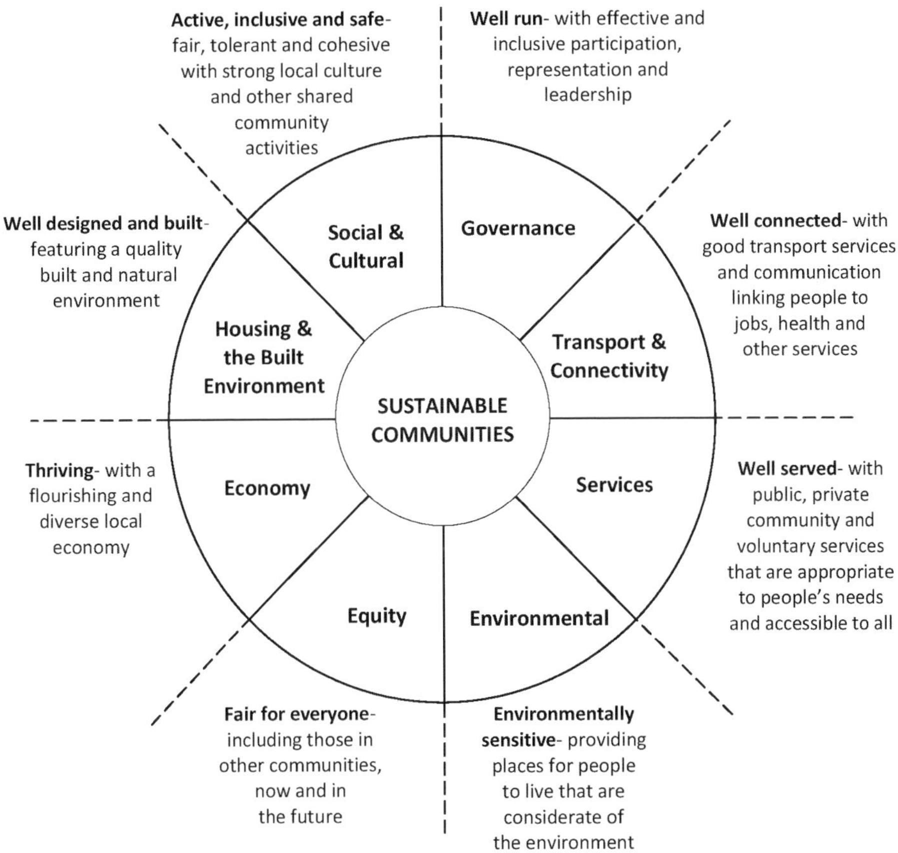

Fig. 1: The Egan Wheel presentation of skills for implementing social sustainability (Manzi et al., 2010, p. 17)

ence of "the quality and design of the built environment" on social sustainability is mentioned, no concrete outcome is presented that could indicate how this influence can actually be studied. The collection of articles evidences the gap as concerns the relationship between the design and the physical aspects of urban spaces, and social sustainability.

Among the examples of research attempting to study how the physical characteristics of urban spaces influence social life we can cite that of Gehl (1989; 2013), who conducted street-life observation in Copenhagen in view of the extension of pedestrian zones. Gehl studied how social change has led to changes in the patterns of use of public spaces in the historic centre of Copenhagen. He sees public spaces as places for "direct communication" and "cultural exchange". As he sees it, the city resembles a "party" for which he advocates the free enjoyment of all (Gehl, 1989).

The Copenhagen studies included several projects. One was the research project for studying public life in Strøget, a pedestrian street located in the historic centre of Copenhagen, which began in 1967. In *How to Study Public Life*, Gehl and Svarre (2013) explain how the Strøget project was used as an urban laboratory to observe the patterns of use of public space. Observations would document how the street functioned normally and during certain particular days and events. Gehl's methods are mainly based on the behavioural observation of pedestrians. In this methodological framework, the researcher would trace individual public space users or observe large groups of users, writing field notes and taking pictures to document the routes used, the times, pleasures and problems (ibid., 2013) that occurred.

For example, the relationship between pedestrian flow (number of people/minute) and the activity level of the street (number of people on 100 metres of street) was studied to evaluate the changes in street life throughout the year. Naturally, a low rate of flow shows that people are standing, moving slowly and talking, which indicates a greater possibility of social interaction. Gehl discovered that during summer or when a cultural event is taking place and in the absence of automobiles, public places offer a greater possibility for social interaction (ibid., 2013). In his series of studies in Copenhagen, Gehl also ascertained that there is a direct relation between "the physical qualities of public space and the volume and character of life there" (Gehl, 1989, p. 15). Doubtless, Gehl's works are among the most important contributions to research on public space and its relation with social life, and although his publications are not directly focused on the relationship of social sustainability and urban design, his methods for studying public spaces are widely used in the field.

Porta and Renne's (2005) research attempts to introduce indicators for measuring social sustainability in urban settings. Their work is the result of literature review and field research in Western Australia. They introduce the concept of *formal indicators* to quantitatively evaluate the design of streets in terms of their ability to promote certain activities and encourage people to walk or drive. Through these indicators, they attempt to quantify the design component of spaces on urban fabric and street scales.

On an urban fabric scale, they suggest indicators of *accessibility, land-use diversity, legibility* of public and private realms, *natural surveillance* (security), *permeability* (street connectivity), *employment density, number of buildings* and *number of lots* to assess social sustainability. At this level, for example, through front and back mapping, they identify areas of the street that have active frontage, indicating safety. Regarding the level of permeability, they suggest that urban layout should contain a high proportion of four-way intersections.

On street scale, Porta and Renne's (2005) measurement system suggests a set of indicators showing the architectural qualities of the urban spaces in the streets of Joondalup and Fremantle (Western Australia). One of the suggested street indicators is *sky exposure*, in an attempt to understand the urban environment's ability to encapsulate the pedestrian, and to evaluate the level of street intimacy. Other indicators are *facade continuity, softness* (transparency of spaces which makes a street safe and welcoming), social width (allowing human interaction), *visual complexity, number of buildings, sedibility* and *detractors* (such as large blank walls, aggressive automobile facilities, parking lots and billboards).

Their research suggests that the traditional urban fabric of Fremantle was more user-friendly than the newly developed Joondalup area. They conclude with ten rules that advise designing narrow streets, not isolating buildings, designing continuous frontages, increasing the number of small buildings instead of building a few large ones, putting retail businesses on the ground floor, avoiding parking lots, creating a soft transition from the street to the building, avoiding blank walls and large billboards, putting trees on wide streets, and providing sedible spaces.

The conclusions of this measurement system are largely based on quantified visual values and take other human senses much less into consideration. Although their criteria provide a description of the streetscape, qualities such as *street intimacy* or *safe and welcoming streets* are extremely subjective at cultural and individual levels. Therefore, this method can be used as a basis for further qualitative studies based on user opinions and perceptions. As for its applicability to other places, considering the time and funding needed for such surveys, it would seem most applicable at the urban fabric level, mainly carried out on the basis of maps. Given that assessments in street scale are largely based on the work of an operator quantifying data hidden in several pictures of streets, the results can be influenced by the subjective judgments of the operator. Nonetheless, this a good example of the strengths and weaknesses of currently used methods of studying the relation between urban form and social sustainability.

In the field of urban heritage conservation, the state of literature is no different from that of urban planning. The review conducted by Ryberg-Webster and Kinahan (2014) shows the gaps in urban heritage conservation research. Viewing urban preservation as a key driver of urban revitalization, Ryberg-Webster and Kinahan believe that heritage is linked to sustainability and can be used in the transformation of cities. They refer to several urban conservation research works, suggesting that built heritage can develop a *sense of place*, enhance *quality of life* and offer a *unique community attachment*. However, they acknowledge that there is a dearth of empirical research to support these claims. Arguing that preservation should be present at economic and community development debates, they state that preservationists should “come to the table with new ideas and data to support their arguments” (Ryberg-Webster and Kinahan, 2014, p. 29).

The works reviewed in the above are based on indicator-based methods supported by behavioural observations, interviews, and observation of the built environment. Each example focuses mainly on one or two of these techniques. Using a mixture of interview and participant observation techniques and observation of the physical characteristics of the built environment can link physical and social components of public space. The same argument can be made regarding qualitative and quantitative methods. For example, in urban fabric and district level studies, quantitative data can provide more useful evidence, while at the street level, a qualitative understanding from the perspective of users is more helpful. Briefly, when the research question is related to social life, the triangulation of data collected through different methods can be used to establish a useful research framework.

The outlook for public space research

Social sustainability involves setting the needs and limits of a society in an ethical framework. As mentioned earlier, it takes into consideration principles such as *social justice, social cohesion, participation,* and the rights of future generations to enjoy the environmental and cultural resources. Conceptually speaking, public space values and nurtures those same principles by advocating equal accessibility and the openness to all of shared urban spaces, and by providing physical space for communication among diverse groups of people. The authors reviewed also point out the unique power of historical public spaces as urban heritage – sources of public history and collective identity.

Thanks to the works of urban theorists, there is no need today, to justify the importance of the physical components of public space in social sustainability – at least at a theoretical level. However, when it comes to empirical research, there remains a challenge: indeed, the weakness of current public space research is more apparent in methodological matters than in theoretical matters.

The reviewed examples of research in urban planning have in fact been developed to assess and implement the shared principle of social sustainability and public space. Through the assessment of equal openness and accessibility, land-use diversity, activity level, user-friendliness and safety of urban spaces, an attempt is made to concretize values such as *diversity, equality, health,* and *safety* in urban social life. Nevertheless, the field lacks a more comprehensive methodological framework, if it is to embrace and integrate the social and physical aspects of historical public spaces.

The empirical examples usually categorize the characteristics of public spaces in terms of measurable indicators, on the basis of which the ability of the physical space to host public life is assessed. By means of interviews and observation of the built environment, these methods obviously help formulate a functional assessment of public spaces so far as meeting user needs is concerned. However, the implementation of social sustainability/public space principles requires more practical methods that would explain and assess the *qualitative* characters of public spaces and how they actually contribute to social sustainability. In order to scientifically prove the ability of historical public spaces to foster characteristics such as *place attachment* and *collective identity,* further research is definitely needed in the field of urban heritage conservation. Public space research is by nature interdisciplinary, and its epistemological and methodological approach has been enriched by other disciplines; nevertheless, further methodological developments are necessary to enhance our knowledge of the relationship between human beings and physical spaces, and how the sense of belonging to a shared place can strengthen the sense of belonging to a community.

It is certain that the knowledge provided by various case studies is extremely helpful in understanding the correlations involving social sustainability and historical public spaces. However, different cultural contexts may have different understandings of the concept of social sustainability and the meaning of public space. As a result, along with the findings of previous case-study research, we need methods based on local observations, with attention paid to how social sustainability is related to local economic and environmental sustainability.

References

Albert, M.-T. 2013. Heritage studies. Paradigmatic reflections. In: Albert et al., op cit., pp. 9–17.

Albert, M.-T., Bernecker, R. and Rudolff, B. (eds). 2013. *Understanding Heritage: Perspectives in Heritage Studies*. Berlin, De Gruyter. (Heritage Studies Vol. 1.)

Bandarin, F. 2012. From paradox to paradigm: Historic Urban Landscape as an urban conservation approach. In: *Managing Cultural Landscapes*. London/New York, Routledge, Taylor and Francis Group, pp. 213–31.

Colantonio, A. and Dixon, T. 2011. *Urban Regeneration and Social Sustainability: Best Practice from European Cities*. Oxford, UK, Wiley-Blackwell.

Gehl, J. 1989. A changing street life in a changing society. *Places Journal,* Vol. 6, No. 1, pp. 8–17.

Gehl, J. and Svarre, B. 2013. *How to Study Public Life*. Washington DC/Covelo, Calif./London, Island Press.

Hayden, D. 1995. *The Power of Place: Urban Landscapes as Public History.* Cambridge, Mass., MIT Press.

Madanipour. 2003. *Public and Private Spaces of the City.* London, Routledge.

Manzi, T., Lucas, K., Jones, T. L. and Allen, J. 2010. *Social Sustainability in Urban Areas*. London/Washington DC, Earthscan.

MIT. 2013. *Places in the Making: How Placemaking Builds Places and Communities*. Cambridge, Mass., Department of Urban Studies and Planning, Massachusetts Institute of Technology.

Newman, P. and Kenworthy, J. 1999. *Sustainability and Cities, overcoming automobile dependence*. Washington DC/Covelo, Calif., Island Press.

Orum, A. M. and Neal, Z. P. 2009. *Common Ground? Readings and Reflections on Public Space,* New York/London, Routledge.

Parkinson, J. 2012. *Democracy and Public Space, The Physical Sites of Democratic Performance.* New York, Oxford University Press.

Porta, S. and Renne, J. L. 2005. Linking urban design to sustainability: formal indicators of social urban sustainability field research in Perth, Western Australia. *Urban Design International,* Vol. 10, No. 1. pp. 51–64.

Ring, K. (ed.). 2013. *Selfmade City, Self-Initiated Urban Living and Architectural Interventions.* Berlin, Jovis Publishers.

Ryberg-Webster, S. and Kinahan, K. L. 2014. Historic preservation and urban revitalization in the twenty-first century, *Journal of Planning Literature,* Vol. 29, No. 2, pp. 119–39.

The American Heritage Dictionary of the English language. 2000. http://www.thefreedictionary.com/democracy (Accessed 4 December 2014.)

Turner, M. 2013. UNESCO Recommendation on the Historic Urban Landscape. In: Albert et al., op cit., pp. 77–87.
UNESCO. 2011. Recommendation on the Historic Urban Landscape, including a glossary of definitions. http://portal.unesco.org/en/ev.php-URL_ID=48857&URL_DO=DO_TOPIC&URL_SECTION=201.html (Accessed 11 December 2014.)
UNDP. 2014. *Human Development Report. Sustaining Human Progress: Reducing Vulnerabilities and Building Resilience.* New York, United Nations Development Programme. http/hdr.undp.org/en/2014-report (Accessed 13 December 2014.)
WCED. 1987. *Report of the World Commission on Environment and Development. Our Common Future.* (Brundtland Report). New York, United Nations. http://www.un-documents.net/wced-ocf.htm
Whyte, W. H. 1980. *The Social Life of Small Urban Spaces.* Washington DC, Conservation Foundation.

The Social Function of Cultural Heritage: Conservation Practices on the Basis of Sociocultural Sustainability

Juliana Forero

Introduction

Contemporary development paradigms have acknowledged the power of culture and social categories to enhance development processes in a sustainable way (Winter, 2012). Nevertheless, sustainable development and heritage management still face a constant struggle between the conservation of heritage and economic growth and modernization.

Cultural heritage has become an object used and consumed for the sake of sustainable development (Winter, 2012; Ballart and Tresserras, 2005). In the shape of education, leisure and tourism, heritage is now part of the regular consumer demand of contemporary societies. Its recognition as a social, economic and cultural resource has led to a broader conscious interpretation, not only of its value, but also of its vulnerability (Hong and Forero, 2012; Winter, 2012; Ballart and Tresserras, 2005). While debates on integrating tradition and modernity have begun to take place (Bandarin and Oers, 2012; 2014), in many cases, architecture and modernization are still leading international development trends, leaving aside urban issues such as social change, the recognition and transmission of local memory (Duché, 2010).

In this context, different sustainable approaches for the understanding, management and planning of heritage have been formulated in both the Western and the Eastern worlds. In the West, environment and the economy were until recently established as the main factors involved in achieving sustainable development.[1] In the

1 During the second half of the twentieth century the idea of sustainability occupied increasing space in debates on development. In the 1970s, with the United Nations Conference on the Human Environment in Stockholm (1972), the concept of sustainable development came into use, emphasizing concern for environmental and economic aspects. With the aim of the international community to achieve worldwide sustainable development, various global meetings were held and international agreements signed. However, sustainable development discourse is subject to multiple questions. As Vinterhav (2009, p. 30) has pointed out, the definition of the term is too wide and general: "what are really the needs of the present? And what do we know about the future? How much can we plan for? ... We can only assume, or guess". In this context, Moss and Grunkemeyer (2010) developed an alternative definition for sustainable development: First, it is *inclusionary,* involving diverse populations. Second, it is *long term,* promoting intergenerational equity. Third, it brings about a *balance* between social, environmental and economic considerations. Fourth, it is *multidimensional,* pur-

East, due to the fact that most Asian and Pacific countries have developed under differing economic and technological conditions, the area's very strong and varied cultural and social backgrounds have greatly benefited from the recognition of local cultural and social expressions and needs for their own development alternatives in the post-1990s era, making it possible for sustainable development to in fact be achieved (Duxbury and Jeannotte, 2010*a;* 2010*b;* Nurse, 2006).

The sociocultural dimension of development refers to situations in which people and communities do not need to transgress their own values and beliefs when facing the changes normally brought about by development (Duxbury and Gillette, 2007; Duxbury and Jeannotte, 2010*a;* 2010*b;* Yung et al., 2011). Cultural heritage concerns a set of actions adapted to social, urban, cultural, economic and environmental realities that makes it a resource for development, as well as the representation of sociocultural dynamics in the production and perception of space. Although in academic productions the recognition of heritage as an element in sustainable development is still insufficient (Hong and Forero, 2013), within the international exchange of practices and regulations, culture and heritage have gradually become a main focus point of debate. For the forthcoming 2016 UN-HABITAT III Conference, in the context of the Post-2015 Sustainable Development Goals, a New Urban Agenda will be set that fully acknowledges the role of culture in sustainable development, and UNESCO will also present a Global Report on Culture and Heritage in Sustainable Urban Development in support of this idea.

International and regional guides for cultural heritage management are testimony to how the notions of cultural heritage have changed throughout the twentieth century (UNESCO, 2008; 2011; Ahmad, 2006). Although after the beginning of the twenty-first century many advances were made towards the recognition of the sociocultural aspects of heritage, in other aspects dealing with the conception, diffusion, preservation and management of this heritage, exclusively architectural and aesthetic perspectives continue to exert a strong influence on heritage management (Choay, 2007; Hong and Forero, 2012). As Jukka Jokilehto (2010) has pointed out: "One of the limitations of the existing international doctrine tends to be that it is mainly focused on architecture, even when related to historic urban areas. For example ... the Council of Europe document of 1975, which introduced the concept of integrated conservation, is called the European Charter of the Architectural Heritage. Similarly, even with due emphasis

posefully linking together goals and measurements of progress known as indicators (ibid. p. 243). Moreover, Omann and Spangenberg (2010) established that sustainable development also involves an important demand for a population's quality of life and well-being, involving a decent standard of social cohesion, healthy environment, living conditions, and full participation, as well as the integration of economic, environmental, social and cultural objectives. This integration of policies and methodologies for development includes community perspectives of life on an institutional level, as well as urban development and planning frameworks. Such institutional approaches as involve communities still need to be developed (Omann and Spangenberg, 2010).

on integrity including human functions, the 1976 UNESCO Recommendation still defines the notion in relation to 'historic and architectural areas', which is taken to mean 'any groups of buildings, structures and open spaces'. Similarly, the World Heritage Convention places historic urban areas under the category of 'groups of buildings'. What we are missing here are the notions that would make an urban area 'urban' beyond architecture (if possible)" (ibid., p. 57).

The 1979 Burra Charter based the guidelines for conservation management of heritage sites on their cultural significance, adding the notion of landscape modified by human activity. This principle was also recalled by the Xi'an Declaration (2005), the Hoi An Protocols for Best Conservation Practice in Asia (2005), Vienna Memorandum (2005), the Declaration of Foz do Iguaçu: Reflections about the notion of the Spirit of Place (2008), and the Quebec Declaration on the Preservation of the Spirit of Place (2008). The UNESCO Recommendation on Historic Urban Landscape (2011) acknowledged different layers of the heritage landscape of the city, dealing with the constant relationship between development and conservation and linking urban, historical, natural and social values.

Although these different declarations have progressively recognized the need to integrate the historic and cultural dimensions of heritage, there is no specific approach to the social function of heritage.

The theoretical and philosophical approaches to the debate proposed in this document are based on critical heritage studies and post-Western perspectives. These approaches bring comprehensive positions to the definition and analysis of cultural heritage, irrespective of institutional and power discourses, by recognizing alternative understandings of heritage, based on multicultural expressions and academic viewpoints thereof. At the same time, they address heritage matters based on studies of how the relationships between humans and space are established, how humans perceive space, and the social and cultural conditioning that results from communities' mental image of their environment, allowing each society the independence to adapt its development process according to its own conditions (Winter, 2012; Gabrielli, 2010).

Considering heritage as a core element for development, this paper identifies and analyses the social function of cultural heritage in the context of sociocultural sustainability principles. The following sections present a theoretical construct of the relationship between sociocultural sustainability and cultural heritage, followed by a description of the social function of heritage, an analysis of its main components and modes of action.

Sociocultural sustainability and cultural heritage

Sociocultural sustainability concerns the sum of cultural knowledge and the social uses and limitations of that knowledge by a specific population (Tiwari, 2007). Here, sustainability lies in the continuity of the development of a society and a culture that promotes quality of life, social integration and interaction (Omann and Spangenberg, 2010). It "encourages holistic and integrative ways of thinking in community planning practice, emphasizing interconnectedness, cross-sectorial collaborations, and plural perspectives that encompass both the community's physical form and its people" (Duxbury and Jeannotte, 2010*a*; 2010*b*). Debates on sustainable development point out that sociocultural sustainability also integrates the creativity of people and communities to solve the problems they discover during development processes (Rantala et al., 2012). According to Duxbury and Gillette (2007), this also implies the taking into account of traditions, values, heritage and place, the arts and the diversity of a specific population.

Cultural heritage is witness to the different cultures that throughout history have lived in specific territories, modeling the space from its origin to the present (Harrison, 2010*a*). This highlights the existence of an intangible cultural identity in the surrounding environment: a dynamic environment resulting from the cultural dynamism of

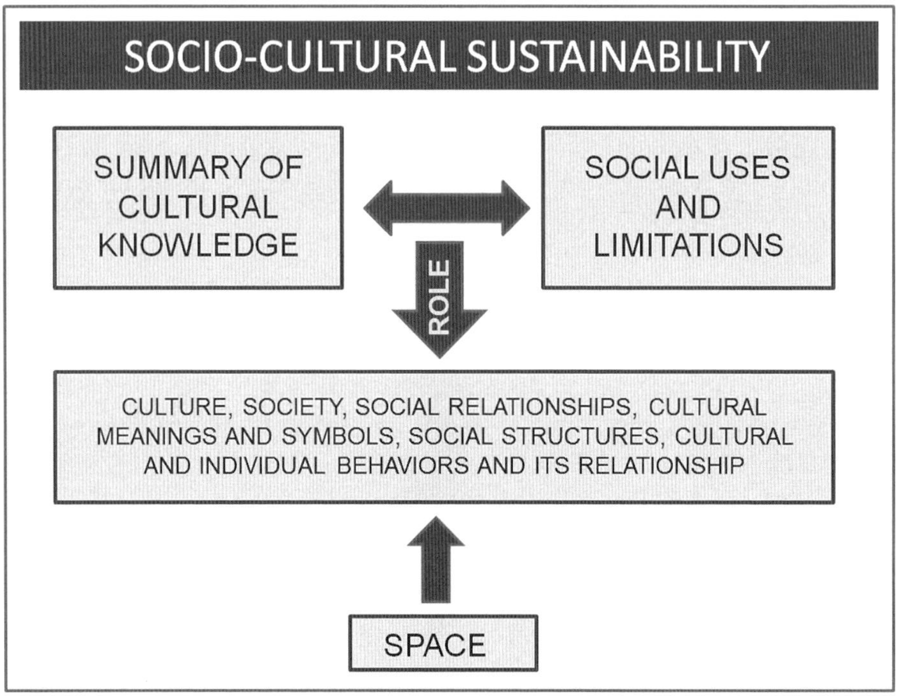

Fig. 1: Sociocultural sustainability definition framework (own illustration)

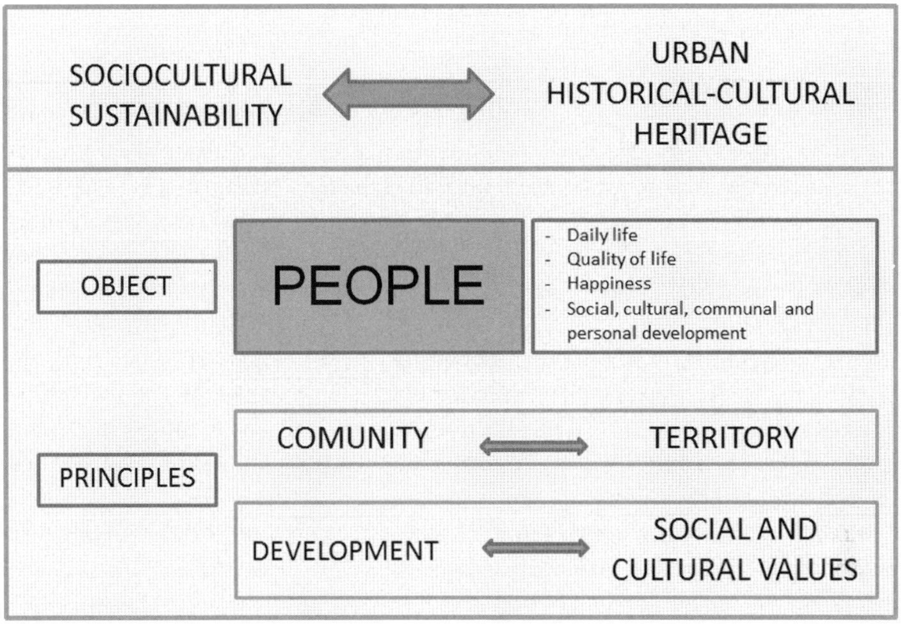

Fig. 2: Sociocultural sustainability and the urban/cultural heritage relationship framework (own illustration)

successive generations and cultures. Heritage consists of all the real and imaginary, cultural and natural, tangible and intangible elements having guided societies and communities in the past and that remain part of the present and continue to guide the future (Edson, 2007).

Sociocultural sustainability for development and cultural heritage preservation have a common basis: people and their life experience, present and future. They both aim for the improvement of a community's quality of life, happiness, life prospects, and of the individual's living conditions, expressed and developed in personal, social and cultural, economic, environmental and political dimensions (Colantonio, 2008; Colantonio and Dixon,2009, Hopwood and O'Brien, 2005; Duxburyand Gillette, 2007; Duxbury, 2012; Manzi et al., 2010; Nurse, 2006; Harrison, 2010*a;* Queról, 2010; UNESCO, 2008; Tweed and Sutherland, 2007).

Likewise, social sustainability and cultural heritage share two basic principles that, although developed from different perspectives, in practice are intimately related: (1) the recognition of the relationship between a community and its territory; (2) the engagement of cultural and social values during the development processes. These are not understood in terms of a completed, static status, but as a historical, social and cultural process under permanent construction and change (Hong and Forero, 2012; 2013; Bandarin and Oers, 2012).

Under this umbrella are acknowledged heritage elements such as peoples' personal, social and communal experiences in their daily lives. At the same time, heritage and the way it is practiced and understood is determined by the social and cultural basis of a society, a community and a group of people (Edson, 2007). This means it is a matter of reintegrating culture into a wider perspective, in which society itself reaffirms its own system of values concerning its development and transformations for the future. It also means articulating values of culture, community development, economy and environment (Trotte et al., 2012).

When cultural heritage becomes an issue in the context of social sustainability, different communities have the opportunity to undermine the orders of power through the recognition of their own identity, memory and territory, as well as to inhabit the city with the feeling that it is their own. This results in development processes where the socio-historical dimensions of the peripheries are recognized, affording citizens' inclusive living conditions. The happiness, welfare and quality of life of residents and communities foster a realization of how important their heritage is and thus an appreciation of the importance of defending those things that represent them culturally. In this sense, heritage protection "is not anymore a concern of an elite, and the states do not have any more total control of the decisions regarding the territory" (Neely, 2011).

In other words, the relationship between sociocultural sustainability and cultural heritage is also composed of the relationships, networks and norms that make collective actions possible in changing environments (Duxbury and Gillette, 2007; Putnam, 1993; Coleman, 1988).

The social function of cultural heritage

The existence of a cultural heritage is prompted by reasons of a social order: heritage values are a necessary part of the life experience of the community, and the elements of which it is made up are those cultural or historic objects that define and differentiate a community, enrich and produce happiness for its residents and enhance citizens' self-pride and sense of belonging (Queról, 2010).

The social function of cultural heritage is based on the set of values, the construction processes, and the use of singular or collective attributes giving significance to objects (movable or immovable) and sociocultural practices (tangible and intangible). These values and processes reflect how, influenced by multiple cultural perspectives, people shape their territory and construct dynamics of differentiation and change (MCC, 2011). The significance of heritage lies in the fact that it involves values, the presence and use of cultural artefacts and territories, and gives sustainable possibilities for the different generations of a social group or a community to redefine or enhance its heritage (UNESCO, 2010).

The social function of cultural heritage concerns social cohesion, integration and education, as well as social and cultural distinction processes in multicultural societies (Alofs, 2008). In other words, cultural heritage and the way it is practiced and understood, is determined by the sociocultural basis of a society, a community and a group of people.

Edson (2007) defines heritage as a social phenomenon. However, "the explanatory value of heritage, as it is often conceived and promoted, is low when it comes to investigating the conditions of social stability or identity validation" (Edson, 2007, p. 343).

Heritage is a social phenomenon with specific social functions that cannot be explained without involving the social conditions of the communities (ibid.). It requires a definition of time and space relationships, material and immaterial resources, and interaction between the identity of local communities and processes of change.

The social importance of heritage preservation lies in its testimonial values of different phenomena, which link all categories in the development process, including the cultural values and social well-being of a society in the course of its history. International agreements on the importance of conserving cultural heritage (UNESCO and ICCROM, 2006; 2012), consider that it:

- embraces multiple and complex messages and values (historical, artistic, political, religious, social, spiritual, cultural, scientific, natural, etc.);
- represents the identity of a social group: people together need common references to feel attachment to the territory and the community;
- is a vehicle to understand multiculturalism and diversity, promoting healthy sociocultural exchanges;
- is a source of economic development, where sustainable cultural interchange and cultural tourism can improve communities' economic resources;
- is unique and unrepeatable.

Cultural heritage, based on cultural elements that are necessary for the existence of society, enhances social cohesion, social harmony and pacific (non-violent) cohabitation (coexistence) processes.

Elements of action and analysis

There are three fundamental elements in the recognition of the social function of heritage in the sociocultural sustainability framework: (1) the dialogue between formal and informal heritage; (2) the understanding of heritage as a whole involving material and immaterial components without fragmenting the social and symbolic representations of heritage; (3) heritage practices and the acknowledgement of the cultural rights of populations.

1) Formal and informal cultural heritage preservation: Who defines cultural heritage?

Conservation processes as part of governmental and communal initiatives demonstrate that heritage is not a neutral concept. On the contrary, it is laden with political and ideological content. When it comes to heritage management, it is fundamental to answer the following questions: who decides and who defines what is heritage? Who decides what needs to be preserved and how? How do governments and communities wish to acknowledge cultural heritage and from what perspectives? What are the ideological and cultural backgrounds contained in these conceptions and decisions? (Harrison,2010*b;* Mac Gregor, 2008).

Formal heritage, also called official heritage, concerns processes of heritage identification, management and preservation that are determined by specific legislation and governmental definitions and regulations (Harrison, 2010*a*). It also refers to objects, places and practices that have been classified as formal, by inclusion in a registration list of cultural heritage that is institutionally recognized, in which parameters are established in given legal terms. However, the parameters by which an element is evaluated and included in the list are not necessarily the same as those the community acknowledges as their own (ibid.).

Informal heritage, also called unofficial heritage, is distinguished by the fact that it is local. According to Rodney Harrison (2010a) "unofficial objects, places and practices of heritage may not be recognised by governments or be listed on official heritage registers but they are considered to be significant or culturally meaningful by communities and collectives in the ways in which they constitute themselves and operate in the present, drawing on aspects of the past" (Harrison, 2010*a*, p. 240). Informal heritage, rather than being subject to a set of discourses by experts and institutions attempting to describe and promote it, is represented through the relationships within the community, the objects, places and memory that integrate the population in its day-to-day life experience. In that sense, this informal patriotism is generally less studied, but is the most widely known among the members of a community, who possess an integrated understanding of the place where their heritage is located. At the same time, unofficial heritage enhances the transformation of societies, as it implies the recognition of a community's genuine interpretation of its past, its present and its future (ibid.).

2) Material-immaterial heritage: Both inseparable

"For every object of tangible heritage there is also an intangible heritage that 'wraps' around it – the language we use to describe it, for example, or its place in social practice or religion" (Harrison, 2010*a*, p. 10). Heritage is formed by a set of tangible and intangible elements in permanent and inseparable interaction. There is no built heritage that has significance *per se*, as well as there is no heritage practice discon-

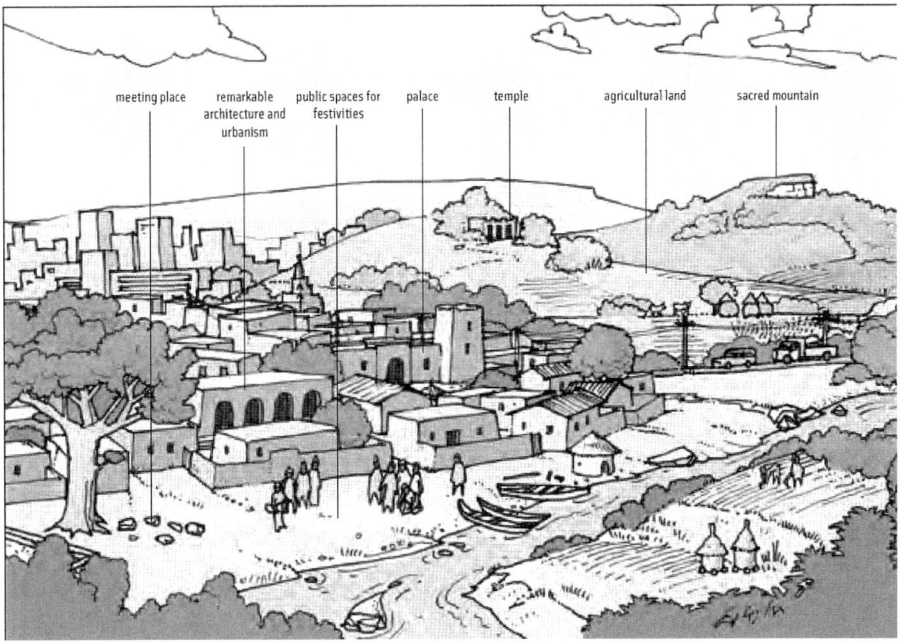

Fig. 3: Material and immaterial heritage interaction (Craterre-ENSAG et al., 2006)

nected from a place. Heritage is both tangible and intangible; it cannot be only one of the two (Harrison, 2010*a;* Villaseño and Magar, 2012; Mac Gregor, 2008).

Among different academic, political, local and international institutional spaces, the concept of heritage has been divided into material and immaterial, creating confusion about their significance and social function (Clarke and Johnston, 2008). Heritage protection has mainly been oriented towards conservation of the object rather than towards protecting the significance given to it by the people, and as a result, protection of the collective memory, which gives the object its value, has been neglected (Jaramillo, 2011; Benton, 2010).

According to different heritage analysts, this division has reinforced the exclusion of the communities' cultural expressions and ways of living, leading to heritage practices that go beyond a simple classification between material and immaterial heritage (Clarke and Johnston, 2008; Jaramillo, 2011; Benton, 2010).

Recently, the principal tendency has been to reduce the importance of this distinction, to understand material and immaterial heritage in an integrated and more comprehensive way, and to recognize that both aspects of cultural heritage must be related to the cultural values of the society that produces them (Craterre-ENSAG et al., 2006; Queról, 2010), which is closer to the historic urban landscape approach.

3) The management of cultural heritage

The management of cultural heritage concerns two principal activities: first, when a community as a collective group recognizes certain shared values, emphasizing the connection it has with the members of that community and its space (West, 2010); and second, the formal and informal heritage management practices and recognition of the community's cultural rights (Sanchez, 2005; Mac Gregor, 2008).

Heritage practices are passed on from one generation to another. They are related to the non deliberate or unintentional ways a community chooses which heritage expressions should be preserved, how to safeguard culture and traditions and what can be forgotten; in other words, which memories should be kept so as to construct others on top, and which can be demolished. As Harrison establishes: "Management and Implementation are customs and habits with collective social memory we use as objects of heritage (artifacts, buildings, sites, landscapes) alongside practices of heritage (languages, music, community commemorations, conservation and preservation of objects of the memories of the past) to shape our ideas about our past, present and future" (Harrison, 2010*a*, p. 9).

Heritage practices are social procedures accumulated and renewed, as well as producers of economic and sociocultural outputs that different social and cultural sectors appropriate in an unequal manner (García-Canclini, 1999). In this context, regarding management of cultural heritage, the discourse of formal heritage is one of the main elements that influences government criteria when it comes to choosing the patrimonial goods to be managed and protected (Harrison, 2010*a*), because formal heritage is that which favours the economy through the benefits of tourism, patriotism and primarily those parameters necessary for the inclusion of heritage in the local, national and international lists (Harrison, 2010*a;* García-Canclini, 1999).

Heritage management and the recognition of the population's cultural rights are closely linked when it comes to development processes. The implementation of a given development model can respect or transgress the cultural rights of the community that is being impacted. These rights are essential for community development, peace, poverty eradication and the construction of social cohesion (Sanchez, 2005; Mac Gregor, 2008).

Cultural heritage expresses the solidarity that brings together persons who share cultural goods and practices with which they identify, thus creating a space of social complicity. The practices designed to define heritage, to preserve and transmit it, almost always bring a society together without dividing it into classes, ethnic groups or provoking other social ruptures (García-Canclini, 1999).

In this context, in the process of promoting cultural heritage, the modern state has had to convert local realities into political cultural abstractions, represented by identity symbols fostering memory and urban communities' territorial attachment to their environment. Thus during the last decades the interaction between state and society has emphasized the social function of heritage as a way to improve quality of life, social cohesion and the overall well-being of citizens (ibid., 1999).

Conclusions

Acknowledging the social function of heritage in the course of development allows heritage to be interpreted as a dynamic socio-historical process, which also serves as a framework enabling greater quality of life, well-being and the enhancement of cultural values for communities within a specific territory. Heritage is moved to a level where the community takes possession of it and uses it as a strategy for appropriating its own development destiny.

Thanks to its core elements of analysis and development, the relationship between sociocultural sustainability and cultural heritage, rather than hierarchical, is a non-directional radial relationship in which all elements are interdependent and in permanent interaction, thus generating sustainable development processes. Sociocultural sustainability approaches to heritage conservation make it possible for heritage to be interpreted not as something static, but as a dynamic socio-historical process with the community and the territory at the heart of the analysis.

It is important to acknowledge that sociocultural sustainability and cultural heritage studies create an important framework for heritage conservation and management, combining top-down and bottom-up perspectives founded on the principle of reconciling specialized and sociocultural knowledge of the community. Heritage management cannot be reduced to the notion of urban services and the material aspects of heritage, nor to purely spiritual and cultural elements; it is possible to integrate the two aspects.

Sociocultural sustainability approaches for heritage preservation constitute an alternative model for sustainable development, one which best corresponds to specific cultural, social, as well as political contexts.

In the international context today, some of the most important approximations to the social function of cultural heritage are the Historic Urban Landscape (HUL) approach, as well as the increasing calls to officially acknowledge culture as a fundamental component of sustainable development, as expressed in declarations such as the UNESCO Declaration on Education and Sustainable Development (2005), Agenda 21, the Resolution on Culture and Sustainable Development at the 68th session of the United Nations General Assembly (2013), the Hangzhou Declaration (2013), and the forthcoming UN-HABITAT III 'New Urban Agenda', among others. These approaches update the heritage concept, linking it more closely with its social basis and recognizing the social implications of heritage as a tool for sustainable development. An analysis of the practical outcomes of these declarations would bring to the fore the international implications of a programme of heritage conservation based on social function.

References

Ahmad, Y.2006. The scope and definitions of heritage. *International Journal of Heritage Studies*, Vol. 12, No. 3, pp. 292–300.

Alofs, L. 2008. *The Aruba Heritage Report*. Aruba, UNESCO.

Ballart H. J. and Tresserras J. J. 2005. *Gestion del patrimonio cultural*. Barcelona, Ariel.

Bandarin, F. and van Oers, R. 2012. *The Historic Urban Landscape. Managing Heritage in an Urban Century*. Chichester, UK, Wiley-Blackwell.

Bandarin, F. and van Oers, R. 2014. *Reconnecting the City: The Historic Urban Landscape Approach and the Future of Urban Heritage*. Chichester, UK, Wiley-Blackwell.

Benton, T. 2010.*Understanding Heritage and Memory*. Manchester, UK, Manchester University Press.

Choay, F. 2007. Alegoria del patrimonio. Barcelona: Gustavo Gill.

Clarke, A. and Johnston, C. 2008. *Time, Memory, Place and Land: Social Meaning and Heritage Conservation in Australia*. Quebec, ICOMOS.

Colantonio, A. 2008.*Traditional and Emerging Prospects in Social Sustainability*. Oxford, UK, Oxford Institute for Sustainable Development/Oxford Brookes University.

Colantonio, A. and Dixon, T. 2009.*Measuring Socially Sustainable Urban Regeneration in Europe. Creating Sustainable Environments*. Oxford, UK, Oxford Institute for Sustainable Development (OISD)/Oxford Brookes University.

Colantonio, A. and Dixon, T. 2009. *Urban Regeneration in Europe*. Oxford, UK, Oxford Institute for Sustainable Development School of the Built Environment/Oxford Brookes University.

Coleman, J. S. 1988.Social capital in the creation of human capital. *American Journal of Sociology*, Vol. 94, pp. 95–120.

Craterre-ENSAG and Convention France-UNESCO. 2006. *Cultural Heritage and Local Development: A Guide for African Local Governments*. Grenoble, France, Craterre-ENSAG/Convention France-UNESCO.

Duché, D. 2010.*From Individual Structures to Urban Landscape management: the French Experience*. Paris, UNESCO World Heritage Centre, pp. 89–98.

Duxbury, N. 2012.*Cities, Culture and Sustainable Development*. Coimbra, Portugal, Universidade de Coimbra.

Duxbury, N. and Gillette, E. 2007. *Culture as a Key Dimension of Sustainability: Exploring Concepts Themes, and Models*. Vancouver, Creative City Network of Canada.

Duxbury, N. and Jeannotte, M. S. 2010*a*. *Culture, Sustainability and Communities: Exploring the Myths*. Coimbra, Portugal, Centro de Estudos Sociais.

Duxbury, N. and Jeannotte, M. S. 2010*b*. From the Bottom-Up: Culture in Community Sustainability Planning. Milan, ESA Sociology of Culture Research Network, 7–9 October.

Edson, G. 2007. Heritage: pride or passion, product or service? *International Journal of Heritage Studies*, Vol. 10, No. 4, pp. 333–48.

Erlij, M. 2006. *Protección del patrimonio construido urbano*, Vol. 9, No. 13, pp. 19–23.

Gabrielli, B. 2010.*Urban Planning Challenged by Historic Urban Landscape*. Paris, UNESCO World Heritage Centre, pp. 19–26.

García-Canclini, N. 1999. *Los usos sociales del patrimonio en patrimonio etnológico*. Andalucía, Consejería de Cultura, Junta de Andalucía, pp. 16–33.

Harrison, R. 2010*a*. *Heritage as Social Action*. Manchester, UK, Manchester University Press, pp. 241–77.

Harrison, R. 2010*b*. *Understanding the Politics of Heritage*. Manchester, UK, Manchester University Press.

Hong, L. and Forero, J. 2012. New perspectives to understand the cultural heritage through the social-cultural. Florence, Italy, *Esempi di Architettura*, pp. 566–88.

Hong, L. and Forero, J.2013. *Recognizing Cultural Heritage for Social-Cultural Sustainability: the Case Study of the Park Mirador de los Nevados*. Coimbra, Portugal, Coimbra University.

Hopwood, B., Mellor, M. and O'Brien, G. 2005. Sustainable development: mapping different approaches. *Sustainable Development,* Vol. 3, pp. 38–52.

ICOMOS. 1979. Burra Charter. ICOMOS Australia.www.doeni.gov.uk/niea/burra_charter.pdf

ICOMOS. 2005. Xi'an Declaration. Xi'an, China, ICOMOS.ww.international.icomos.org/xian2005/xian-declaration.htm

ICOMOS. 2008*a*. Declaration Foz do Iguaçu: Reflections about the notion of the Spirit of Place. Foz do Iguaçu, Paraná, Brazil.www.international.icomos.org/centre.../declaration-iguaçu-eng.pdf

ICOMOS. 2008*b*. Québec Declaration on the Preservation of the Spirit of Place. Quebec, ICOMOS. whc.unesco.org/document/116778

Jaramillo, M. 2011.*Beyond the Protection of Material Cultural Heritage in Times of Conflict*. Rome, ICCROM, pp. 23–8.

Jokilehto, J. 2010. Reflection on Historic Urban Landscapes as a Tool for Conservation. Paris, UNESCO World Heritage Centre, pp. 53–64.

Mac Gregor, J. A. 2008.El efecto del adjetivo intangible en la cultura. *Revista de Vinculación y Ciencia,* Vol. 6, No. 24.

Manzi, T., Lucas, K., Lloyd-Jones, T. and Allen, J. 2010.*Under Social Sustainability: Key Concepts and Developments in Theory and Practice*. London, Earthscan.

MCC.2011. *Formulación e implementación de planes especiales de manejo y protección*. Bogotá, Ministerio de Cultura, Republica de Colombia.

Moss, M. L. and Grunkemeyer W. T. 2010. Building shared visions for sustainable communities. *Community Development,* Vol. 41, No. 2, pp. 240–54.

Neely, M. J. 2011. Gestión urbana en el contexto de la reconstrucción patrimonial. *RevistaAméricaPatrimonio,* Vol. 2, pp. 80–91.

Nurse, K. 2006.*Culture as the Fourth Pillar of Sustainable Development*. London, University of the West Indies.

Omann, I. and Spangenberg, J. H. 2010. *Assessing Social Sustainability: The Social Dimension of Sustainability in a Socio-Economic Scenario*. Sousse, Tunisia, Université du Centre.

Putnam, R. 1993.*Making Democracy Work: Civic Traditions in Modern Italy*. Princeton, NJ, Princeton University Press.

Queról, M. A.2010. *Manual de gestión del patrimonio*. Madrid, Akal.

Rantala, M.,Hujala, T. and Kurttila, M.2012. Measuring and monitoring sociocultural sustainability in the action of forest biodiversity cooperation networks. *Silva Fennica,* Vol. 46, No. 3, pp. 441–59.

Sanchez, M. 2005. *La gestión municipal del patrimonio cultural*. Málaga, Spain, Universidad de Málaga.

TiwariSudarshan, R. 2007. *Transforming Patan's Cultural Heritage into Sustainable Future: Case Studies of the Past and the Present*. New York, United Nations University Press, pp. 62–106.

Trotte, F., Brunet, P. and Barone, L. 2012.*Culture and Innovation*. European Union, Sostenuto Project.

Tweed, C. and Sutherland, M. 2007. Built cultural heritage and sustainable urban development. *Landscape and Urban Planning,* Vol. 83, No. 1, pp. 62–9.

UNESCO. 2008. *Historic Districts for All: a Social and Human Approach for Sustainable Revitalization*. Paris, UNESCO.unesdoc.unesco.org/images/0015/001583/158331e.pdf

UNESCO. 2010. *Managing Historic Cities*. Paris, UNESCO World Heritage Centre. (World *Heritage Papers No. 27.*) whc.unesco.org/documents/publi_wh_papers_27_en.pdf

UNESCO. 2011. Recommendation on the Historic Urban Landscape, including a glossary of definitions. http://portal.unesco.org/en/ev.php-URL_ID=48857&URL_DO=DO_TOPIC&URL_SECTION=201.html

UNESCO and ICCROM. 2006. *Introducing Young People to the Protection of Heritage Sites and Historic Cities*. Rome, UNESCO/ICCROM.
UNESCO and ICCROM. 2012. *Introduciendo a los jóvenes en la protección del patrimonio cultural y los centros históricos*. Bogotá, UNESCO/ICCROM/MInisterio de Cultural de la República de Colombia.
Villaseñor, I., MagarMeurs, V. 2012.*Assessing the Performance of Conservation Activities*. Recife, Brazil, ICCROM/LATAM/CECI- Olinda& Rome, pp. 1–14.
Vinterhav, J. 2009. *The Urban Game: Social Aspects on Sustainable Urban Development and Citizen Participation in Nanjing, the People's Republic of China*. Uppsala, Sweden, Swedish University of Agricultural Science.
West, S. 2010.*Understanding Heritage in Practice*. Manchester, UK, Manchester University Press.
Winter, T. 2012. Clarifying the critical in critical heritage studies. *International Journal of Heritage Studies,* Vol. 16, No. 6, pp. 1–14.
Yung, E. H. K., Chan, E. H. W. and Xu, Y. 2011. Sustainable development and the rehabilitation of a historic urban district: social sustainability in the case of Tianzifang in Shanghai. *Sustainable Development,* Vol. 22, No. 2, pp. 95–112.

IV Theory, Methods and Practices

Sustainability in Heritage Management Strategies

Cultural Heritage Management and Sustainability

Ron van Oers

Cultural heritage management: A profound transformation

Over the last two decades the field of cultural heritage management has undergone a profound transformation. This has been related to an alignment of several powerful forces of change, including runaway urbanization, a looming environmental crisis due to overexploitation of natural resources coupled with the impending impacts of climate change, an explosive growth of international tourism, as well as changing notions of what constitutes heritage (Bandarin and Van Oers, 2012, pp. 75–122). The discipline has reacted to this profound and rapidly changing landscape by developing new charters, guidelines, approaches and tools, all aimed at addressing developmental pressures on heritage resources by creating broader awareness and new alliances, and by incorporating, rather reluctantly, the idea that heritage could be a vector of sustainable development. While this transformation is still going on, along with the debates that accompany it, nevertheless, an emerging change in attitude – some would argue a new paradigm – can already be discerned.

In particular, since the early 1990s several groundbreaking ideas and debates have led the charge to transform our thinking about heritage and its management. The most important include the inclusion of the concept of cultural landscapes (1992), the debate on authenticity in Nara, Japan (1994), the focus on cultural significance in ICOMOS Australia's Burra Charter (revised, 1999), the adoption of the Intangible Cultural Heritage Convention (2003) and the Convention on Cultural Diversity (2005) (Bandarin and Van Oers, 2012, pp. 49–51). These all signalled the start of a gradual shift away from an essentially nineteenth-century approach to heritage management, centred on the strict preservation of monuments as the means to construct the nation-state (Muñoz Viñas, 2005, p. 30) and executed by centralized governments by way of specialized agencies with predefined ideas and *fragmentation* of tasks. This approach has run its course and is currently being replaced by a post-modern phase that is characterized by *integration:* of different value systems in the main heritage discourse, of community-driven processes in decision-making, and of heritage management in locally-rooted development projects – or, in the words of philosopher Ken Wilber (2000, pp. x–xi), from "universal formalism" towards "pluralistic relativism" in order to respect "the rich differences between cultures, peoples, and places".

In truth the international conventions and charters that have been laid down by organizations such as UNESCO and ICOMOS over the course of the twentieth century have played a very valuable role in that they assisted in the global establishment of professional standards of practice for the protection of the world's cultural and natural heritage. Without this basis, the current shift would not have been possible; in fact, it would be pointless. Nevertheless, when looking at international standards – primarily based on the Western conservation canon – the fundamental questions arise, *whose values are we addressing and whose heritage is it?* As such, it has become imperative that the universality of practice, adoption of international standards and the nationally recognized icons do not overwhelm local communities and their traditional values to be found in everyday places.

Cultural heritage as understood nowadays has increased significantly in breadth and depth, in meaning and importance, and is primarily understood as a living entity covering far more than simply structures and sites. While based on the international recognition of its value, the concept of "living heritage" as a resource for local community-based sustainable development has become the lens through which cultural heritage management is currently being conceived. Again, this shift is still under way.

Although a globalizing tendency indeed, the practice of international organizations such as UNESCO, ICOMOS, ICOM and ICCROM should not be judged too harshly. They have laid the foundation of a shared way of working that is apparent, understandable and replicable, so that its validity is testable, as well as one that allows comparative evaluation of findings and management recommendations. Importantly, however, it should be added that these methods and guidelines must then be applied in ways that are appropriate and sympathetic to the specific cultural context to be found locally. To this effect, national and local laws, regulations and institutional frameworks, formal or customary, need to be in place to ensure that international best practice can be embedded in an enabling environment to assist in further nurturing and blossoming to the benefit of local communities. Bridging this gap is *the* critical management challenge of cultural heritage today.

Sustainability and culture: New life for an old concept

Generally, the idea of sustainability is attributed to the report published in 1987 by the United Nations World Commission on Environment and Development, which was chaired by Norway's Prime Minister Gro Harlem Brundtland. The key message it contained has been quoted *ad nauseam* (WCED, 1987). However, almost two decades before that, in 1969, the International Union for Conservation of Nature (IUCN) adopted its mandate, which spoke of "the perpetuation and enhancement of the living world – man's natural environment – and the natural resources on which all living things depend", referring to management of "air, water, soils, minerals and living species including man, so as to achieve the highest sustainable quality of life" (Adams, 2006, p. 1). Since then the theme of sustainability has been central to a series of United Nations conferences and declarations, the most significant of which include the

Conference on the Human Environment in Stockholm, Sweden, in 1972;[1] the World Commission on Environment and Development of 1987 (which issued the Brundtland Report already mentioned); the Conference on Environment and Development in Rio de Janeiro (Brazil), in 1992;[2] the Millennium Summit in 2000 that issued the Millennium Declaration with its eight Millennium Development Goals;[3] the World Summit on Sustainable Development in Johannesburg (South Africa), in 2002;[4] and the Conference on Sustainable Development (Rio+20), in Rio de Janeiro in 2012, which issued the report *The Future We Want*.[5]

After this decades-long parade of high-level intergovernmental meetings around the theme of sustainability, two things became clear (Bandarin and Van Oers, 2012, p. 84). First, that sustainable development is politically savvy: it is an attractive and flexible concept, a convenient container to lodge a variety of ideas or viewpoints relating to economic and environmental management. Second, due to this convenience and flexibility, it has been used and abused so often that effectively it has lost its meaning, while the question of how to operationalize its potential remains unanswered. Therefore, in spite of the criticism the world's leaders decided not to abandon it, as it has taken so long to build the concept into the mindset of the international community (Adams, 2006, p. 3), but instead to revamp it. To this end, during the first decade of the twenty-first century the international community started to discuss a *modus operandi* that would put past lessons into practice in order to capitalize on the promise of sustainability. This resulted, in December 2010, in the adoption by the United Nations General Assembly of Resolution 65/166 on Culture and Development, which for the first time established a clear role for culture in the development process for consideration in the Post-2015 Development Agenda.[6]

This constituted an important departure from previous considerations, where sustainability involved only the three "pillars" of environment, economy and society, but wherein culture was excluded as a significant component in and by itself. UNESCO, however, had long argued that sustainable development and the blossoming of culture are interdependent,[7] and finally it seems this has now been recognized. It may need emphasizing that culture, in its broadest sense, comprises the entire spectrum of equity and access, the safeguarding of heritage, the economics of cultural production,

---

1 For the Declaration of the United Nations Conference on the Human Environment (1972) see http://www.unep.org/Documents.Multilingual/Default.asp?documentid=97&articleid=1503

2 http://www.un-documents.net/k-001962.htm

3 http://www.un.org/millenniumgoals/

4 http://www.johannesburgsummit.org/html/basic_info/basicinfo.html

5 http://www.uncsd2012.org/

6 http://www.un.org/depts/dhl/resguide/r65_en.shtml

7 Intergovernmental Conference on Cultural Policies for Development, Stockholm, April 1998, which adopted UNESCO's Action Plan on Cultural Policies for Development. http://www.unesco.org/cpp/uk/declarations/cultural.pdf

and the promotion of innovation and creativity. It involves, but is not limited to, local knowledge; indigenous typologies of nature, space, and society; knowledge of animals and plants, including local pharmacology; hunting and agricultural cycles and practices; food preparation, preservation and eating habits; music and dance; artistic and handicraft traditions; writing systems; notions about the nature of man and the universe; religious and ritual practices; symbolic, social and material values of natural, built, and intangible expressions of heritage, including that of associated artefacts, tools, costumes, utensils and documents; as well as traditional safeguarding practices including taboos and other restrictions (see Engelhardt, 2014, p. 247). When considering this broad spectrum, the cultural dimension of development becomes clear: no matter which of the original three pillars is taken as an entry point, cultural factors will determine to a very large extent policy development, programme design and project management – and by that token they are key to the success or failure of development initiatives.

In anticipation of the approval by the United Nations General Assembly of the Post-2015 Sustainable Development Goals, UNESCO has reorganized parts of its institutional and operational capacity in order to strengthen its Culture and Development policy with an emphasis on sustainability. To achieve this it has grouped its cultural policies along two main axes: Heritage and Creativity. Its flagship Convention concerning the Protection of the World Cultural and Natural Heritage (1972) and Convention for the Safeguarding of the Intangible Cultural Heritage (2003) support the safeguarding and conservation of natural, cultural and intangible heritage, which are basic components of social identity and cohesion, as well as collective memory and dialogue among communities. On the other hand, the Convention on the Protection and Promotion of the Diversity of Cultural Expressions (2005) supports the creative economy and its cultural industries. Together they constitute a suite of policies and practices aiming to guide innovations in socio-economic development, regeneration and resilience-building as part of the operationalization of the sustainability concept through culture.

Returning to the topic of this paper and relating sustainability to the management of heritage resources, the essential questions are the following. If heritage should become one of the drivers of sustainable development, what then is it that we do not want to lose when development takes place? Who stands to benefit from this process, and who to lose? And how can we optimize positive impacts and mitigate negative ones?

Two case studies in China, on the cities of Macao and Shanghai, illustrate some of the resulting dilemmas and implications of these questions. Both are wealthy cities, in terms of per capita income as well as heritage resources, and both are developing at high speed and are thereby illustrative of the type and scale of pressure that is prevalent in much of the larger cities of Asia. However, the approaches to heritage management taken by Macao and Shanghai are starkly different, with correspondingly different outcomes in terms of the sustainability of management efforts and of successful heritage protection.

Case Study 1: Macao

Macao's cultural heritage of Outstanding Universal Value

The inner city of Macao represents an outstanding example of an architectural ensemble that developed out of the encounter between the European and Chinese civilizations over approximately four and half centuries (between the sixteenth and the mid-twentieth). The historical route through the centre, with a series of urban spaces and mixture of vernacular architectural ensembles, links the ancient Chinese port with the Portuguese city. Moreover, Macao bears a unique testimony to the first and longest-lasting encounter between the West and China. It was the focal point for traders, but also for Roman Catholic and Protestant missionaries, and developments in the different fields of learning, such as literature and medicine, among others. The impact of this encounter can be traced in the mixture of different types of architecture with a fusion of styles and technologies from the different cultures, which characterizes the historic core of Macao (ICOMOS, 2005; see also Coates, 2009, pp. 31–52).

This encounter can also be detected in the existing culture of the place, its traditions, and even its special creole language, *patua,* which mixes influences from Portuguese, Cantonese and Malay as well as African languages. Macao has been associated with the exchange of a variety of cultural, spiritual, scientific and technical influences between the Western and Chinese civilizations. These ideas directly motivated the introduction of crucial changes in China, ultimately ending the era of the imperial feudal system and establishing the modern republic (ICOMOS, 2005). The International Council on Monuments and Sites (ICOMOS), the scientific advisor on cultural heritage to the World Heritage Committee, recognized Macao's exceptional cultural-historic significance as being of Outstanding Universal Value, which is the main criterion for inscription on the World Heritage List. Based on this positive recommendation, the Committee decided to award World Heritage status to the Historic Centre of Macao and inscribed it in 2005.

However, next to the recognition of the Outstanding Universal Value of Macao, ICOMOS also issued a warning with an associated recommendation, being that the management system had to be improved by better correlating the city's economic development with appropriate management strategies and plans to safeguard its heritage resources and "to make every effort to develop the management system so as to retain the existing structural and visual integrity, and to maintain the principal sightlines of the nominated area within its contemporary setting" (ICOMOS, 2005, p. 62). In other words, the particular construction of high-rise buildings as part of the continuing development of the city were identified as potential threats to the unimpaired views to and from the historic centre, which had endured for centuries. The suggestion put forward by ICOMOS was not to curb the city's development, but to ensure that any development would be planned and designed in accordance with the city's outstanding cultural heritage assets and related World Heritage status, and to enhance, not to diminish or destroy, the experience and enjoyment of these assets.

Less than four years after its inscription on the World Heritage List, Macao found itself in front of the World Heritage Committee, when in January 2009 a joint World Heritage Centre/ICOMOS reactive monitoring mission condemned a scheme for proposed high-rise buildings that were threatening to negatively affect the visual integrity of the historic centre. In the triumphant period following inscription it seems that the government officials had forgotten about the ICOMOS warning issued at the time. Subsequently, the World Heritage Committee at its 35th session in Seville (Spain) noted the "apparent inadequacy of the current management system" and requested the development of a comprehensive statement on Macao's cultural-historic significance with related values, or a draft Statement of Outstanding Universal Value, and appropriate legal and planning tools, including a comprehensive urban plan (UNESCO, 2009).

Macao's "Dutch Disease"

Macao, a Special Administrative Region (SAR) of 29 km^2 under the sovereign rule of China since December 1999, enjoys one of the fastest growing economies in the world, primarily due to its gambling industry. In 2012 it attracted 28 million visitors, the majority from mainland China, who in taking their chances at the gaming tables brought in more than US$ 33 billion in revenues, constituting 40 per cent of its gross domestic product (Master, 2012, p. 19; *The Economist*, 2013, p. 51). But while this bonanza has undoubtedly improved the overall living conditions of the resident population of approximately half a million souls, it has also led to a seriously congested transport network, a struggling middle class, and steep increases in prices for real estate and food – the latter almost twice as much as what residents of Hong Kong, just an hour away by ferry, pay for their groceries. This perverse effect is the result of lots of money entering an economy at a faster rate than it can handle and has been coined the "Dutch Disease". First observed in the 1960s in the Netherlands when it experienced a huge influx of gas revenues, this generally leads to a stagnation of the economy, which becomes saturated and loses its competitive edge and capacity for innovation; or put differently, economists characterize it as "too much wealth managed unwisely" (Ebrahim-zadeh, 2003).

Despite regular handouts in cash as a form of "wealth share", in 2013 raising the allowance per capita to 7,000 *patacas* (about US$ 875), Macao's residential population is growing increasingly frustrated over the lack of a more diversified economy and an appropriate social infrastructure for the city, with rising inequality and struggling small and medium-size businesses. Although the casino industry pays very well, the working conditions are often unfavourable to leading a regular family life, while there are limited other opportunities for good employment. In this regard it is important to remember that in this globalized urban age, the young, the bright and the talented

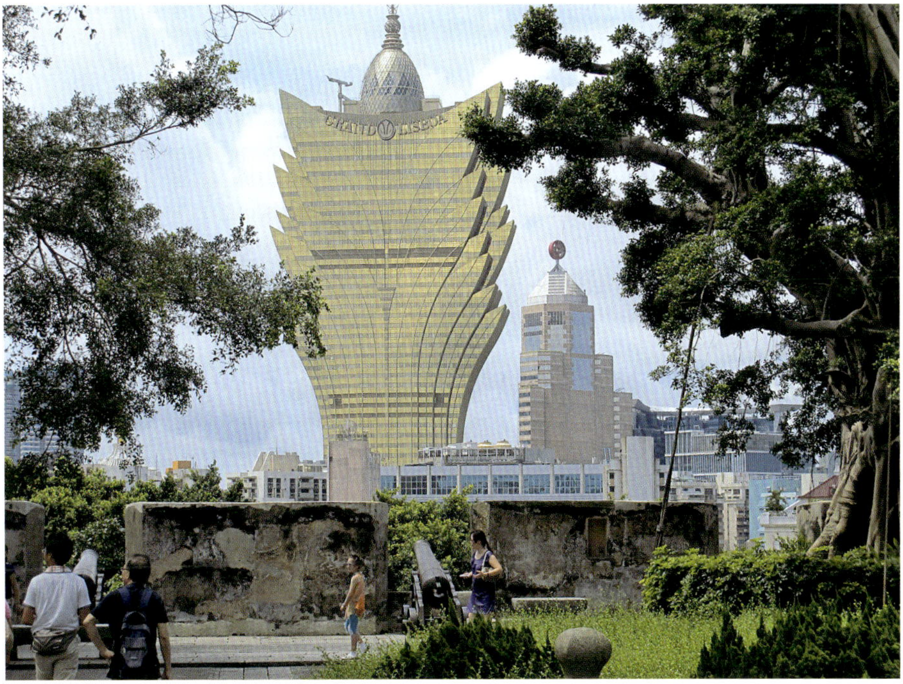

Fig. 1: With Gotham rising and money talking, the guns of high culture become aimless, which prompts the need for a renewed dialogue between the benefits of heritage conservation and possible types of urban development. © Ron van Oers, June 2013.

have plenty of options to move to places where living and working conditions are more diversified and accessible, which nowadays means places that are affordable for young families and that offer a rich urban culture to stimulate and motivate, where leisure time can be enjoyed. In these areas Macao, in spite of all the money in its coffers, is not doing a good job, with "four times as many gambling tables per 1,000 residents than there are hospital beds" (Master, 2012, p. 19).

In spite of the enormous influx of money at present, Macao's economic base is very vulnerable and urgently needs diversification. The preparation and submission of the nomination dossier in January 2002 to obtain World Heritage status for its historic centre was no doubt motivated by a wish to safeguard the city's extraordinary built heritage, and perhaps also to increase cultural tourism.[8] While seeking greater

8 World Heritage nominations are prepared, on a voluntary basis, by countries that have ratified the 1972 World Heritage Convention, thereby becoming "States Parties", and are inscribed (or not) by the World Heritage Committee, an elected body of twenty-one States Parties on a rotating basis. UNESCO is the multilateral agency that administers the Convention and oversees the process.

tourism appeal and related revenues has become something of an accepted norm within the World Heritage process, generally speaking this should not be the primary reason for undertaking heritage conservation. After all, the true nature of conservation goes beyond tourism development and lies in the ambition and challenge to develop a more sustainable environment through wise resources management. Even so, Macao to date has not capitalized on this potential and the historic centre remains surprisingly devoid of tourism-related activities and crowds,[9] which are so characteristic of World Heritage sites on mainland China. Some may think that this absence may be beneficial for its heritage buildings and spaces, given some of the excesses seen in many other sites, but the truth is that these buildings and spaces are largely non-functional and thereby receive little or no attention. Indeed, in practice heritage management oscillates between these two extremes and it is hard to strike the right balance, as in the case of Macao.

After the World Heritage Committee's decision in 2009 requesting a comprehensive urban plan for Macao, Tongji University's College of Architecture and Urban Planning (CAUP) assisted Macao's government in developing this urban plan with the principal sightlines of the nominated area within its contemporary setting (see Zhang Song, 2012). In January 2011 Macao submitted a Statement of Outstanding Universal Value to the World Heritage Committee, while it also reported that two studies completed in April 2010 would form the basis of Macao's Urban Plan, describing the characteristics of the existing urban plan, as well as several detailed studies on building control of districts around the inscribed World Heritage property. While this was examined by the World Heritage Committee at its 37th session in June 2013 in Cambodia, Macao was raising the bar again to attract ever more rich tourists with the world's most luxurious hotel and casino under development, its top suite costing US$ 130,000 per night (*Financial Times*, 2013, p. 16).

Case Study 2: Shanghai

Integrated conservation at Sinan Mansions

Sinan Mansions, a conservation and renovation project of 4.2 ha (Phase 1) in the former Luwan District, is located in central Shanghai's Hengshan Road-Fuxing Road Historic and Cultural Area. It consists of a group of detached houses with gardens that were originally built in the 1920s, supplemented by Shanghai *lilong* (local-style, traditional lane houses; li = house, long = alley), which stem from the 1920s to 1940s, and other early twentieth-century modern residential complexes. As a whole, this

9 Although Macao received more than 2 million visitors in April 2013 (from: *Macau Daily Times*, 24 May 2014), the overwhelming majority go straight into the casinos.

highly diverse but compact site with its gardens forms a significant architectural ensemble that relates to the early development phase of Shanghai, when the city started its expansion brought about by the foreign concessions – in this case the French Concession – which makes this an important historical and authentic Shanghai neighbourhood (Xu Yibo, 2012, pp. 17–19).

During the last half-century, the site and its buildings suffered from extensive use, overcrowding and lack of maintenance, coupled with aggressive real estate and infrastructure development in their direct surroundings. In 2002–03 the Shanghai municipal and district governments, in alliance with a private developer from Hong Kong, elaborated a conservation and renovation project with the overall aims of protecting the particular identity and character of the site, rehabilitating its individual buildings and spaces, revitalizing the neighbourhood and its functions, and safeguarding the memories, history and culture in this central part of Shanghai. The renovation project technically upgraded and transformed the residential neighbourhood into a mixed-use complex with middle-income and high-end residential, commercial and public facilities through revealing and further developing the site's spirit of place, i. e. the historical, social and cultural values relating to Shanghai's overall development and specific culture. Three types of key intervention have been undertaken to achieve this goal.[10]

First, the overall function and layout of the site were optimized through recognition and utilization of its strategic central location, with its open garden setting in highly urbanized and densely built-up surroundings, and through surgical interventions that removed some structures that had no historical or sociocultural significance, but that partly re-created the spacious layout of its original design which had been lost throughout a century of neglect and over-use.

Second, an environmental conservation, rehabilitation and redesign of the complete site, with extensive replanting, gardening and improvement of circulation and accessibility as a public space for the neighbourhood.

Third, all remaining on-site buildings were architecturally rehabilitated and structurally strengthened, including those of high architectural value (i. e. the detached European-style villas) as well as those of lesser architectural value (i. e. Shanghai *lilong* housing), involving the exterior surfaces, structural frames and interiors, with partial redesign to upgrade and retrofit technical utilities (electric wiring, plumbing, fire and termite protection, waterproofing, accoustic treatment, modern kitchen and bathroom for the *lilong*), to create better daylight penetration and to comply with the latest environmental standards concerning energy efficiency.

10 Communication with architect Cheng Zichun, Director of Jiang Architects & Engineers responsible for the Sinan Mansions Conservation and Renovation Project, Shanghai, April 2014.

Shanghai's local heritage of exceptional value

The technical project, after planning and design, started in January 2004 and took seven years to complete; it was finalized in November 2010. The project was a tripartite public-private partnership between the municipal and district governments of Shanghai and a private developer from Hong Kong, who was later bought out by the government. The total cost of the project was US$ 500 million,[11] which is an enormous sum of money in China, even for a relatively rich city like Shanghai, begging the question of what motivated the city to invest so much in the project of Sinan Mansions?

The property involves an area of the former French Concession in Shanghai that was part of the city's third expansion in 1914. Sinan Mansions originated as a group of detached houses with lush gardens in 1921 built by a Belgian developer to accommodate Chinese as well as Western people living in Shanghai. During that period the French Catholic Church owned large tracts of land around the centre of Shanghai, where many public facilities such as parks, a hospital and a Catholic church were constructed, eventually forming an integral residential community. When the war with Japan broke out in 1937, refugees crowded into Shanghai's foreign concessions, which resulted in a population explosion in the city. During the 1930s and 40s Shanghai-style *lilong* housing and other types of high-density residential buildings were constructed on site to accommodate a burgeoning population.[12] As such, this site experienced an organic evolution reminiscent of the different phases of Shanghai's urban history and cultural development, where East met West, and rich met poor, co-inhabiting the same space and creating the fusion of cultures that Shanghai was – and still is – internationally famous for.

But the property is also witness to some of the darker pages in China's history, relating to colonial occupation and war and suffering, which fortunately did not result in a complete demolition and redevelopment of the site, but was recognized as an important historical value to be safeguarded. During its relatively short but turbulent history of a century, several artistic and politically influential people famous in China and abroad made the site their home, including Premier Zhou Enlai (from 1946 to 1947), and Beijing opera singer Mei Lanfang (from 1932 to 1958), adding to the overall sociocultural significance of the place: 'every building has a story to tell', as the popular saying about Sinan Mansions goes.

In addition to historical and sociocultural values, the property also contains an important architectural value. A variety of modern Shanghai residential building types are to be found in this rather compact plot, including large-scale and regular detached houses with garden, semi-detached houses with garden, row houses,

11 Communication with Mr Stephen Liu, Managing Director of Sinan Mansions, Shanghai, April 2014.
12 Communication with Prof. Shao Yong, College of Architecture and Urban Planning (CAUP), Tongji University, Shanghai, April 2014.

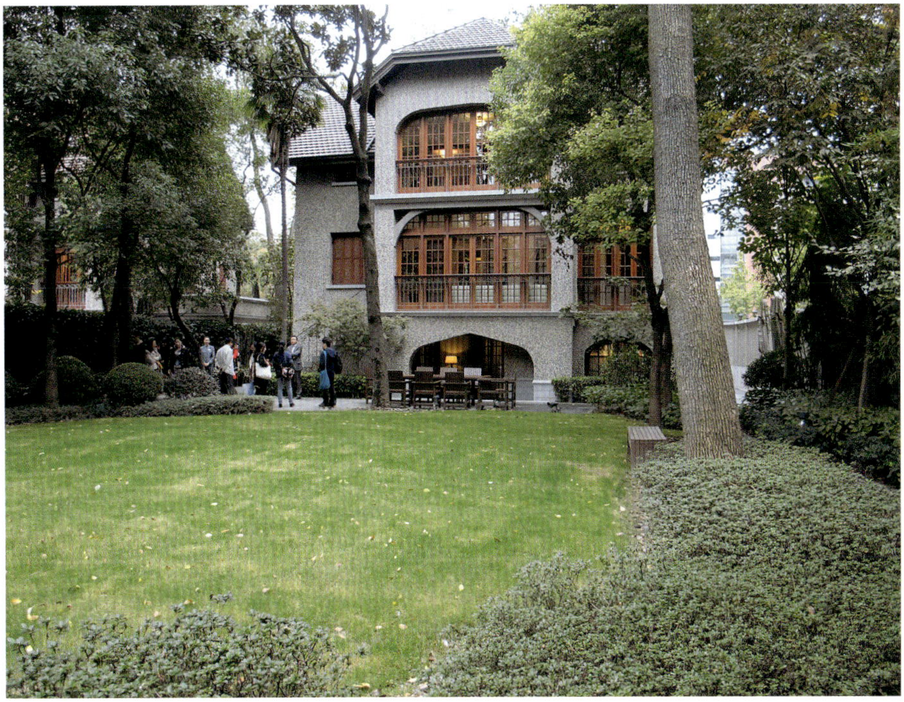

Fig. 2: Sinan Mansions, a premium mixed-use property, with successful revitalization of spacious colonial-era residential living in the heart of the dynamic metropolis of Shanghai.
© Ron van Oers, November 2013.

Shanghai *lilong* housing with garden, and modern style apartments. This diversity of on-site residential buildings originated from the need to accommodate people from various levels in society. The detached houses with gardens were built according to the colonial lifestyle of Western people, in a villa-type architectural style, with a grand layout and elegant decoration and finishes. In sharp contrast, the Shanghai *lilong* housing was a high-density residential building type, with a relatively compact floor plan adapted to the Chinese lifestyle and suited to Chinese people with low or moderate incomes. The villas expressed Western values such as individuality and having "your own place under the sun", while the *lilong* expressed the Eastern values of communality and sharing life with your extended family and those of others. The different lifestyles expressed through architecture and building styles coexisted and exchanged their respective values, which makes this type of neighbourhood rare in Shanghai. Here Chinese people came into contact with modern Western lifestyles and habits, and eventually Eastern and Western cultural values were exchanged, mixed and merged into a particular aspect that defines Shanghai's spirit of place, of which this property is a living example. Next to local significance, the property has thereby national significance as well and has become a mandatory stop for delegations from other Chinese cities, as well as delegations from overseas, to experience the site's successful rehabilitation and revitalization.

Conclusion: *A Tale of Two Cities*[13]

Sinan Mansions originated as a residential neighbourhood that was carefully planned and designed. The conservation and renovation project has meticulously studied, analysed and restored the historical features of the site and its different buildings, though not through a "hard" restoration back to the original plans, but through recognition of the site's organic evolution, and distinguishing those elements and aspects that have added value, historical and sociocultural, to the property. The previous use and function was residential; currently the property has mixed-use functions, being residential (middle-income and high-end housing), commercial (offices, restaurants, hotel), and public (exhibition centre). The commercial and public functions have been introduced to upgrade and adapt the neighbourhood to contemporary city life, to revitalize the larger area in this central part of Shanghai and to make the conservation and rehabilitation plan financially feasible and sustainable. The increased revenues from high-end commercial functions (e. g. hotel, restaurants and bars, cultural centre) paid for the technical interventions and site rehabilitation – and continue to pay for regular maintenance. In this way an effective and successful merger was created between historic site preservation and commercial operations, in which public welfare and local quality of life have been improved and new sociocultural functions have revitalized the neighbourhood, all sustainably financed by on-site activities, while the tangible and intangible heritage of the place has been safeguarded. Sinan Mansions is protected and listed at both national and municipal levels and has a conservation plan for the whole site.

The contrast with Macao could not be starker. When the last Portuguese administration was confronted with the prospect of returning the city to China, in 1999, it initiated a flurry of public art and building conservation projects in the historic town aiming to safeguard the Portuguese colonial legacy in this part of the world (De Pina-Cabral, 2002). Many of these restoration and renovation projects served to beautify colonial-style buildings and spaces, but they remained empty shells, literally, with neither input from, nor use to local residents. Even though a process of World Heritage listing was successfully completed, no comprehensive urban planning was initiated that included a vision and strategy for the sustainable management of its cultural heritage. The current impasse in discussions between heritage preservationists and

13 *A Tale of Two Cities* (1859) is a novel by Charles Dickens, set in London and Paris before and during the French Revolution. *Source:* Wikipedia.

the city's entrepreneurs and developers does not bode well for the future of Macao: the breakneck speed of development leaves its heritage of Outstanding Universal Value with fewer and fewer spaces for enjoyment and inspiration. However, Macao does not need to choose between conservation or development, from a radical all-or-nothing position – the way forward lies in leaving the trenches in which both groups in Macanese society currently find themselves and starting a dialogue between the city's planners, entrepreneurs and preservationists, including engaged citizenry, about what can and should be done, where, and how. After all, each party stands to lose a great deal if Macao fails to keep its competitive edge, greatly broadened and enhanced by its distinct culture and heritage – indeed its UNESCO World Heritage status – which affirms this uniqueness through one of the world's most powerful brand names.

To achieve sustainability in today's urban heritage management means not only putting protective measures in place through legislation and conservation plans, but going beyond this by creating mutually beneficial partnerships in order to enlarge constituencies that support conservation efforts and reduce conflicts. Developing a more sustainable urban environment means striving for a continuum between past, present and future, where productivity increase and resilience are generated by harnessing the population's diversity and creativity. Citizens' welfare and quality of life can only be enhanced when development respects and builds on urban communities' ecological balance and social identity, both embedded in the natural, cultural and immaterial heritage of the city. Sustainable cities utilize their heritage resources as drivers of cultural creativity, innovation and urban regeneration (Van Oers and Pereira-Roders, 2013).

Given the extraordinary pressures of urbanization and urban development in China at the moment, the revitalization project of Sinan Mansions is setting an important standard. If mayors and city governments are willing and capable of considering the future planning and design of the city in the light of its historic development, local culture and inherited characteristics and qualities, then the identities that have been built up over a hundred years or more can be safeguarded, nurtured and enhanced in a quest for a distinct urban environment, modern but truly local. Instead of squandering a heritage for the sake of short-term gains and riches, these distinct identities will allow local population groups and visitors to better enjoy the labours and fruits of previous generations, while adding their own layer in time – this, after all, constitutes the essence of sustainability in heritage management.

References

Adams, W. M. 2006. *The Future of Sustainability: Re-Thinking Environment and Development in the Twenty-First Century.* Report of the IUCN Renowned Thinkers Meeting, 29–31 January. Gland, Switzerland, IUCN.

Bandarin, F. and Van Oers, R. 2012. *The Historic Urban Landscape. Managing Heritage in an Urban Century.* Chichester, UK, Wiley-Blackwell.

Coates, A. 2009. *A Macao Narrative*. Hong Kong, Hong Kong University Press (first published in 1978 by Heinemann).
De Pina-Cabral, J. 2002. *Between China and Europe: Persons, Culture and Emotion in Macao*. London/New York, Continuum.
Ebrahim-zadeh, Ch. 2003. Dutch disease: too much wealth managed unwisely. *Finance and Development*. Washington DC, International Monetary Fund, Vol. 40, No. 1.
Engelhardt, R. A. 2014. Valuing cultural diversity. In: F. Bandarin and R. Van Oers (eds), *Reconnecting the City. The Historic Urban Landscape Approach and the Future of Urban Heritage*. Chichester, UK, Wiley & Sons, pp. 245–8.
Financial Times. 2013. Macau wakes up to the riches in luxury hotels. 29 April, p. 16.
ICOMOS. 2005. Advisory Body Evaluation Macao (China), No. 1110, April, pp. 58–62. http://whc.unesco.org/archive/advisory_body_evaluation/1110.pdf (Accessed 16 December 2014.)
Macau Daily Times. 2014. 24 May. http://macaudailytimes.com.mo/ (Accessed 16 December 2014.)
Master, F. 2012. Focus on gambling leaves Macau with 36 casinos and one public hospital. *International Herald Tribune*, 23 October, p. 19.
Muñoz Viñas, S. 2005. *Contemporary Theory of Conservation*. Oxford, UK, Elsevier Butterworth-Heinemann.
The Economist. 2013. US$ 38 billion in revenues for 2012, or "more than six times the Las Vegas strip's takings": 7 September, p. 51.
UN. 1972. Declaration of the United Nations Conference on the Human Environment. http://www.unep.org/Documents.Multilingual/Default.asp?documentid=97&articleid=1503 (Accessed 16 December 2014.)
UN. 1992. United Nations Conference on Environment and Development (1992) Agenda 21. (A/CONF.151/26.) http://www.un-documents.net/k-001962.htm (Accessed 16 December 2014.)
UN. 2010. United Nations Resolution 65/166. Culture and Development, 20 December 2010; http://www.un.org/depts/dhl/resguide/r65_en.shtml (Accessed 16 December 2014.)
UNCSD. 2012. *The Future We Want*. Outcome Document adopted at Rio+20 Conference, Rio de Janeiro, Brazil, 20–22 June. New York, United Nations Commission on Sustainable Development. (A/CONF.216/16.) http://www.uncsd2012.org (Accessed 16 December 2014.)
UNESCO. 1998. *UNESCO's Action Plan on Cultural Policies for Development;* http://www.unesco.org/cpp/uk/declarations/cultural.pdf (Accessed 16 December 2014.)
UNESCO. 2009. Convention Concerning the Protection of the World Cultural and Natural Heritage. World Heritage Committee Thirty-third Session (Seville, Spain). Paris, UNESCO World Heritage Centre (WHC-09/33.COM/7B.)
Van Oers, R. and Pereira-Roders, A. 2013. Road map for application of the HUL approach in China. *Journal of Cultural Heritage Management and Sustainable Development,* Vol. 3, No. 1. pp. 4–17.
WCED. 1987. *Report of the World Commission on Environment and Development. Our Common Future.* (Brundtland Report). Transmitted to the General Assembly as an Annex to document A/42/427 – Development and International Co-operation: Environment. New York, United Nations. http://www.un-documents.net/wced-ocf.htm
Wilber, K. 2000. *Sex, Ecology, Spirituality: The Spirit of Evolution,* 2nd edn. Boston, Mass., Shambhala Publications, pp. x-xi.
Xu, Yibo. (ed.) 2012. *A Sight amid Phoenix Trees: Sinan Mansions on Century-old Sinan Road of Shanghai*. Shanghai, Shanghai People's Fine Arts Publishing House.
Zhang, Song. 2012. Research on the conservation planning of historic urban landscape: a case study of the Historic Center of Macau. *WHITRAP Newsletter,* Shanghai, World Heritage Institute of Training and Research for the Asia and the Pacific Region, March, No. 21. pp. 4–8.

World Heritage and Sustainable Tourism: A Multifaceted Relationship

Carol Westrik

Introduction

As of summer 2014, there were 1,007 World Heritage properties. During the 38th session of the World Heritage Committee (Doha, Qatar) the magic number of 1,000 sites was surpassed. This milestone was accompanied by several reports of the possible negative impact of tourism on both existing World Heritage properties and new nominations. With the prediction of ever-increasing numbers of tourists, this is a cause for concern if the properties are not addressing this issue in a sustainable manner. Therefore, UNESCO's World Heritage and Sustainable Tourism Programme is an important tool as it aims to integrate sustainable tourism principles into the mechanisms of the World Heritage Convention.

World Heritage Convention

The 1972 Convention concerning the Protection of the World Cultural and Natural Heritage is one of the most successful United Nations Conventions. UNESCO has 195 Member States of which 191 are States Parties to the World Heritage Convention (UNESCO, 2014*b*; 2014*d*). The aim of the Convention is to ensure the "identification, protection, conservation, presentation and transmission to future generations of the cultural and natural heritage" (UNESCO, 1972, Article 4). In order to be able to do this, sustainable management of the property, including the impact of tourism, is indispensable. Tourism can help with the protection, conservation, presentation and transmission of the World Heritage property if well managed. It can also have a negative impact on the site if for example the number of tourists is higher than the carrying capacity of the site. With an ever-increasing number of tourists every year, it is imperative to ensure that World Heritage properties have a sustainable tourism management system. This is not always the case, however, as the concept of sustainable tourism in relation to World Heritage is not always clear. Furthermore there is no specific mention of sustainable tourism management in the *Operational Guidelines*. (UNESCO, 2013*a*). Sustainable tourism should look at all the facets of tourism, be it for visitor infrastructure, visitor experience, or interpretation of the site. There is also the aspect of visitors actively engaging with the site, for example by joining reconstruction projects or exploring its history via events organized on site. General applicable tools for assessing and developing sustainable tourism in the context of World Heritage are therefore urgently needed.

For a site to become a World Heritage property it has to be of Outstanding Universal Value, meaning that its cultural and/or natural significance is so exceptional that it goes beyond national boundaries and is of importance for all humanity (ibid., para. 9). Currently, there are 1,007 World Heritage properties, of which 779 are cultural, 197 natural and 31 mixed (UNESCO, 2014*g*). The *Operational Guidelines* emphasize the international importance of those sites:

"The cultural and natural heritage is among the priceless and irreplaceable assets, not only of each nation, but of humanity as a whole. The loss, through deterioration or disappearance, of any of these most prized assets constitutes an impoverishment of the heritage of all the peoples of the world. Parts of that heritage, because of their exceptional qualities, can be considered to be of 'Outstanding Universal Value' and as such worthy of special protection against the dangers which increasingly threaten them" (UNESCO, 2013*a*, para. 4).

The Convention further highlights the link between heritage and socio-economic conditions. It underlines the fact that the heritage is increasingly threatened with destruction by both traditional causes of decay and changing social and economic conditions (UNESCO, 1972). And in forty-six cases the Outstanding Universal Value is indeed deemed to be in danger of being lost (UNESCO, 2014*a*). Those sites are placed on the List of World Heritage in Danger. The reasons may be natural phenomena such as earthquakes and fires, or they can be man-made, for example political conflict, new developments or tourism. Therefore, UNESCO's World Heritage and Sustainable Tourism Programme (2011) is a very timely and crucial initiative.

Sustainable tourism

Tourism is becoming a bigger industry every year. Even despite the historic milestone of 1 billion people travelling the world in 2012, there was a 5 per cent growth in 2013, equivalent to an additional 52 million international tourists (UNWTO, 2014*b*).

The World Tourism Organization (UNWTO) is the United Nations agency responsible for the promotion of responsible, sustainable and universally accessible tourism. It promotes tourism as "a driver of economic growth, inclusive development and environmental sustainability" (UNWTO, 2014*c*). UNWTO is also committed to "promoting tourism as an instrument in achieving the United Nations Millennium Development Goals (MDGs), geared towards reducing poverty and fostering sustainable development".[1] Furthermore, UNWTO and UNESCO have reached an agreement in which they commit themselves to working together on "national, regional and

1 UNWTO's membership includes 156 countries, six Associate Members and over 400 Affiliate Members (UNWTO, 2014c).

global initiatives in the areas of sustainable tourism and the safeguarding of natural and cultural heritage" (UNWTO, 2014*b*). UNWTO has a recognized definition of sustainable tourism:

"tourism that takes full account of its current and future economic, social and environmental impacts, addressing the needs of visitors, the industry, the environment and host communities" (UNWTO, 2014*a*).

However, this is not specifically related to World Heritage properties. And whereas it gives a good indication, it does not make the link between sustainable tourism and maintaining the Outstanding Universal Value. It is, therefore, important to know precisely what is meant by "sustainable tourism" when used in a World Heritage context. Having a Statement of Outstanding Universal Value is crucial in this respect as it identifies all the unique elements and attributes of a property. And sustainable management should work towards maintaining these values.

The Global Sustainable Tourism Council (GSTC) Criteria for Destinations (GSTC C–D) and the related performance indicators have taken the UNWTO destination level indicators into consideration and have been field-tested around the world (GSTC, 2014). The "destination" aspect is crucial. Although a World Heritage property should have clear boundaries, it is not a world by itself. It is part of a larger community, including local communities and businesses. When visitors come to a World Heritage property, they will often stay at accommodation in the vicinity, use local and regional transport and catering facilities. This has an impact on the direct environment of the site. Therefore, it is crucial to take the World Heritage destination into consideration when looking into the sustainable (tourism) management of the property. The challenge is to achieve partnerships with all those stakeholders, setting out rights and responsibilities. One way to do this is to establish a destination management planning (DMP) forum, which can be used to reach agreement on the way forward regarding sustainable tourism in the destination.

Thus generally applicable tools for assessing and developing sustainable tourism in the context of World Heritage are urgently needed. Clear criteria and indicators must define what is sustainable in the context of that specific World Heritage property, in order to create a baseline, make informed decisions and develop sustainable tourism strategies encompassing the needs and interests of all relevant stakeholders. This means that there must be a clear link between the Outstanding Universal Value and the definition of sustainable tourism for that property. As yet, there are no practical tools for this. However, this will change in the near future.

World Heritage and sustainable tourism

The issue of tourism at World Heritage properties is not a recent one. It is probably fair to say that as long as there has been World Heritage there have been visitors to it, even long before the sites received World Heritage status. It is also interesting to note that the first publication in the World Heritage Papers was a practical manual on managing tourism at World Heritage sites (UNESCO, 2002).

However, the *Operational Guidelines* do not mention sustainable tourism as such. There is reference to tourism in relation to the nomination dossier and the emblem, but it would be beneficial if tourism were listed in a wider context, such as under sustainable management, considering the potential impact of tourism and the fact that it has been identified as an issue for World Heritage. It is consequently crucial to make the transition from words on paper to actual practical tools in the field in order to safeguard the Outstanding Universal Value of sites. And this is precisely what the UNESCO Sustainable Tourism Programme is trying to do.

UNESCO World Heritage Tourism Programme

In 2001 the World Heritage Committee adopted tourism as one of four themes because of the "growing threats on World Heritage sites from tourism which, if sustainably managed could offer socio-economic development opportunities" (25 COM XVII.10). It was not until 2010 that the World Heritage Committee requested the World Heritage Centre to "convene a new and inclusive programme on World Heritage and Sustainable Tourism, with a steering group comprising interested States Parties and other relevant stakeholders" (34 COM 5F.2).[2] The World Heritage and Sustainable Tourism Programme (WH&ST Programme) was adopted in 2012 with a corresponding Action Plan (2013–2015) by the World Heritage Committee (36 COM 5E). The Programme aims to "create an international framework for the cooperative and coordinated achievement of shared and sustainable outcomes related to tourism at World Heritage properties" (UNESCO, 2014*f*). It is based on dialogue and stakeholder cooperation where planning for tourism and heritage management is integrated at a destination level, the natural and cultural assets are valued and protected, and appropriate tourism developed. And it is this emphasis on the destination approach which is important, as demonstrated above.

Part of the WH&ST Programme are the "How To" Guides. These guides are intended to function as a tourism management tool, taking into account the local context and needs (WHC-14/38.COM/5E). They should provide an incentive to achieve sustainable tourism management of the property as part of the larger management system (UNESCO, 2014*f*). There are a total of ten guides, of which the first three are the basic ones. The first is about understanding tourism at your destination; the second focuses

2 The World Heritage and Sustainable Tourism Programme is guided by a Steering Group, comprised of States Parties representatives from the UNESCO Electoral Groups (Argentina, China, Germany, Lebanon, Slovenia and United Republic of Tanzania,), the World Heritage Centre, the Advisory Bodies to the World Heritage Centre (ICCROM, ICOMOS, IUCN), and UNWTO (36 COM 5E).

on developing a strategy for progressive change, including the DMP; and the third deals with developing effective governance. The guides should be useful at all World Heritage properties, adaptable as they are to the specific context and challenges of each property.

Towards a Nordic-Baltic pilot region for World Heritage and sustainable tourism

The "How To" Guides have been tested in a project by the Nordic World Heritage Foundation (NWHF) entitled *Towards a Nordic-Baltic Pilot Region for World Heritage and Sustainable Tourism.*[3] This project is obviously being executed in close cooperation with the World Heritage Centre and the Nordic-Baltic region. This region was the first to help implement UNESCO's World Heritage and Sustainable Tourism Programme.

The aim of the project is to contribute to tools for assessing and developing sustainable tourism at World Heritage properties. Crucial to the project was the participation of fifteen pilot sites in the Nordic-Baltic region. They ensured the transition from text to tool by testing the "How To" Guides. Existing information was used where possible in order not to duplicate what was out there and to keep the workload of the participating pilot sites to a minimum. It is important to emphasize that the sustainable management of tourism should be part of an overall management system and not stand on its own.

The project looked at Periodic Reporting, since it is an existing monitoring tool of the World Heritage Convention. Periodic Reporting serves several purposes, among them assessing the status of Outstanding Universal Value, providing updated information regarding the state of conservation of the property, and providing a mechanism for regional cooperation and exchange of experiences between States Parties (UNESCO, 2013*b*, para. 201). However, when looking at the questionnaire of the second cycle of Periodic Reporting, it became clear that it is difficult to extrapolate specific information regarding sustainable tourism, since the questionnaire does not specifically address the subject. In order to do this, additional questions will have to be developed. Furthermore, it was felt that the current questions might serve the purpose of analysis, but they did not provide more details on sustainable tourism which could be useful as a conservation tool for the site itself or even for sharing with other World Heritage properties. It was therefore suggested to provide more space for brief explanations and added information.

---

3 In 2003 the NWHF was the first organization to be recognized as a UNESCO Category 2 Centre specifically focusing on the implementation of the World Heritage Convention. One of their Strategic Objectives is to promote sustainable development through tourism. http://nwhf.no/index.cfm?oa=content.display&con=11

The first specific result of the NWHF project was the checklist for World Heritage properties regarding their sustainable tourism management: what works well and what can be done better? Thus if the answer to a statement is yes or non-applicable, that area may be considered taken care of. A negative answer, however, indicates an area of attention. This should subsequently help with the next step of the process, the "How To" Guides. The areas of attention identified should correspond to a specific guide. For example, thanks to the checklist, if it became clear that tourism infrastructure is not as good as it could be – this corresponds with guide six, *Managing the Development of Tourism Infrastructure*. It is important to highlight that it is useful to go through all the "How To" Guides at some point, as they might contain useful information and insights, even if the area is considered to have been adequately dealt with.

Challenges for World Heritage properties regarding tourism

The fact that tourism can be both a blessing and a curse for World Heritage properties is clear. The first cycle of Periodic Reporting for Europe and North America (2001–2006) highlighted the importance of dealing with tourism in a sustainable manner. Visitor/tourism pressure (60 per cent) was identified as the most commonly reported threat to sites, except in the case of Eastern Europe. The outcomes state that:

"In all sub-regions, reports stated that there is a need for further support and development regarding visitor management. World Heritage status has brought with it the benefits of a higher profile in the tourism market but it has also left some site managers unable to cope with the pressures of rapidly rising tourism numbers. Many sites have underlined the double-sided effect of tourism increase following World Heritage inscription" (UNESCO, 2007).

The results furthermore show that only 40 per cent of the sites in the region had adopted a tourism or visitor management plan (ibid.). It will be interesting to compare these figures to those of the second cycle of Periodic Reporting (2012–2015), currently in process (WHC-14/38.COM/10 A). It was furthermore stated that "tourism management could also be seen in a wider geographic context of national or international cooperation, sharing knowledge and capacity with adjacent heritage sites and/or between sub-regions to balance the negative impacts of tourism" (ibid.).

Nevertheless, when looking at feedback on the second round of Periodic Reporting, it became clear that more attention to sustainable tourism in the World Heritage context is still needed. The impact of tourism is once again among the main factors affecting World Heritage properties (UNESCO, 2013*b*). In 2014, 20 per cent of the properties reported on to the World Heritage Committee were brought to the Committee's attention due to tourism-related issues (WHC-14/38.COM/7). Furthermore, as stated, the outcomes of the NWHF project indicate that the questionnaire of the second round of Periodic Reporting does not fully function as a tool for sharing knowledge concerning sustainable tourism between the World Heritage properties in the region, as was so hopefully expressed in the report of the first round.

Certain State of Conservation reports in 2014 illustrated the challenges that tourism can bring to World Heritage properties. Venice and its Lagoon (Italy) and the Old City of Dubrovnik (Croatia) were reported on because of the potential negative impact of tourism.

Venice and its Lagoon (Italy)

Venice and its Lagoon were inscribed on the World Heritage List in 1987.

"Founded in the 5th century and spread over 118 small islands, Venice became a major maritime power in the 10th century. The whole city is an extraordinary architectural masterpiece in which even the smallest building contains works by some of the world's greatest artists such as Giorgione, Titian, Tintoretto, Veronese and others" (UNESCO, 2104*e*).

Civil society alerted UNESCO about the state of conservation of the property. According to the 2014 World Heritage Committee, the city faces "irreversible transformations due to proposals for large infrastructure, navigation and construction projects, such as new off-shore platform, new terminals, tourist port and large leisure facilities which can seriously jeopardize the OUV of the property" (WHC-14/38.COM/7B.Add). It was therefore recommended that a sustainable tourism strategy be developed within the framework of the management system. The World Heritage Committee encouraged the State Party to "develop jointly with the major tourism and cruise companies alternative solutions to allow cruise tourists to enjoy and understand the value of Venice and also its fragility" (38.COM/7B.27). However, on 8 August 2014, just over a month after the World Heritage Committee's session, the large interministerial committee announced its intention to use a channel in the lagoon to bring the vast cruise ships into the port of Venice instead of sending them through the city, which would entail widening, straightening and dredging it. As this could have serious implications for the environment, it is still subject to an official environmental impact assessment (Da Mosto, 2014).

The Territorial Plan (PAT) aimed to exclude all ships incompatible with the historic city and with the lagoon. This has, however, not been achieved. Even more so, the regional court of Veneto region suspended the law reducing the number of cruise ships (WHC-14/38.COM/7B.Add). The fact that the regional court suspended the law shows the different values that are being placed on heritage by national, regional and local authorities. What complicates matters is that responsibilities over the Venice Lagoon are divided among the national, regional and local authorities. This further highlights the importance of applying a destination approach, including the DMP.

City of Dubrovnik (Croatia)

Another example of a World Heritage property dealing with the impact of tourism is the City of Dubrovnik, which is one of the earliest World Heritage properties, as it was inscribed in 1979 and extended in 1994.

"The 'Pearl of the Adriatic', situated on the Dalmatian coast, became an important Mediterranean sea power from the 13th century onwards. Although severely damaged by an earthquake in 1667, Dubrovnik managed to preserve its beautiful Gothic, Renaissance and Baroque churches, monasteries, palaces and fountains" (UNESCO, 2014*c*).

As in the case of Venice, civil society played an important role in transmitting information concerning the state of conservation of the City of Dubrovnik to the World Heritage Centre. Subsequently, the Centre requested the State Party to "provide clarifications on a large project in the vicinity of the World Heritage property, as well as on the progress in regulation of cruise ship tourism". The State Party reported that the Ministry of Tourism plans to develop a new Croatian Tourism Development Strategy until 2020, which will address all relevant issues, and this tourism strategy will be part of the overall management plan.

Consequently, the World Heritage Committee was recommended to provide "more concrete details on the foreseen solutions to the problem associated with high tourist numbers visiting the property in a very short time" (WHC-14/38.COM/7B.Add). The World Heritage Committee subsequently requested the submission of the management system of the property which should include a "tourism strategy and legal regulations of cruise ship tourism, as well as the project documentation and the respective heritage impact assessment" (38.COM/7B.25).

New nominations

However, not only existing World Heritage properties have tourism challenges. During the same Committee session in 2014, two new inscriptions received specific recommendations concerning their tourism management: Pyu Ancient Cities (Myanmar) and Trang An Landscape Complex (Viet Nam).

Pyu Ancient Cities (Myanmar)

The Pyu Ancient Cities property consists of the remains of three partly excavated brick, walled and moated cities, situated in an irrigated landscape in the dry zone of a river basin. They represent the Pyu Kingdoms (200 BC and AD 900). ICOMOS questioned the preparedness of the property for an increase in tourism as there was "no active consideration of the potential impacts of tourists, no monitoring of visitor numbers and no understanding of the carrying capacity of the sites" (WHC-14/38. COM/inf.8B1). They therefore recommended that a tourism plan/strategy should be developed taking into account the current situation and ways of monitoring the impacts of tourism. Interestingly enough they also requested a look into the means by which the local people might benefit from tourism. This tourism plan is crucial, as Myanmar is experiencing a sudden increase in tourism and ICOMOS noted that the property does not appear to be prepared. They therefore recommended deferring the nomination. The Committee decided that this nomination was worthy of inscription, since the property has a management plan, but it did note that this plan had to be "complemented through the ongoing development of a tourism management strategy/plan to prepare for an increase in visitors" (38.COM/8B.28).

Trang An Landscape Complex (Viet Nam)

This mixed World Heritage property in North Viet Nam is contained mostly within three protected areas in the Trang An limestone massif. It is a humid tropical tower karst landscape in the final stages of geomorphic evolution, composed of a variety of classical karst cones and towers and a network of enclosed depressions inter-connected by an intricate system of subterranean waterways (38.COM/8B.14).

ICOMOS considered that the main threats to the property "are lack of adequate regulation for development of facilities for tourism and reconstruction" and that it had "no adequate regulation for development of facilities for tourism" (WHC-14/38. COM/inf.8B1). They were of the opinion that tourism could have significant and irreversible consequences on the authenticity of the property and that involvement of the local communities in the overall management of the property was desirable. They therefore recommended deferring the nomination. The Committee decided that there was "an effective, well enforced, and adequately resourced tourism management" but nevertheless requested the State Party to "submit a revised management plan and zoning plan which includes a tourism management plan" and to effectively implement it (38.COM/8B.14).

The UNESCO WH&ST Programme could certainly play an important role in dealing with the tourism challenges identified for the above-mentioned World Heritage properties as it provides practical tools to develop tourism infrastructure and involve local communities.

Conclusion

Two aspects of tourism emerge clearly: it can assist with the protection, conservation, presentation and transmission of a World Heritage property but it can also be damaging to the property. It is therefore crucial to have a sustainable management plan for tourism included in the management system of the property; however, this is not always the case. Currently, there are no practical tools specifically for sustainable tourism management of World Heritage properties, but this is about to change. UNESCO's World Heritage and Sustainable Tourism Programme aims to create an international framework for tourism at World Heritage properties. The "How To" Guides provide knowledge and ideas for establishing a structure for sustainable tourism management and making things happen practically. Furthermore, this programme is based on stakeholder cooperation at destination level. The destination aspect is crucial, as a World Heritage property exists in a wider context with various stakeholders. The establishment of a destination management planning (DMP) forum can assist in creating partnerships with all stakeholders, setting out rights and responsibilities. Finally, it is interesting to note the increasing importance of civil society when it comes to alerting the World Heritage Centre of potential issues relating to the state of conservation of World Heritage properties.

References

Da Mosto, J. 2014. New route for Venice cruise ships would damage the lagoon. *The Art Newspaper,* online only, 20 August. http://www.theartnewspaper.com/articles/New-route-for-Venice-cruise-ships-would-damage-the-lagoon/33434 (Accessed 30 August 2014.)

GSTC. 2014. *Global Sustainable Tourism Council Criteria for Destinations.* http://www.gstcouncil.org/sustainable-tourism-gstc-criteria/criteria-for-destinations.html (Accessed 9 September 2014.)

NWHF. 2014. *What is NWHF?* Oslo, Nordic World Heritage Foundation. http://nwhf.no/index.cfm?oa=content.display&con=11 (Accessed 21 September 2014.)

Tsui, B. (ed.). 2010. *Saving our Vanishing Heritage. Safeguarding Endangered Cultural Heritage Sites in the Developing World.* Palo Alto, Calif., Global Heritage Fund.

UNESCO. 1972. *Convention concerning the Protection of the World Cultural and Natural Heritage.* Paris, UNESCO World Heritage Centre.

UNESCO. 1994, rev. edn. 2013. *Operational Guidelines for the Implementation of the World Heritage Convention.*

UNESCO. 2002. *Managing Tourism at World Heritage Sites: a Practical Manual for World Heritage Site Managers.* Paris, UNESCO World Heritage Centre. (World Heritage Papers No. 1.)

UNESCO. 2007. *Periodic Report and Action Plan, Europe 2005–2006.* Paris, UNESCO World Heritage Centre. (World Heritage Papers No. 20.)

UNESCO. 2013*a,* (rev. edn). *Operational Guidelines for the Implementation of the World Heritage Convention.* Paris, UNESCO World Heritage Centre.

UNESCO. 2013*b. Report. Mid-cycle Review Meeting for National Focal Points of the Europe and North America Region Second Cycle of the Periodic Reporting Exercise on the implementation of the World Heritage Convention.* UNESCO, Paris World Heritage Centre. http://whc.unesco.org/en/events/1081/ (Accessed 9 September 2014.)

UNESCO. 2014*a*. List of World Heritage in Danger. http://whc.unesco.org/en/danger/ (Accessed 9 September 2014.)

UNESCO. 2014*b,* Member States. http://www.unesco.org/new/en/member-states/member-states-information/ (Accessed 15 September 2014.)

UNESCO. 2014*c*. Old City of Dubrovnik. http://whc.unesco.org/en/list/95 (Accessed 9 September 2014.)

UNESCO. 2014*d*. States Parties: Ratification Status. http://whc.unesco.org/en/statesparties/ (Accessed 15 September 2014.)

UNESCO. 2014*e*. Venice and its Lagoon. http://whc.unesco.org/en/list/394 (Accessed 9 September 2014.)

UNESCO. 2014*f*. World Heritage and Sustainable Tourism Programme. http://whc.unesco.org/en/tourism/ (Accessed 9 September 2014.)

UNESCO. 2014*g*. World Heritage List. http://whc.unesco.org/en/list/ (Accessed 15 September 2014.)

UNWTO. 2014*a*. Definition. http://sdt.unwto.org/content/about-us-5 (Accessed 19 September 2014.)

UNWTO. 2014*b*. *UNWTO Annual Report 2013*. Madrid, World Tourism Organization. http://www2.unwto.org/publication/unwto-annual-report-2013

UNWTO. 2014*c*. Who we are. http://www2.unwto.org/content/who-we-are-0 (Accessed 9 September 2014.)

World Heritage Committee Documents

WHC-14/38.COM/5E

WHC-14/38.COM/7B.Add

WHC-14/38.COM/inf.8B1

WHC-14/38.COM/10 A

WHC-14/38.COM/7

World Heritage Committee Decisions

25.COM/XVII.10

34.COM/5 F.2

36.COM/5E

38.COM/7B.25

38.COM/7B.27

38.COM/8B.14

38.COM/8B.

Heritage Impact Assessments as a Tool to Open Up Perspectives for Sustainability: Three Case Studies Related to Discussions Concerning the Visual Integrity of World Heritage Cultural and Urban Landscapes

Michael Kloos

Introduction

Since the UN Conference on Environment and Development (Earth Summit) in Rio in 1992, where the action programme Agenda 21 was adopted, the idea of sustainability has become the central political concept for the world community. In total, 180 countries have obligated themselves to the principle to balance economic development with social and ecological needs (UNESCO, 2009, p. 28). Meanwhile, UNESCO has defined culture as a fourth vector of sustainability in this context. Cultural heritage in general and World Heritage sites in particular are presented in official discourses and policies as a key element for the sustainable development of human societies.

However, in recent years a relatively large number of World Heritage sites, especially cultural and urban landscapes, have witnessed serious disputes. Particularly recent discussions about the "visual integrity" of such World Heritage properties, referring to significant modifications of city images or landscape scenery (e. g. due to the erection of high-rise tower blocks or new traffic infrastructure), often led to bitter and extremely emotional discussions. Such disputes frequently brought about serious tensions between local and international decision makers, thus jeopardizing UNESCO's intention to use cultural heritage as a vector for sustainable development.

Drawing on recent fundamental research and practical experiences by the UNESCO Chair in World Cultural and Urban Landscapes at RWTH Aachen University, this paper explores possibilities of using Heritage Impact Assessments (HIAs) to support the sustainable development of World Heritage cultural and urban landscapes. Against the background of three different case studies, it is argued that communication is a key element for achieving sustainable development of such complex World Heritage sites on a large scale. Finally, recommendations are provided as to how HIAs can be used as a catalyst to support mutual communication between various stakeholders.

Conflicts about visual integrity as a challenge to the sustainable development of cultural and urban landscapes

For several years, the UNESCO Chair in World Cultural and Urban Landscapes at RWTH Aachen University has evaluated and moderated in conflicts in World Heritage sites facing high pressure to change. A head of such conflicts was the case of the former World Heritage cultural landscape Dresden Elbe Valley (Germany), which was inscribed on the UNESCO World Heritage List in 2004. Due to the conflict about the Waldschlösschen Bridge, the property was withdrawn from the World Heritage List only five years later, in 2009. What was entirely new in the case of Dresden is that a local government was ready to openly confront the decisions of UNESCO as an international organization. For example, besides other high-ranking politicians, Georg Milbradt, the former Minister President of Saxony, attacked the decisions of the World Heritage Committee in public as "close to blackmailing", putting Dresden's citizens under pressure and "punishing" them (Schorlemmer, 2008; Kloos, 2014, p. 71).

The UNESCO Chair was commissioned at the beginning of this conflict to carry out an independent evaluation concerning the impact of the planned bridge on the Outstanding Universal Value of Dresden's World Heritage property. To evaluate this complex case, a previously developed and tested methodology for carrying out Heritage Impact Assessments (HIAs) consisting of three different steps was applied. First, the

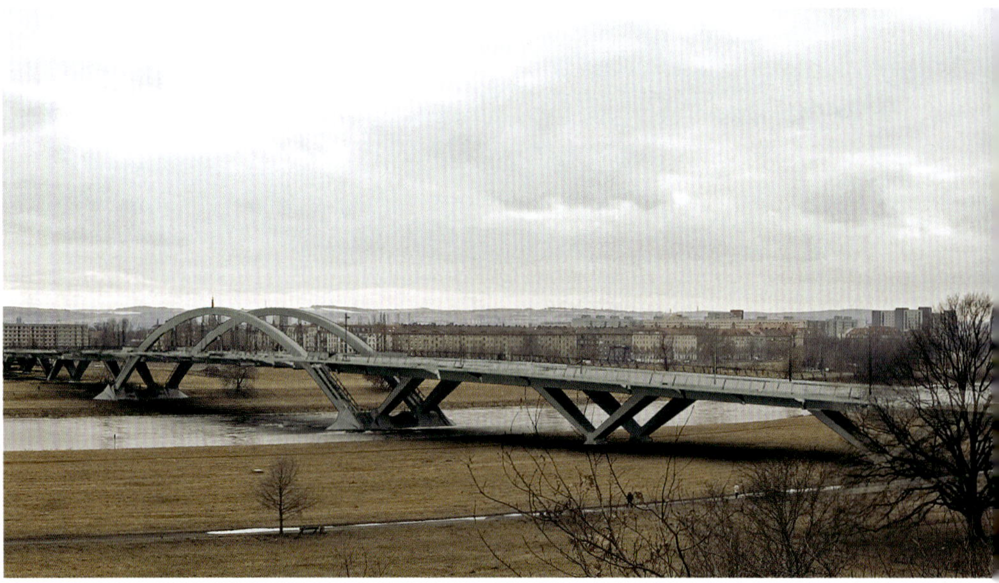

Fig. 1: Visualization of the Waldschlösschen Bridge (© Institute for Urban and Regional Planning, RWTH Aachen University)

inscription criteria, especially the Outstanding Universal Value, were carefully assessed. Second, a thorough analysis of the cultural, historical and symbolic values of the World Heritage property was carried out in order to define and qualify important viewpoints and sightlines. As a third step, a 3D-computer model of the site was generated. This was the basis for producing very precise visualizations, which were generated by superimpositions of GPS-related digital camera photographs and the 3D-computer model. As a result, the transformations of the landscape scenery or city silhouettes could clearly be shown and their impact evaluated and assessed according to the World Heritage site's criteria of inscription.

It was clearly mentioned in the nomination dossier of the former Dresden Elbe Valley World Heritage cultural landscape, that the existing sight connections were considered an important part of its Outstanding Universal Value (ICOMOS, 2003). As the visualizations showed that at least some of these sight connections would be severely disturbed, the HIA led to the result that the planned bridge would have an irreversible negative impact on the preservation and sustainable development of the World Heritage property (Kloos et al., 2006, p. 111). As a reaction to this report the UNESCO World Heritage Committee inscribed Dresden Elbe Valley on the List of World Heritage in Danger (Ringbeck and Rössler, 2011). This was the beginning of a three-year discussion which finally ended up with the World Heritage Committee's decision to withdraw Dresden Elbe Valley from the World Heritage List. Consequently, the HIA

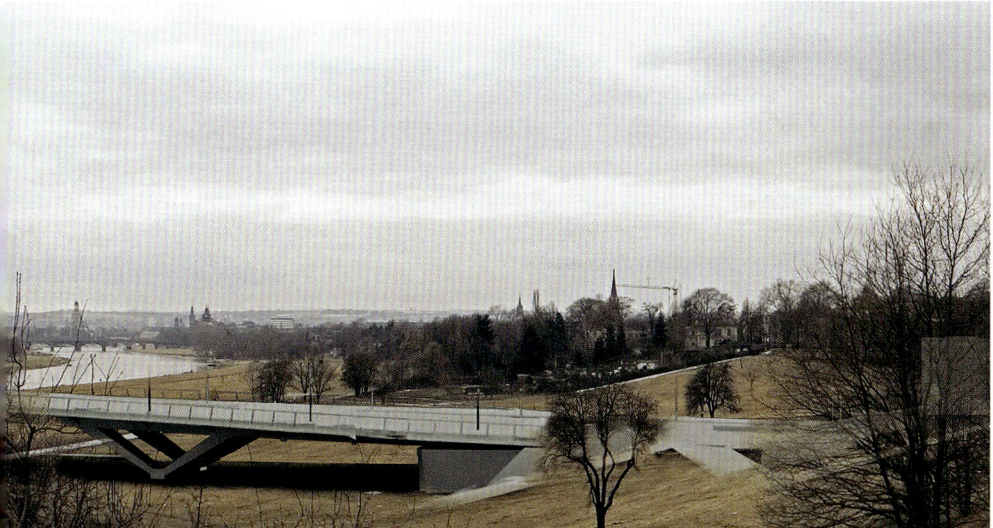

could neither contribute to the moderation of the conflict nor to the sustainable development of Dresden Elbe Valley. Ultimately, the HIA had even been an important factor in the delisting of the property.

But why could the HIA not contribute to solving this conflict? Retrospectively it can be stated that the following two reasons were crucial in this respect:

(1) Lack of time

The German Commission for UNESCO and the City of Dresden agreed to commission the HIA only six weeks before the planned tendering of the bridge. Consequently, the remaining time span for the evaluation was extremely short. The immediate results of the evaluation could not be discussed with the commissioner of the study, the City of Dresden. Similarly, alternative solutions or modifications of the bridge design could neither be elaborated nor communicated during the study.

(2) Lack of communication

Finally, the City of Dresden had financed an HIA, but its representatives were left with a negative result while solutions and "ways out" could not be shown. Confronted with this situation, both Dresden's representatives and important decision-makers of the Federal State of Saxony concentrated on proving alleged shortcomings of the methodology of the HIA, rather than intensifying communication with the World Heritage Committee and its Advisory Bodies. As a result, the ultimate goal – finding a solution for the question of the Waldschlösschen Bridge – was eclipsed by a serious conflict between local and international decision-makers.

To summarize, it can be stated that the HIA could not contribute to overcoming the lack of communication, that is, the lack of willingness to communicate which in turn led to the escalation of the conflict between the two parties. Future HIAs carried out by the UNESCO Chair, however, could contribute significantly to moderating similar conflicts at World Heritage sites. To explore the possibilities of using HIAs as a tool to support the sustainable development of World Heritage cultural and urban landscapes, two of these studies are examined in more detail in the following sections.

HIAs as a tool for mediation and to stimulate communication: the case of the Golden Horn Metro Bridge (Istanbul)

In 2010 the question of whether a new metro bridge could be built in Istanbul had to be evaluated. The newly planned bridge was meant to link the two European parts of Istanbul's inner city. These plans arose because Istanbul is a rapidly growing metropolis. Currently the city has approx. 13 million inhabitants, but in only ten years this number could have passed the 20 million mark. Consequently, the extension of Istanbul's public transport system serves as a key element for both coping with the

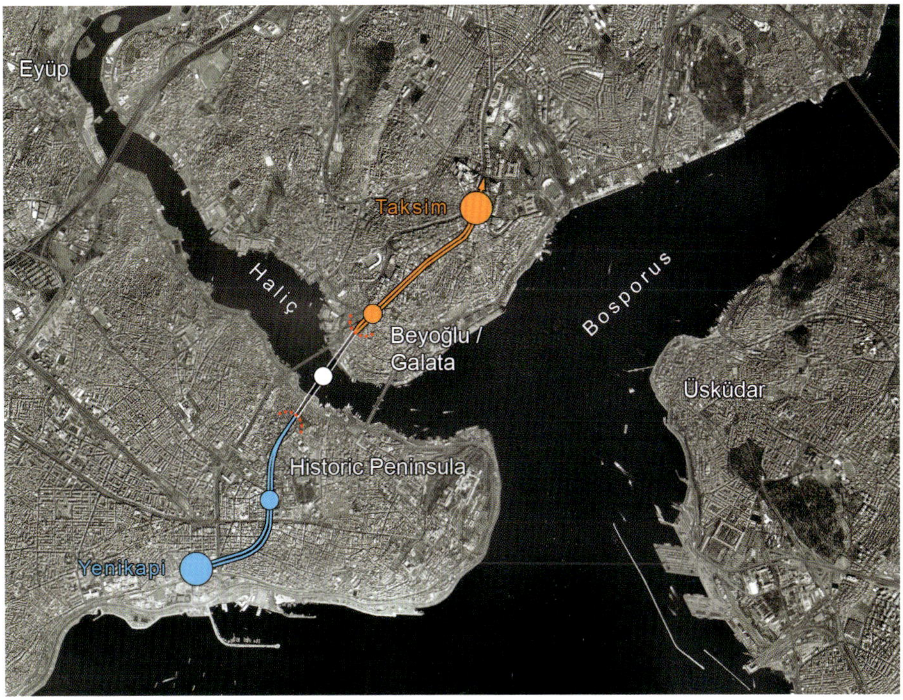

Fig. 2: Planned metro line and location of the bridge (white point on map) (© Institute for Urban and Regional Planning, RWTH Aachen University)

environmental problems of the city and managing its sustainable development. As a result, there was no dispute between the UNESCO World Heritage Committee and local stakeholders as to whether this new metro link would be necessary or not. It was also clear that the bridge proposal could not be replaced by a tunnel due to the extremely complicated geological conditions at the envisaged construction site.

However, discussions evolved about the bridge design, which was initially presented to UNESCO as a cable-stayed construction supported by two pylons each over 80 metres in height. Additionally, a covered metro stop with a length of 180 metres was integrated on the bridge. Due to the dominance of the bridge, UNESCO and its Advisory Bodies feared that this project would have a negative impact on Istanbul's historical city silhouette. Concerns especially appeared that the bridge would stand in concurrence to Süleymaniye Mosque, one of Istanbul's four World Heritage areas and a significant part of the Historic Peninsula's characteristic urban landscape.

Prior to commissioning the HIA in December 2010, Istanbul Metropolitan Municipality and the Turkish State Party respectively had been repeatedly requested by the World Heritage Committee to submit additional information concerning the "large-scale development and infrastructure projects [in Istanbul] and to carry out

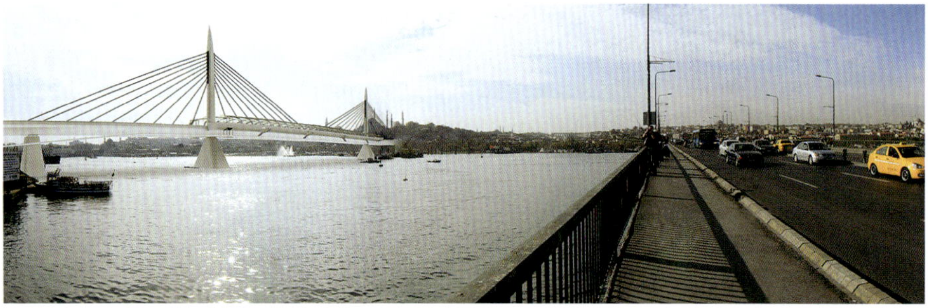

Fig. 3: Visualization of the planned Golden Horn Metro Bridge – Süleymaniye Mosque visible in the background (© Institute for Urban and Regional Planning, RWTH Aachen University)

impact studies to international standards" on them (Kloos et al., 2011, p. 86). However, the planned project had already been approved by Istanbul Metropolitan Municipality in 2005. Consequently, construction work gradually commenced in parallel to the Committee's requests. Work on the foundations of the bridge, reaching to a depth of more than 100 metres, had already been finished before the HIA was started. Alongside this, the two metro tunnels which were meant to connect the planned bridge with Istanbul's metro network had already been finished several years before. In short, prior to the HIA there were a large number of misunderstandings and serious frictions between the State Party and the UNESCO World Heritage Committee and it was no longer possible to think about alternative locations for the bridge. Moreover, the time span for finishing the HIA was even shorter than for Dresden. As a result, the point of departure for the HIA on the planned Golden Horn Metro Bridge was even more inconvenient than in the case of the Waldschlösschen Bridge.

Confronted with these difficult conditions, a Preliminary Report was carried out on this case as a first step of the assessment. This report was meant to inform all stakeholders at local and international levels as transparently as possible about the stage of the construction work, as well as the potential impact of the planned bridge and the expected outcomes of the HIA End Report.

As the first visualizations carried out during the Preliminary Report clearly showed that the planned bridge would negatively affect the integrity of Süleymaniye Mosque, one of the main goals of the ongoing process was to avoid further escalation of the conflict, so that a similar situation to Dresden, where the HIA commissioners were also confronted with a negative result but alternatives could no longer be developed, would not occur. Hence, it was jointly decided with local stakeholders that an international expert panel should be integrated into the evaluation process, with the goal of working together on possible options to minimize the impact on Süleymaniye Mosque in parallel to the compilation of the HIA. Concerning the expert panel, it was crucial to bring in both expertise in international World Heritage policy as well as additional skills and experience in structural engineering. Against this background, Dr Birgitta Ringbeck (German Representative to the World Heritage Committee), Dr Christopher Young (English Heritage), Prof. Dr Moawiyah Ibrahim (Jordan Representative to the World Heritage Committee) and Prof. Dr Jörg Schlaich (schlaich bergermann und partner) were asked to join this international expert panel.

The involvement of these international experts turned out to be an extremely useful step in the whole working process. Prof. Dr Schlaich developed several alternatives to the existing bridge design that were immediately discussed in two working sessions in Frankfurt and Istanbul. Among other things, this cooperation of local and international stakeholders led to the result that the pylons of the bridge could be lowered. A second suggestion was to modify the planned metro halt on the bridge in order to make it appear lighter and smaller. Moreover, a new concept for the lighting and colour of the bridge was suggested, with the goal of reducing its dominance in Istanbul's inner city. Finally, the design of the surroundings of both bridgeheads was adjusted in order to preserve important archaeological sites and improve the integration of the bridge into its sensitive environment.

Afterwards both the original and the new proposal for the bridge were evaluated and compared in the HIA-End Report in order to inform the Committee that first steps to modify the bridge had already been undertaken. Additionally, the process of evaluation and modification of the existing bridge design was fully documented in the Report by schlaich bergermann und partner. As a general recommendation it was stressed in the HIA-End Report that the documented state of affairs should be seen as an intermediate rather than an end result, since the whole working process had had to be managed within an extremely constricted period. Consequently, it was also suggested in the End Report that the bridge design should be further developed during its construction under the supervision of international experts, including representatives of the World Heritage Centre. Ultimately, the World Heritage Committee accepted these suggestions. Thus the HIA and the associated communication strategy turned out to be a crucial contribution to mediation of the conflict over the Golden Horn Metro Bridge.

HIAs as a tool to activate sustainable urban development: The case of Cologne Cathedral (Germany)

Although a serious confrontation as in Dresden could be avoided in Istanbul, it was already too late to actively influence the reconciliation of Istanbul's rapid development with the preservation of the city's extremely valuable cultural heritage. The conflict had mainly been solved at a political level. In Cologne, however, it proved possible to achieve such an active contribution to the city's sustainable development with the help of an HIA. Here, it had to be evaluated whether the so-called ICE High-Rise Cluster – an ensemble of five high-rise tower blocks planned in the immediate vicinity

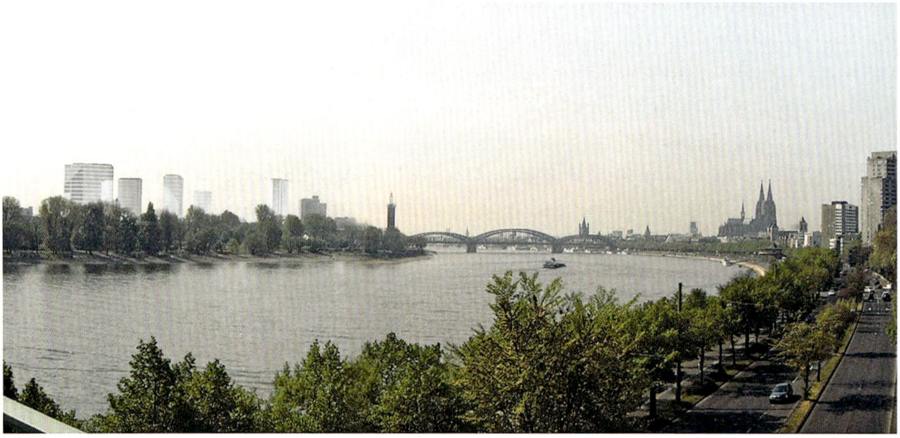

Fig. 4: Visualization of the cluster (left) and the cathedral (right) (© Institute for Urban and Regional Planning, RWTH Aachen University)

of Cologne Cathedral on the opposite side of the Rhine next to Köln-Deutz railway station – would have a negative impact on this UNESCO World Heritage site. Prior to the assessment, in 2004, the UNESCO World Heritage Committee had already included the cathedral on the List of World Heritage in Danger (Ringbeck, 2006). Similarly to the cases of Dresden and Istanbul, friction between local and international decision-makers was soon evident. The former mayor of Cologne, Fritz Schramma, for example, stated that it cannot be that "a city must not develop further only because it has a cathedral" (Kloos, 2014, p. 402). Besides, the majority of the local press clearly supported the high-rise concept (Ringbeck, 2006).

The HIA concerning this case had been commissioned by the Federal Republic of North Rhine Westphalia, which was in charge of compiling a report on the case of Cologne Cathedral for the World Heritage Committee. Based on a thorough cultural and historical analysis of Cologne's city structure and its distinctive silhouette, several of the visualizations generated clearly showed that the dominance of the cathedral's characteristic silhouette would suffer under the planned high-rise scheme. This referred especially to habitual views from the right bank of the Rhine, which were identified in the study as an important element of the experience of Cologne's city silhouette. As a result, it was recommended that the ICE High-Rise Cluster should be reviewed and the buffer zone around Cologne Cathedral should be enlarged by a monitored zone in order to avoid similar conflicts in the future (Ringbeck, 2006; Kloos et al., 2005).

The HIA was presented at the 2005 UNESCO conference on World Heritage and Contemporary Architecture: Managing the Historic Urban Landscape in Vienna (Austria). At the same conference a representative of the City of Cologne, *inter alia*, offered to revise two tower blocks of the planned high-rise scheme and to enlarge the buffer zone around the Cathedral. Nevertheless, the World Heritage Committee's Decision taken in 2005 still considered withdrawing Cologne Cathedral from the World Heritage List. According to the Committee, the so-called Jahn Tower had to be revised in particular, although at that point it had not been called into question by the City of Cologne (Ringbeck, 2006).

However, in parallel to this situation it gradually became clear that the economic concept of the Jahn Tower had failed because potential tenants were missing. This new situation opened up the possibility for a new general approach to resolve this situation. Based on a decision of the Cologne City Council in December 2005, intending to change the high-rise scheme to achieve full compliance with the latest decision of the World Heritage Committee, it was agreed that a moderated workshop should be organized by the City of Cologne. This workshop was meant to integrate some sixty representatives of relevant groups of Cologne's city population and three renowned urban planning offices (Stadt Köln, 2006). The multi-stage workshop, conceived and moderated by Prof. Kunibert Wachten, was organized as a cooperative planning process with a time span of seven weeks. The three urban planning offices were requested to present intermediate states of their plans during three different sessions which were organized as a mixed system of panel discussions and work in smaller groups. During these sessions, the invited representatives acted as an expert panel, providing recommendations and ideas for the elaboration of the various proposals. This working method allowed the urban planning offices to outline their plans successively. At the same time, the ideas and thoughts of the representatives of Cologne's city population were integrated into the proposals during the working sessions, thus generating a broad consensus concerning the project (Stadt Köln, 2006, p. 9).

This multi-stage cooperative workshop led to the result that the existing planning scheme consisting of five high-rise tower blocks could be replaced by a more compact and lower ensemble of buildings (Stadt Köln, 2009, p. 24). A particularly interesting aspect of this result was that the newly suggested planning scheme was not only far more flexible in terms of its use than the originally planned tower blocks but also more efficient in economic terms. Besides, Cologne Cathedral was removed from the

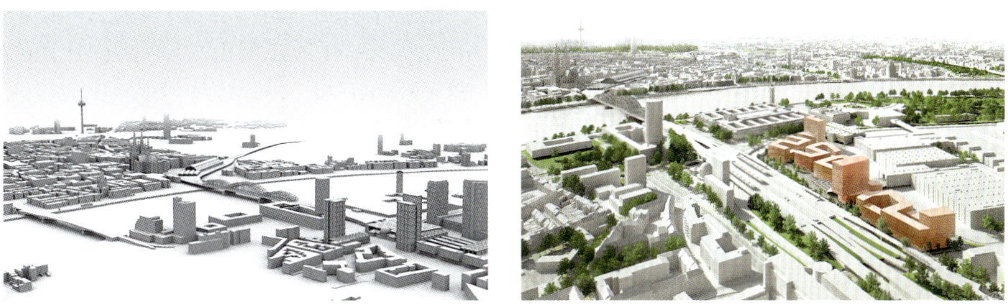

Figs 5a, 5b: Originally planned ICE High-Rise Cluster and the scheme that was finally realized after a cooperative workshop (© v-cube/© HH Vision/STRABAG-ECE)

List of World Heritage in Danger by the UNESCO World Heritage Committee after the City of Cologne had decided to carry out this new scheme. Meanwhile, the concept has been further refined and it will probably be realized soon. Hence, the compilation of the HIA and the cooperative workshop had been important steps towards a solution aligning economic, societal, ecological and cultural aspects. In general, the intensive discussions about Cologne's cultural heritage turned out to be a valuable contribution for the city's sustainable development.

Conclusion: Communication as a key element to achieve sustainability and HIAs as a tool to support communication

To summarize, it can be stated that the three above-mentioned cases concerning the visual impact of new planning schemes on UNESCO World Heritage cultural and urban landscapes show that communication is a key element in achieving the sustainable development of such complex properties on a large scale. This is completely congruent with the definition of sustainable development provided in the Brundtland Report, where the concept of sustainability is defined as follows:

"Sustainable development meets the needs of the present without compromising the ability of future generations to meet their own needs" (WCED, 1987).

According to this definition, sustainability is a notion oriented towards the present needs of humanity but obviously directed to the future at the same time. "Sustainability" therefore remains largely undefined in terms of its content. Hence, there is no silver bullet leading to more sustainability and it is impossible to define fixed criteria that lead to sustainable development. Elaborating concepts for sustainability therefore means, as stated by the geographer Urs Müller, to "negotiate between various values in a democratic manner and to incorporate various conceptions into this process. The focus of sustainable development is", according to Müller, "the communication itself" (Müller, 2006; Kloos, 2014, p. 445).

Which targets are (or will be) related to sustainable development or to sustainable management, is therefore largely dependent on the stakeholders concerned and on further place-related factors in which the World Heritage Convention is implemented. As a result, an indispensable precondition to elaborating sustainable development is a broad understanding between all stakeholders. This is indeed true for UNESCO World Heritage cultural and urban landscapes, which have a large degree of complexity, making controversial opinions concerning their preservation and development almost inevitable.

HIAs can stimulate such discussions in the context of sustainability. However, the above case studies show that the following three aspects should always be taken into account:

Use HIAs in time

Currently, HIAs are mostly commissioned fairly late in disputes concerning World Heritage sites. As a result, it is often no longer possible to solve conflicts completely and to achieve results with optimum quality. This is clearly shown by the cases of Dresden and Istanbul. Consequently, HIAs should be commissioned and compiled before relevant decisions are made. In the best scenario, they should be used in parallel to the development of new planning schemes in order to evaluate the potential impact on their environment as soon as possible.

Use HIAs as an active tool to offer solutions rather than constraints

As HIAs are often commissioned late in disputes, they frequently have to be carried out in an atmosphere of conflict influenced by various stakeholders and interest groups. It is therefore very important to communicate transparently and as early as possible about the development of HIAs, their methodology and the expected results. The case of Dresden clearly shows that HIAs can even lead to additional frictions when negative results are expected. In such cases the focus should be on possible (alternative) solutions besides the assessment itself in order to give latitude for future decisions. The cases of Istanbul and Cologne show that such a concept of HIAs helps to solve existing conflicts and can even lead to more sustainability in the end results.

Use HIAs together with communication strategies

A very efficient instrument to turn HIAs into tools to support sustainability is to use them together with tailor-made communication strategies. This is especially necessary if HIAs lead to the result that the Outstanding Universal Value of World Heritage properties will be negatively affected. In this context, moderated cooperative workshops

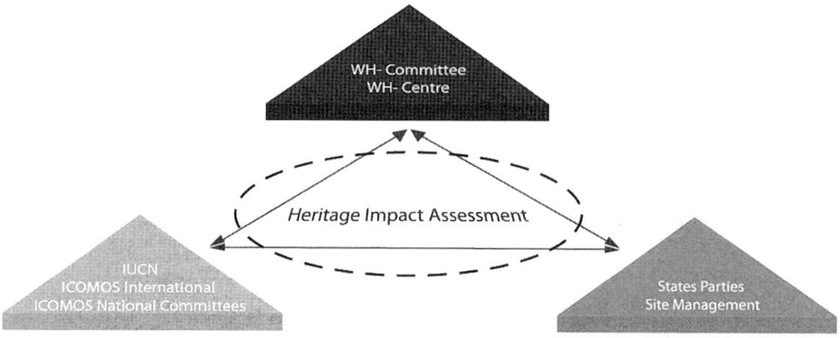

Fig. 6: Heritage Impact Assessments as a communication tool (© Michael Kloos)

integrating representatives of politics, architectural or urban planning offices, as well as other disciplines and stakeholders, are a helpful tool in reaching a consensus. Cooperative workshops are also helpful in setting out the framework for future steps of planning and management in sensitive World Heritage sites and their surroundings. However, recent experiences with cooperative workshops also show that it is vital to select the participating architectural and planning offices carefully, as they actively influence these processes by bringing in their ideas and skills. Consequently, their expertise in urban planning should be combined with a high affinity for the preservation of cultural (or natural) heritage.

In general, all the cases discussed show that HIAs are a valuable instrument in raising awareness of cultural (or natural) heritage as an important asset of collective identity. Thus they are a tool to meet the needs of the present without compromising the ability of future generations to meet their own needs. In other words, they are a tool to open up perspectives for sustainability.

References

ICOMOS. 2003. *Advisory Body Evaluation Dresden Elbe Valley* (1156.pdf). http://whc.unesco.org/archive/advisory_body_evaluation/1156.pdf (Accessed 28 October 2014.)

Kloos, M. 2014. *Landscape 4. Landscape Ideas in Northern Europe and Visual Integrity of UNESCO World Heritage Cultural and Urban Landscapes*. PhD thesis electronically published at RWTH Aachen University. http://darwin.bth.rwth-aachen.de/opus3/volltexte/2014/5078/

Kloos, M., Korus, C., Nadrowska, M. and Wachten, K. 2006. *Gutachten zu den visuellen Auswirkungen des "Verkehrszugs Waldschlösschenbrücke" auf das UNESCO-Weltkulturerbe "Elbtal Dresden"*. Aachen, Germany, RWTH Aachen University.

Kloos, M., Manleitner, N., Rekittke, J. and Wachten, K. 2005. *Unabhängiges Gutachten zur "Stadtbildverträglichkeitsuntersuchung zu Hochhausplanungen in Köln"*. Aachen, Germany, RWTH Aachen University.

Kloos, M., Tebart, P. and Wachten, K. 2011. *Independent Assessment of the Visual Impact of the Golden Horn Metro Crossing Bridge on the World Heritage property "Historic Areas of Istanbul"*. Aachen, Germany, RWTH Aachen University.

Müller, U. 2006. Die Macht der Bilder in der nachhaltigen Entwicklung. In: U. Müller-Böker (ed.), N. Backhaus et al., *Kraft der Bilder. Vorstellungen über Nachhaltigkeit – ein Entscheidungsspiel*. Zurich, Druckerei der Zentralstelle der Studentenschaft Zürich.

Ringbeck, B. 2006. Welterbe Kölner Dom: Chronologie eines Streites. Rat der Stadt Köln beschließt Änderung des umstrittenen Bebauungsplans. *Denkmalpflege im Rheinland*, Vol. 23, No. 2.

Ringbeck, B. and Rössler, M. 2011. Between international obligations and local politics: the case of the Dresden Elbe Valley under the 1972 World Heritage Convention. *Informationen zur Raumentwicklung*, Vol. 3, No. 4.

Schorlemmer von, Sabine. 2008. Compliance with the UNESCO World Heritage Convention:
Reflections on the Elbe Valley and the Dresden Waldschlösschen Bridge. *German Yearbook of International Law*, Vol. 51.

Stadt Köln and scheuvens + wachten. 2006. *Städtebauliche Entwicklung im Umfeld Bahnhof Köln-Messe/Deutz. Dokumentation des Werkstattverfahrens*. Cologne/Dortmund.

Stadt Köln. 2009. *Rechtsrheinisches Entwicklungskonzept/Teilraum Nord (REK-Nord): Deutz-Nord/ Mülheim-Süd/Buchforst*. Cologne, DFS Druck Brecher GmbH.

UNESCO. 2009. *World Heritage Cultural Landscapes. A Handbook for Conservation and Management*. Edited by N. Mitchell, M. Rössler and P.-M. Tricaut. Paris, UNESCO World Heritage Centre. (World Heritage Papers No. 26.) http://whc.unesco.org/en/series/26/

WCED. 1987. *Report of the World Commission on Environment and Development. Our Common Future*. (Brundtland Report). New York, United Nations. http://www.un-documents.net/ wced-ocf.htm (Accessed 23 March 2013.)

Annex

The following annex is a compilation of websites with further information, documents, resolutions and declarations on Heritage and Sustainability. The editor would like to indicate that the accessibility of the websites was last checked in January 2015.

Council of Europe, 2000, European Landscape Convention, http://conventions.coe.int/Treaty/Commun/QueVoulezVous.asp?NT=176&CM=8&CL=ENG

ICOMOS, 2011, Paris Declaration on Heritage as a Driver of Development, http://www.international.icomos.org/Paris2011/GA2011_Declaration_de_Paris_EN_20120109.pdf

International Federation of Arts Councils and Culture Agencies (IFACCA), 2013, Culture as Goal in the Post-2015 Development Agenda, http://media.ifacca.org/files/cultureasgoalweb.pdf

UNESCO, 1972, Convention Concerning the Protection of the World Cultural and Natural Heritage, http://whc.unesco.org/archive/convention-en.pdf

UNESCO, 1982, Mexico City Declaration on Cultural Policies, http://portal.unesco.org/culture/en/files/12762/11295421661mexico_en.pdf/mexico_en.pdf

UNESCO, 1997, Declaration on the Responsibilities of the Present Generations Towards Future Generations, http://portal.unesco.org/en/ev.php-URL_ID=13178&URL_DO=DO_TOPIC&URL_SECTION=201.html

UNESCO, 2001, Universal Declaration on Cultural Diversity, http://portal.unesco.org/en/ev.php-URL_ID=13179&URL_DO=DO_TOPIC&URL_SECTION=201.html

UNESCO, 2002, The Budapest Declaration on World Heritage, http://unesdoc.unesco.org/images/0012/001257/125796e.pdf

UNESCO, 2003, Convention on the Safeguarding of Intangible Heritage, http://unesdoc.unesco.org/images/0013/001325/132540e.pdf

UNESCO, 2005, Convention on the Promotion and Protection of the Diversity of Cultural Expressions, http://portal.unesco.org/en/ev.php-URL_ID=31038&URL_DO=DO_TOPIC&URL_SECTION=201.html

UNESCO, 2005, Vienna Memorandum on "World Heritage and Contemporary Architecture – Managing the Historic Urban Landscape", http://whc.unesco.org/archive/2005/whc05-15ga-inf7e.pdf

UNESCO, 2011, Future of the World Heritage Convention, http://whc.unesco.org/archive/2011/whc11-18ga-11-en.pdf

UNESCO, 2011, Recommendation on the Historic Urban Landscape, http://portal.unesco.org/en/ev.php-URL_ID=48857&URL_DO=DO_TOPIC&URL_SECTION=201.html

UNESCO, 2011, Strategic Action Plan for the Implementation of the World Heritage Convention 2012–2022. Future of the World Heritage Convention. Document WHC-11/18.GA/11, http://whc.unesco.org/archive/2011/whc11-18ga-11-en.pdf

UNESCO, 2012, Culture: a driver and enabler of sustainable development, Thematic Think Peace, https://en.unesco.org/post2015/sites/post2015/files/Think%20Piece%20Culture.pdf

UNESCO, 2012, Kyoto Vision, http://whc.unesco.org/document/120133

UNESCO, 2012, Reports of the World Heritage Centre and Advisory Bodies. World Heritage Convention and Sustainable Development. Document WHC-12/36.COM/5C, http://whc.unesco.org/archive/2012/whc12-36com-5C-en.pdf

UNESCO, 2013, The Hangzhou Declaration – Placing Culture at the Heart of Sustainable Development Policies, http://www.unesco.org/new/fileadmin/MULTIMEDIA/HQ/CLT/images/FinalHangzhouDeclaration20130517.pdf

United Cities and Local Governments (UCLG), 2008, Agenda 21 for Culture, 8 May 2004, http://www.agenda21culture.net/index.php/documents/agenda-21-for-culture

United Cities and Local Governments (UCLG), 2010, Culture: Fourth Pillar of Sustainable Development, http://www.culturaldevelopment.net.au/wp-content/uploads/2010/11/Culture4pillar-policy.pdf

United Nations (UN), 2000, Resolution 55/2. United Nations Millennium Declaration, http://www.un.org/millennium/declaration/ares552e.htm

United Nations (UN), 2010, Keeping the promise: united to achieve the Millennium Development Goals – Outcome Document of the 2010 MDG Summit, http://www.un.org/en/mdg/summit2010/pdf/mdg%20outcome%20document.pdf

United Nations (UN), 2011. Resolution 65/166. Culture and development, http://www.un.org/en/ga/search/view_doc.asp?symbol=A/RES/65/166

United Nations (UN), 2012, Resolution 66/208. Culture and development, http://daccess-dds-ny.un.org/doc/UNDOC/GEN/N11/471/30/PDF/N1147130.pdf?OpenElement

United Nations (UN), 2012, The Future we want, outcome document of the UN Rio + 20 Summit, http://www.uncsd2012.org/content/documents/727The%20Future%20We%20Want%2019%20June%201230pm.pdf

United Nations, Open Working Group proposal for Sustainable Development Goals, http://sustainabledevelopment.un.org/content/documents/1579SDGs%20Proposal.pdf

Notes on Contributors

Albert, Marie – Theres is Chair of Intercultural Studies, studied educational science, sociology and educational economics at TU Berlin. She earned her Dr. phil and qualified as a university lecturer (Habilitation) in Educational Sciences at TU Berlin on the strength of her thesis, entitled "The Limits of 'culturalist' Pedagogical Conceptions in Light of Critical Cross-Border Developments". Since 1994, she has served as Head of the Chair of Intercultural Studies at the Brandenburg University of Technology Cottbus-Senftenberg, and since October 2003, is Chair holder of the UNITWIN/UNESCO Chair in Heritage Studies. She is the initiator and former Head (1999–2010) of the Master's programme "World Heritage Studies", and since 2010, initiator and Head of the PhD programme "International Graduate School: Heritage Studies at Cottbus-Senftenberg University". Her research endeavours focus on issues such as protecting tangible and intangible heritage, identity and development, in addition to educational development in the developing countries. She is the editor of the "World Heritage Studies" series and the "Heritage Studies" series, which critically evaluate theories related to world heritage.

Bandarin, Francesco is Professor of Urban Planning at the University IUAV of Venice. He served as Director of the UNESCO World Heritage Centre from 2000 to 2011 and as UNESCO Assistant Director-General for Culture from 2010 to 2014. He was trained as an Architect (Venice, 1975) and as an Urban Planner (UC Berkeley, 1977). He has written numerous publications, and co-authored The Historic Urban Landscape: Managing Heritage in an Urban Century, 2012 and Reconnecting the City, 2014, both published by Wiley-Blackwell, London.

Boccardi, Giovanni graduated in Architecture from the University of Rome (1988), with a dissertation on the restoration of monuments, and obtained a Master Degree on Sustainable Heritage from the University College of London. As a free-lance and then UNESCO staff, he worked for several years in various regions of the world, implementing conservation projects. In 2001, Mr. Boccardi joined the UNESCO World Heritage Centre in Paris where he was responsible for programmes in the Arab and Asia Units, as well as for sustainable development issues. Recently, he has been appointed Head of the newly established Unit for Emergency Preparedness and Response in the Culture Sector of UNESCO.

Engels, Barbara has worked since 2002 as scientific officer at the German Federal Agency for Nature Conservation (BfN). Her work covers international cooperation with a focus on World Natural Heritage as well tourism and nature conservation. She is a member of the German delegation to the World Heritage Committee and an elected member of the German National Commission for UNESCO (DUK). Barbara Engels is also a member of the IUCN World Commission on Protected Areas (WCPA).

Erlewein, Shina studied Social and Cultural Anthropology at Free University Berlin as well as History and Society of South Asia and Gender Studies at Humboldt University of Berlin. In 2014, she graduated from the PhD programme Heritage Studies at BTU Cottbus-Senftenberg with the thesis, entitled "Screening Intangible Heritage: The Role of Audio-Visual Media in the Representation of Intangible Heritage. The Case of Kutiyattam Sanskrit Theatre in India". Her research interests lie in the field of heritage studies and cultural policy, visual and media anthropology, cultural studies, religion, performance studies and intercultural communication.

Forero, Juliana is an anthropologist, PhD in Urban Studies from Huazhong University of Science and Technology (China) and MA in Social Anthropology from Andes University, (Colombia). She has worked in cultural heritage management at the City Hall of Bogota and the Ministry of Culture of Colombia. Since 2008 Juliana has been in China, associated with the laboratory of Sustainable Development of the School of Urban Planning (HUST) and the Cultural Bureau of Hubei Province, working on cultural heritage conservation and sustainability in the cities of Wuhan, Guangdong and Qinzhou. Since 2013 Juliana has been programme specialist for research at the World Heritage Institute of Training and Research for the Asia and the Pacific Region (WHITRAP-UNESCO) focusing her research on the social function of heritage, community participation, public policies, as well as notions of memory, territory and identity, the concept of Western and Asian shifts of cultural heritage, and historic urban landscapes.

Hosagrahar, Prof., Jyoti holds the UNESCO Chair for Culture, Habitat, and Sustainable Development at the Srishti School of Art, Design, and Technology, Bangalore. She is a professor at Columbia University, New York; Chair of the PhD programme at Srishti; and Founder-Director of Sustainable Urbanism International, an NGO in Bangalore, India, and a research unit at GSAPP, Columbia University. Since 2011, Hosagrahar has served as an expert member of the national Advisory Committee for World Heritage Matters under the aegis of the Ministry of Culture, Government of India. She serves on the Executive Committee of ICOMOS India and is on the Scientific Board of the ICOMOS International Scientific Committee on the Theory and Philosophy of Conservation and Restoration. Hosagrahar is a Global Advisor for the UN Global Compact Cities Programme, coauthor of the Policy paper for "Operationalizing Culture in the Sustainable Development of Cities" for GOLD IV of the UN United Cities and Local Governments, and an Expert Group member on Public Space with UNHABITAT. For UNESCO, Hosagrahar has authored "Culture: A Driver and an Enabler of Sustainable Development", Thematic Think Piece for the UN System Task Team on the Post-2015 UN Development Agenda, 2012; and two background papers for the Hangzhou Congress on Culture and Development, 2013.

Kloos, Dr., Michael is an architect and urban planner. Between 1997 and 2003 he realized various awarded buildings in the Netherlands as responsible architect. In 2003, he became Scientific Assistant at Prof. Wachten's Institute for Urban Design and Regional Planning at the Faculty of Architecture at RWTH Aachen University, Germany. Since 2005 he compiles Heritage Impact Assessments and Management Plans for UNESCO World Heritage sites and he has been involved in transnational serial nomination projects. In 2012 he co-established the UNESCO Chair in World Cultural and Urban Landscapes at RWTH Aachen University which aims to support the preservation and sustainable development of Cultural and Urban Landscapes inscribed in the World Heritage List and facing high pressure to change. Recently he finished his PhD thesis, Landscape 4, which investigates questions about the visual integrity of World Heritage sites.

Peters, Manuel is an academic assistant at the Chair of Intercultural Studies/UNESCO Chair in Heritage Studies at BTU Cottbus-Senftenberg. He studied intercultural pedagogy and social sciences in Berlin, Madrid, and Oldenburg. He has a rich variety of experiences in intercultural and political education, media education and as a social worker. His teaching and research interests are in Cultural Studies, Theory and Research in Intercultural Education, Culture in International Relations, Heritage Studies and Migration. For his doctoral thesis he is researching transnational mobilities, i. e. processes of 'self'-formation and 'Bildung' in the context of voluntary engagement in 'development' cooperation.

Rode, Robert, MA, is a researcher whose interests include theories of culture and heritage, cultural approaches to globalization, as well as global institutions. Currently, he is coordinator of the International Graduate School: Heritage Studies at BTU Cottbus-Senftenberg and as scientific assistant at the Intercultural Chair he teaches in the MA programme World Heritage Studies. His doctoral dissertation project focuses on the impact of the United Nations Declaration on the Rights of Indigenous Peoples on heritage conservation practices. He has presented papers on critical approaches to development in heritage studies, indigenous peoples' sacred natural sites, participatory forms of indigenous heritage conservation, the influence of epistemic communities on heritage values, and intangible cultural heritage in Germany, Finland, France and the Netherlands. Prior to his current position, he studied sociology, political science and non-profit-management in Berlin, Madrid, and Melbourne. In his previous positions he worked with charitable foundations in Madrid and the European Commission in Brussels.

Rössler, Mechtild, Dr., geographer and cultural landscape specialist, holds an MA in cultural geography and a PhD from the Faculty for Earth Sciences, University of Hamburg, on the history of planning. In 1991 she joined UNESCO Headquarters in Paris at the Division for Ecological Sciences, and worked on Biosphere Reserves in the framework of the Man and the Biosphere (MAB) programme, and since 1992 at the World Heritage Centre as programme specialist and responsible officer for natural heritage and cultural landscapes. In July 2001 she became Chief of the Europe and North America Section, in December 2010 Chief of the Policy and Statutory Section and in December 2013 the Deputy Director of the World Heritage Centre. In 2014 she was nominated Deputy Director of the Heritage Division, which covers among others the 1954, 1970, 2001 and 1972 Conventions. She lectures at World Heritage study programmes at Turin Polytechnics, University College Dublin and BTU Cottbus-Senftenberg and is carrying out a research project on the History of the World Heritage Convention led by Prof. Cameron of the University of Montreal. She has published 10 books and over 100 articles and contributed to the editorial board of three international journals.

Sabaté, Joaquim is Chair of Town Planning at the Polytechnic University of Catalonia, coordinator of the PhD and Research Master in Urbanism, founder of the International Laboratory of Cultural Landscapes (MIT-UPC) and director of the journal Identities: Territory, Culture, and Heritage. He has lectured in 60 European, Asian, and American Universities. Research activities have focused on the study of theories, methods and tools of urban and regional design, and on the relation between heritage resources and local development, published in over two hundred books, book chapters, and articles in specialized journals.

Turner, Michael, Prof., is the UNESCO Chairholder in Urban Design and Conservation Studies and heads the Research and Innovation Authority at Bezalel, Academy of Arts and Design, Jerusalem. His activities focus on urban sustainability, heritage, social inclusion and urban spaces. He is a member of many professional-academic bodies, and is currently special envoy to the World Heritage Centre Director focusing on Culture for Development and the implementation of the UNESCO Recommendation on Historic Urban Landscapes.

Van Oers, Ron (PhD, Delft University of Technology) worked for more than a decade at UNESCO's World Heritage Centre in Paris in project management and programme design, including coordinating the development of the 2011 UNESCO Recommendation on the Historic Urban Landscape. He is Vice Director of the World Heritage Institute of Training and Research for Asia and the Pacific in Shanghai, and Senior Research Fellow at Tongji University, where he has set up the Historic Urban Landscape research programme.

Warren, Mark is a student of the history and theory of architecture and urban planning. He graduated from Harvard College with a bachelor's degree in history of art and architecture, and was awarded a Fulbright grant from the United States government to study urban and regional planning in Barcelona. He currently resides in Boston, Massachusetts.

Westrik, Carol, Dr., has worked in the field of World Heritage for nearly twenty years. She is an art historian with a specialization in cultural landscapes and has a PhD in post-war reconstruction and development. Carol also conducted a post doc looking at the Netherlands and the World Heritage Convention. She has her own consultancy as heritage advisor, and has seen the workings of the Convention from different angles: State Party, Committee Member, World Heritage Centre, Advisory Body and Category 2 Centre.

Yadollahi, Solmaz is a conservation architect and urban heritage conservationist from the University of Tehran. Currently she is doing her PhD on "The Iranian bazaar as a public place" at the IGS Heritage Studies, BTU Cottbus-Senftenberg. She has been involved in several historic urban revitalization projects in Iran. From 2008 to 2012 she collaborated with the World Heritage Inscription Bureau at the Iranian Cultural Heritage Handicrafts and Tourism Organization (ICHHTO) in the preparation of four successful World Heritage nominations.

Yang, Minja has been President and Professor of the Raymond Lemaire International Centre for Conservation of the Catholic University of Leuven (RLICC/KU Leuven) in Belgium since 2010, a post she assumed upon retiring from 30 years of service in the United Nations, of which 20 at UNESCO. She was formerly Chief of the Angkor Unit launching the major UNESCO Safeguarding & Development Programme after the political settlement in Cambodia, then Chief of the Asia-Pacific Unit of the UNESCO World Heritage Centre, then promoted as its Deputy Director, while concurrently serving as Coordinator for the World Heritage Cities Programme, then Director for Museums prior to her posting as UNESCO Representative to Bhutan, India, Maldives and Sri Lanka & Director of the UNESCO Sub-regional Office in New Delhi. Throughout her career, she focused on capacity-building of local authorities in cultural resources management and in heritage-base Urban Development. She holds a BA in Sociology from Georgetown University (Washington DC), MA in Politics & Social Anthropology, and PhD qualifying diploma in Political Theory from the School of Oriental & African Studies, University of London.

Notes on Peers

Emara, Dr. ElArabi is Associate Professor in the Department of Islamic Archaeology of the Faculty of Archaeology, Cairo University in Egypt, and at Jazan University in Saudi Arabia since 2011. He holds a BA in Islamic Archaeology from Cairo University, an MA in Islamic Archaeology and PhD in Islamic Archaeology from Cairo University, 2004. Dr. Emara was an Islamic heritage expert in The Center for Documentation of Cultural and Natural Heritage (CULTNAT) from 2000 until 2009. He was a member of the Committee preparing the scientific content for the Islamic section of the Eternal Egypt site and also a member of the Committee preparing the scientific content for the database document Islamic Monuments in Cairo. Dr. Emara supervised the archaeological excavations in the Saudi Arabia (ALMANARA) site in Jazan from 2010–2014. He is currently the academic coordinator of the Department of Tourism and Antiquities at Jazan University. Throughout his career, a particular focus in his work has been placed on the documentation of Islamic heritage.

Hüfner, Klaus, Dr., former university professor. Since 1971 he has been a member of the German Commission for UNESCO, also serving on the Board of Directors between 1982 and 2010, as well as holding the Vice-President and President roles in 1989-1998 and 1998-2002 respectively; since 2010, he is an honorary member of the Commission. He holds numerous others honorary posts including: honorary member of the German UNESCO World Heritage Sites Association since 2004; senior research fellow of the Global Policy Forum, New York since 2006; honorary chair of the Berlin Committee for UNESCO since 2007 and coordinator of the IREG Ranking Audit, Warsaw since 2011.

Ruggels, D. Fairchild is Professor of art, architecture, and landscape history at the University of Illinois, Urbana-Champaign. Dr. Ruggles research examines the built landscape of Islamic Spain and South Asia and the complex interrelationship of Islamic culture with Christianity, Judaism, and Hinduism and the precise ways that religion and culture are often conflated in the study of these. She is the author of two award-winning books on gardens: Gardens, Landscape, and Vision in the Palaces of Islamic Spain (2000) and Islamic Gardens and Landscapes (2008). Additionally, she has written, edited or co-edited eight other books, including Women, Patronage, and Self-Representation in Islamic Societies (2000), the award-winning Sites Unseen: Landscape and Vision (2007), Cultural Heritage and Human Rights (2007), Intangible Heritage Embodied (2009), Islamic Art and Visual Culture: An Anthology of Sources (2011), and On Location (2012).

Schaaf, Franziska, MA, studied British Studies, French Studies, Arab Studies and Social Geography at Leipzig University and Université Rennes II, France. She wrote her Master's Thesis on Cultural Memory in Structural Change based on her field research at the Big Pit National Coal Museum at the UNESCO World Heritage Site Blaenavon, South Wales. At the Ernst-Bloch-Center in Ludwigshafen, Germany, she worked as a trainee, and later as a cultural manager and in public relations. Since 2013, she has been a research assistant at the ZAK | Centre for Cultural and General Studies at the Karlsruhe Institute of Technology (KIT), working on cultural heritage in interdisciplinary settings, participation, and sustainability studies. Her research fields include memory studies, industrial heritage, discourse analysis and the human-nature relationship.

Index